Transcribing SILENCE

WRITING LIVES
Ethnographic Narratives

Series Editors:

Arthur P. Bochner & Carolyn Ellis

University of South Florida

Writing Lives: Ethnographic Narratives publishes narrative representations of qualitative research projects. The series editors seek manuscripts that blur the boundaries between humanities and social sciences. We encourage novel and evocative forms of expressing concrete lived experience, including autoethnographic, literary, poetic, artistic, visual, performative, critical, multi-voiced, conversational, and co-constructed representations. We are interested in ethnographic narratives that depict local stories; employ literary modes of scene setting, dialogue, character development, and unfolding action; and include the author's critical reflections on the research and writing process, such as research ethics, alternative modes of inquiry and representation, reflexivity, and evocative storytelling. Proposals and manuscripts should be directed to abochner@cas.usf.edu

Volumes in this series:

Erotic Mentoring: Women's Transformations in the University, Janice Hocker Rushing

Intimate Colonialism: Head, Heart, and Body in West African Development Work, Laurie L. Charlés

Last Writes: A Daybook for a Dying Friend, Laurel Richardson

A Trickster in Tweed: The Quest for Quality in a Faculty Life, Thomas F. Frentz

Guyana Diaries: Women's Lives Across Difference, Kimberly D. Nettles

Writing Qualitative Inquiry: Selves, Stories and the New Politics of Academic Success, H. L. Goodall, Jr.

Accidental Ethnography: An Inquiry into Family Secrecy, Christopher N. Poulos

Revision: Autoethnographic Reflections on Life and Work, Carolyn Ellis

Leaning: A Poetics of Personal Relations, Ronald J. Pelias

Narrating the Closet: An Autoethnography of Same-Sex Attraction, Tony E. Adams

Life After Leaving: The Remains of Spousal Abuse, Sophie Tamas

Playing with Purpose: Adventures in Performative Social Science, Mary M. Gergen and Kenneth J. Gergen

Critical Autoethnography: Intersecting Cultural Identities in Everyday Life, Robyn M. Boylorn and Mark P. Orbe

Coming to Narrative: A Personal History of Paradigm Change in the Human Sciences, Arthur P. Bochner

Transcribing Silence: Culture, Relationships, and Communication, Kristine L. Muñoz

Transcribing SILENCE

Culture, Relationships, and Communication

Kristine L. Muñoz

Routledge
Taylor & Francis Group
LONDON AND NEW YORK

First published 2014 by Left Coast Press, Inc.

Published 2016 by Routledge
2 Park Square, Milton Park, Abingdon, Oxon OX14 4RN
711 Third Avenue, New York, NY 10017, USA

Routledge is an imprint of the Taylor & Francis Group, an informa business

Library of Congress Cataloging-in-Publication Data:

Muñoz, Kristine L.
Transcribing silence : culture, relationships, and communication / Kristine L. Muñoz.
pages cm.—(Writing lives ; 15)
ISBN 978-1-62958-023-4 (hardback)—ISBN 978-1-62958-024-1 (paperback)—ISBN 978-1-62958-025-8 (institutional eBook)—ISBN 978-1-62958-026-5 (consumer eBook)
1. Silence. 2. Communication. I. Title.
BJ1499.S5M86 2014
302.2—c23

2014019581

ISBN 978-1-62958-023-4 hardcover
ISBN 978-1-62958-024-1 paperback

Contents

For Kay Quammen Hopper
and in memory of
Robert Hopper
and
Dwight Conquergood

Preface

If at any time there should seem to be an expression unintelligible from one soul to another, it is best not to strive to interpret it in earthly language, but to wait for the soul to make itself understood ... Words may be a thick and darksome veil of mystery between the soul and the truth which it seeks. Wretched were we, indeed, if we had no better means of communicating ourselves, no fairer garb in which to array our essential being, than these poor rags and tatters of Babel.

Nathaniel Hawthorne

The first time I read this observation of Hawthorne's I gasped aloud: No social scientist, he nonetheless put his finger on a key fact of communication. Someone who made his living with the written word observed that language is not enough for humans to understand themselves, each other, or the world around them. He did not go on to say what else we humans have available to make ourselves understood, but several means of making meaning beyond language come to mind:

Most obviously, there is nonverbal communication. A glance can say "Let's get out of here" or "How could you do this to me?" A hug can say "I'm so sorry" or "That was GREAT!" or ... nothing at all, except that hugs are expected in the moment. A foot nudge under the table can say "Stop talking!" or "Remember when we ...?" or "I can't *wait* to get you alone." A sigh can say more about complex experience and profound emotion than any words, however eloquently written or spoken.

There is another realm of communicating without words in and around the words themselves: Saying *y'all* or *ain't* or swear words can be a doorway into, or out of, a particular group of people. Switching from one natural language to another even more clearly does so. A two-second pause after a request for a favor says "I don't want to do that" regardless of which words come out after that pause. The expression *I had to bite my tongue* refers to opinions, observations, instructions, memories—any number of neuronal/emotional connections—that flash through the mind, and then are left consciously and intentionally unsaid. The reasons range from "tact," an abstraction which encompasses both kindness and cowardice, as well as admirable ideals to not interfere or criticize. *What I wish I'd said* ... evokes words that either didn't come to mind in time,[1] or were withheld out of caution, more tact, or inability to get a word in edgewise—an opportunity later regretted. Lies of omission and secrets both involve leaving relevant information unsaid, although "relevance" opens up a whole universe of both cultural and ethical nuance, even before questions of motive come up. Whose skin will be risked or saved by the unsaid that either misleads or conceals? The ethical issues may lie beyond the scope of communication theory[2] because of their origin in the psychological world of intentions and evaluations, but the cultural ones are there to be examined in communication.

A final category of means to construct meaning without words is relationships, those gauzy-wispy, now-you-see-'em-now-you-don't ties we call friendship and romance and family and colleagues. Relationships are made up of both talk and not-talk, including most crucially the usually unspoken agreements to leave some comments unsaid, some events and actions undiscussed, some people unmentioned. Other friends, lovers, or colleagues might be able to give voice to any or all of those particulars, but *this* couple, *these* friends silently agree to leave them unsaid in order to keep the relational boat upright on the waves.

Unsaid words and unspoken agreements are, quite often, human communication at its most complex and elegant. This book is an exploration of that world. It is an excavation of Nathaniel Hawthorne's sense that words are poor, inadequate clothing for the soul—*rags and tatters of Babel*. It is a celebration, on many levels, of everything human beings manage to do with each other outside of, in between, and underneath the words of the languages they speak and write. I love words and languages, and my life is built around them: I live in a bilingual family, I write books and articles and performance evaluations and far too many e-mails. Reading is both a large part of my work and my greatest pleasure. I am a teacher, so in a real sense, I talk for a living (although I like to think I listen as much as I talk). Maybe that eternal focus on words brings with it a hunger to see and hear beyond them, to listen and watch for all the things that go unsaid and all the reasons they do.

Still, exploring the unsaid and unsayable in words creates a dangerous paradox: In the process of writing it down you may ruin whatever is most lovely and valuable about it, precisely because its value lies in the fact of being outside of the spoken and written world. In my observation, the ineffable can also create a more richly colored, though sometimes risky, terrain for human beings—including communication scholars—to wander in. That element of danger is part of the energy that drives this endeavor, along with my certainty that there is much to learn about communication, culture, and relationships that necessarily lives in the unsaid and unsayable.

The narratives in this book are both factual and fictional, and I have tried to be consistent in categorizing them as one or the other. The introduction reviews some of the vast social science literature on silence and the unsaid to anchor the essays that follow in a conceptual structure. After that are eight autoethnographic essays that draw on experiences I really have had. As a still-traditional kind of ethnographer, I tried to stay as close to the real events and, in most cases, the words that created them, as my memory and some concern for the privacy of others would allow. The second section is short fiction, stories about things that did not happen to me or to people I know. They are stories constructed around my observations of silences and unsayables that my own experiences did not stretch to cover, though my imagination (and being an avid reader) did. After each narrative, there are questions for reflection and comments intended to expand on the narrative by tying it to the conceptual framework in the introduction.

The choice to scaffold the narratives within these structures was one of the vast array of learning experiences that writing this book provided. There is debate in autoethnography about whether making analytic points specific violates the spirit of the narrative approach.[3] There are also a variety of ways to scaffold autoethnographic narratives and ethnographic fiction within conceptual frameworks, and the one I use here is among them. The debate will no doubt continue about how explicitly autoethnography should be analytic. I think my choice to do it this way comes from my proclivity to be a teacher: Readers may certainly draw a variety of conclusions and claims from these narratives, but I am uneasy with the possible reaction of, "OK, I liked (or didn't like) the story, what is it supposed to mean?" The reflections and expansions are meant to suggest some possible interpretations and applications of the narratives, without closing off the potential for vastly different others.

One more point I feel compelled to make about the fact of an interpretive social scientist who writes and publishes fiction, calling it scholarship. I learned two things from writing fictional narratives. The first was that disasters, of different types and magnitudes, have a way of bringing into the open that which is ordinarily hidden in silence. Both the intentionally unsaid and the things never mentioned because they were unthinkable tend to surface in moments of catastrophe. Even though I found this out by constructing fictional people and worlds, I also found it an excruciating way to learn about life. Leaving those possibilities unwritten, though—or once written, hidden away on the hard disk—in the end left too much unsaid. Social science, in all its versions, can only go so far in exploring the world. I include these narratives to propose that a fictional narrative must be *accurate,* even if by definition it is not true. Constructing a fictional story is another way to raise questions about the social world, and has the advantage of going beyond the necessarily limited experiences of any one individual. Reading and writing fiction are simply other ways to learn about communication, culture, and relationships.

The second thing I learned was that writing fiction took a great deal of ethnographic research, surprisingly similar to that required to do social scientific ethnography. Novelist Amy Tan (*The Joy Luck Club, Saving Fish from Drowning, The Kitchen God's Wife*) said that doing the research is what she enjoys most about the books she writes. I conclude this book by discussing some issues about writing, as both the central method of ethnography and as the site for so many other affective states of learning: oppression, resistance, confusion, exhilaration, despair.

Being an ethnographer means I have claimed the right to ask people strange, even nosy questions, and to go through life as a perpetual observer and eavesdropper. That license has enriched my journey in many ways, the most profound being the human connections that form in the acts of listening, watching, asking, and interpreting. I have been listening for the unsaid and the unsayable for more than 20 years as I wrote this book, and now will put my trust in words—those *poor rags and tatters of Babel*—to share what I've learned. Fingers crossed.

Acknowledgments

Although his appearances are infrequent and brief in these pages, my father was the first, greatest storyteller I have known. He taught Texas history in junior high school for more than 30 years, and captivated both his students and his children with vivid tales of Santa Ana, Sam Houston, the Galveston Hurricane of 1900. My brother and I hung over the front seat of the car while he drove us to the Houston zoo or the library or to ride the Port Bolivar ferry across Galveston Bay, and the Texas stories came to encompass the private as well as the public. They included his growing up next door to a bootlegger during Prohibition, riding a bicycle out to visit his grandparents in what later became a prosperous part of Houston, and training to be a radio operator on the King Ranch before shipping out to Italy in World War II. Best of all, of course, were the stories he told about the wondrous events of his courting our mother and the cute things we did when we were younger. Much later it dawned on me that there were no stories of his father, apart from the puzzlement that his son Bob would waste time finishing high school when he could have gone to work for Hunt Tool Company like his older brothers did. My mother filled me in on some of them, and I found out why we didn't hear them from Dad: Nate Fitch was a drinker, a womanizer, and a cad. Although he died a millionaire, he left it all to his fourth and final wife, who left it to the Catholic Church. This meant his first wife—my grandmother—couldn't retire until she was 70 years old and that his sons made what they could of their lives—which, except for my father, wasn't much—once Hunt Tool closed down with the rest of the steel industry.

My thanks begin, then, with my parents' stories, both the ones they told and the ones they didn't. I'm also thankful that my father's work as a teacher led me to become one.

I am deeply grateful to the Intergenre Group, sponsored by the Obermann Center at the University of Iowa. That group, one of several interdisciplinary initiatives that are the brainchildren of the much under-appreciated Teresa Mangum, was the catalyst for bringing this collection together and pushing it into the world. Special thanks to Naomi Greyser, Kim Marra, Lisa Heineman, Loyce Arthur, and Sarah Kanouse for the encouragement, support, feedback, and accountability that led to the book actually getting finished and out the door. These women showed what leading the life of the mind could look and feel like, and I am forever in awe of their courage and creativity.

The University of Iowa has been a source of support, strength, and limitless opportunities to grow. Two people in particular have been especially inspirational: Linda Maxson and Raúl Curto. Bruce Gronbeck was a warm, generous colleague and friend during the years we overlapped in the department, particularly during my time as chair. I treasure you all.

Thanks to my two best readers and BFFs, Daena Goldsmith and Erica Muñoz-Fitch. I wanted this book to be useful to college teachers and their students, and they gave unstinting wisdom and practical advice toward that end, along with life nourishment of every possible variety.

Words become once again pale, bedraggled, and inadequate vehicles for expressing my gratitude to Art Bochner and Left Coast Press, Inc. I got invaluable feedback and support from Art, and most importantly his belief that this was a project worth doing. The extent to which I have grown as a scholar in the process of writing this book is matched only by the delight I have gotten from doing it.

The friends and family members who have taught me about culture and relationships, who have told me such good stories and given me so many to tell, are numerous. I particularly appreciate (roughly in order of nation state) Maarit Valo, Pertti Hurme, Maili Porhola, Marko Siitonen, Gabriel Lara, Daniel Chornet, Concha Moreno, Luisa Martin Rojo, Clara Molina, Tato Rodero, John Richardson, Jo Lavis, Charles Antaki, Mary DeValois, Janet Acarregui, Carol Tippe, Becky Scott, Joy Hayes, Carol Schrage, Mary Oquendo, Judy Liskin-Gasparro, and Nina Molinaro. I leave family members unnamed to protect their privacy except for Eric Nelson, who is too important to me to be left unnamed and whose encouragement to keep writing has been uniquely important as well.

I have been abundantly blessed with fine teachers throughout my life, most recently Marilyn Abildskov. Her skilled, subtle guidance is on every page of this volume, and her wit and wisdom inside my soul forever. Gerry Philipsen taught me ethnography, parenthood, humility, integrity, and what it means to be a Christian. Robert Hopper's contributions to my learning are detailed in their own story. Without Dwight Conquergood's gracious encouragement to let people read my non-social science work I would never have kept writing the kinds of essays and stories that appear here, and my life would be much the poorer for that. I hope both of them knew what they meant to me.

All I can say about Jairo Muñoz is that he is my hero, a life partner and garden mate beyond compare. Apart from that, my only words come from Mercedes Sosa: *Gracias a la vida, que me ha dado tanto ...*

Madrid, April 2014

Introduction

Silence and the unsaid

Silence is more than just dead air in human communication. What we experience and describe as "silence" is often, in fact, written or spoken activity that leaves something relevant unsaid. The "relevant" aspect is important: There are too many things that are true in any given moment of conversation that have so little to do with what people are focused on that to bring them up would just be confusing. "Will you marry me?" "You have on brown shoes and a green hat. And, oh yes, I will be delighted to marry you." There are almost as many reasons for leaving something unsaid, beyond relevance, as there are situations and relationships in the human world: It may be taboo or grossly rude to mention that the person you're talking to is difficult to understand, because of an accent, a mental or physical disability, or the fact that he or she is drunk. It may be risky to put thoughts or feelings into words: "I like you, I hate you, I want you to shut up and go away." Something may be relevant but assumed to be so well understood that nothing is gained by saying it out loud. In each of these instances, leaving something unsaid is a kind of

---

Transcribing Silence: Culture, Relationships, and Communication
by Kristine L. Muñoz, 15–43.

silence, even though plenty of talk and other action may be going on. It would be difficult to understand silence without including the unsaid, and vice versa.

Social science research has studied silence explicitly for at least 50 years, sketching the meanings of breaks in flows of communication. Silence has been examined as the tiniest pause within one person's utterance and as several seconds, or even minutes, of silence between the turns of people engaged in conversation. Situations lasting hours or days can be characterized by an expectation of silence, relative or total, within specific cultural groups. Long-term social structures can render less powerful participants silent in families and other organizations, and in important settings like classrooms and courtrooms, for generations. I will open this chapter by sketching some of the vast research into silence, focusing on a few key points and illustrating them with some of the work they are based on, in order to fill out the point I started with: that silence is more than just dead air.

Defining the unsaid and unsayable is more complicated. To claim that something might have been said, but wasn't, requires a different kind of evidence than scientific ways of knowing can provide. That is why this is a book of narratives, rather than a collection of studies based on experiments, interviews, analyses of transcripts, or participant observation. All of these measures could be quite useful, yet the strength of each of them is that they separate complex webs of meaning into bits and pieces. A narrative presents an event in all its details: what happened the night before or two years later, what one or more of the characters were thinking and how they might be wrong about the other people and the situation—and on and on.

An opposing argument is that narratives are not real. People exaggerate when they retell an event, they forget key details, they make stories up and present them as true. However vividly and accurately they are told, narratives by definition happen after the events take place, so they can never capture moments of social life in real time. Consistent with the idea that some things are unsayable, there are narratives that are rarely or never told, for innumerable reasons. Maybe the story would make someone look bad, or destroy the trust crucial for a relationship to survive, or the potential teller believes no one will understand why the story is funny or sad, or why it might be told at all.

Despite these limitations, however, narratives are one of the most powerful communication acts humans are—uniquely, according to some scholars—able to perform. They persuade, they serve as vessels of both individual and collective memory, they teach, they construct understanding from mystery. The power of stories to do those last two things is the reason I approach the complicated issue of the unsaid and unsayable through narratives. First, however, I will ground this exploration in the firmer soil of social science research into silence. At the end of the introduction I list some of the reviews of this literature available elsewhere for those interested in the details of what I sketch briefly here.

Social science and conversation analysis: Turns, pauses, lapses and lulls

Two disciplines grounded in social science inquiry—approaches to social life that generally work deductively, through studies that attempt to minimize possibilities of bias in favor of generalizable, replicable results—are social psychology and sociology. A branch of each of these disciplines has turned to the shapes, sizes, and meanings of silence as part of communication. In social psychology, attitudes toward silence versus talk have been examined as potential matters of concern in communication between people who belong to different groups—racial, national, social class, and so on. In sociology, the development of conversation analysis in the late 1960s revolved around discovery of the microlevel mechanisms through which people (speakers of any language, members of any culture) coordinate their actions in talk. Conversational turn-taking was fundamental to the issues pursued in this vein, and understanding how people worked through interpersonal and institutional matters as basic as opening or closing a telephone call, as complicated as getting a murder suspect to confess, brought the shapes, sizes, and functions of silence in interactional sequences into focus. This research showed time and again, in the most concrete detail, that silence—from micropauses to lengthy lulls in conversation—is central to construction of meaning.

Conversation analysis outgrew its sociological roots very quickly, and is now a prominent line of research in communication, linguistics, social psychology, rhetoric, and other fields. Its focus on microdetails of talk—features that would escape almost everyone's notice in everyday interaction that, once they are pointed out, become inescapably relevant—distinguishes between a pause that happens within one person's turn and ones that happen between turns. In this utterance

A. I think (1.0) ahh, I think so.

the symbol (1.0) stands for a one-second pause, which is experienced in many conversations as being quite long. There are various interpretations of such pauses available to others: maybe A is distracted in mid-utterance by a passing, unrelated thought? Maybe A is hesitant to commit to what seems a very simple agreement with something that came before?

Conversation analysis (CA) stays completely away from anything that might be construed as an inner state: what someone was thinking, what they felt, what their intentions were, whether they were telling the truth. It focuses on what came before, what comes during, and what comes after a turn at talk. Adding hypothetical turns before and after this utterance suggests how sequence shapes the possible meanings of a pause within a turn:

1. Z. Shouldn't Dad be here by now?
   A. I think (1.0) ahh, I think so.
   Z. It's only a 15 minute drive.

2. Z. Do you want to move in with me?
   A. I think (1.0) ahh, I think so.
   Z. Wow, don't be so enthusiastic.

Pauses between turns are also rich with meaning. First, a pause is only a pause if the second speaker is sure the first has finished what he or she was saying (at least in cultures where not interrupting is an important rule of courtesy). Second, reacting to something as a pause depends partly on how quickly the exchange of turns has been proceeding up to that point. If one person is visibly writing down what the other one says, there will be long stretches without talk that are understood to be occupied with the task of writing.

The technical side of silence as approached and documented by CA is a primary theme of the first autoethnographic narrative, "Transcribing the unsaid." Rather than go into more detail about this complex area of study, I will point you to that story, which contextualizes these matters of pauses and turns within one of the most important relationships of my life. I hope the story makes clear that the importance of that relationship started in some untimed, but noticeable to the trained ear, pauses in and between conversational turns.

Once we start to consider silence in sizes and shapes larger than pauses, a rich array of meanings constructed through silence appears. Silence *means* by what it *does*. Consider an extreme case: Two siblings have an argument so serious that they do not speak to one another for several days, or weeks, or years. Neither of them moves through a silent world, of course; each talks to dozens of people during the time they are not speaking to one another. The fact of not speaking must first be logistically arranged. If they live several time zones apart, they may simply stop calling, e-mailing, and visiting. If they live in the same town, they may need to avoid places they might run into each other and find ways to avoid eye or voice contact (perhaps allowing for a civil "Hello" in order to make the situation less painfully awkward) when their paths do cross. Once the physical logistics are in place, the stretch of time they go without speaking will become meaningful in relation to how often they were previously in contact. If they called or texted once a week, a lapse of a month will be noticeable. If they really only exchanged birthday and holiday greetings, it will take at least a year for the lack of speaking to become an actual case of "not speaking." Within these many details of what counts as the siblings not speaking to one another lies the meaning of the silence between them. They will each assign their own meanings, of course: Sibling A knows B is mad at him or her, and does not want to force the issue, so hopes to give B some space to get over being angry. Alternatively, A and B may be in agreement that the argument was so serious that there is no reason to assume they will ever speak again in their lives.

What the silence means, then, is a matter of what it does, both in the relationship between the siblings and in the social world that connects them. It might simply provide a cooling-off period after which the previous communication pattern can resume. It might divide a family, a social group, a jointly managed business, or a company town that relies on the family business into warring factions that eventually split forever.

Staying within the realm of personal relationships (and assuming that personal relationships often have social consequences), the actions performed by smaller silences present other levels of meaning construction. People who feel especially close to others, whether friends, spouses, or family members, sometimes experience that closeness as a freedom to be silent. Social expectations to make small talk, to comment on events as they happen, or to express feelings appropriate to an occasion, are lifted by the bond that allows silence to be a comfortable alternative. Those silences probably do not extend to weeks or years, as the angry kind can, highlighting an important dimension of how silences mean: Silence is relative. What counts as silence depends very much on what people expect to happen, and how quickly, in a particular sequence of events. Those expectations are built on what happened just before the moment that the participants describe, or experience, as "silence." If close relational partners begin a 10-hour drive with a tense disagreement in the first five minutes, and then say nothing until they are joined by others at the end of the journey, the 9:55 in between is unlikely to be the comfortable sort. If, on the other hand, the first five minutes are some kind of small talk or decisions about when and where to stop for gas, after which one person drives and the other reads a book, sleeps, knits, or daydreams while gazing out the window, the 9:55 can be relaxing. For the people involved, it may even be a precious measure of just how uniquely they understand one another and how readily they communicate without saying a word out loud.

Going back to brief silences that happen during conversation, silences that follow questions often constitute what is called a *dispreferred second*. Because questions are expected, most of the time, to draw responses (if not always answers), silence is taken to be the less desirable response. For example:

Mother to child: "Have you done your homework?"

> Silence might mean no. If the child is an adolescent, it might also mean "I don't have to answer that because you are not the boss of me."

Boss to employee: "Do you know that $30,000 is missing from the company account?"

> Silence means yes.

Partner to partner: "Are you having an affair?"

> Silence means yes.

Friend 1 to Friend 2: "Where were you last night? I thought we were going out to dinner and I called your cell phone like a hundred times, but you never answered."

> Silence means Friend 1 won't be pleased with the answer to the question.

Prosecutor to defendant, on trial for murder: "Were you in the home of the victim on September 21st, between 9 p.m. and midnight?"

> Defendant: "On the advice of counsel, I assert my Constitutional right to take the Fifth Amendment."
>
> Although the last response is not silence *per se*, it is likely to be interpreted in exactly the same, dispreferred way as other silences: "Yes, I was there."

This final example brings up a different meaning of silence: I explicitly refuse to answer this question. There are many ways to refuse to answer: "I really don't want to talk about that" or "I'm only answering that question on a need-to-know basis." Most refusals of this kind are implicit, so I will save them for ways of understanding what goes unsaid. Because there are both spoken ways not to answer and silence as a way not to answer, the question arises: Why—or when—do people use silence instead of speech to say no?

A useful theory that takes on this issue is called, somewhat misleadingly, politeness theory.[1] It is not, as its name suggests, an abstraction of rules for where to put your napkin while you eat or when and how to say please and thank you or admonishments never to chew with your mouth full or show up empty-handed as a houseguest. It is a theory that begins from the simple observation that for human beings to live together, they need to cooperate socially, in their communication practices as well as physically, building shelters and gathering food. That cooperation is called *facework*: a standing agreement to play along, most of the time, to some degree, with other people's needs to be seen positively (positive face) and not to be imposed upon by others (negative face). Cooperating with positive face can involve giving compliments, using respectful titles, thanking someone for his kindness, and so forth. It can also involve staying silent about the non-positive aspects of people's identities or actions: how short/fat/ unattractive they are, how rude the noise they just made was, how ignorant, insensitive or unstable their last statement shows them to be, how incredibly boring their stories are. Cooperating with negative face wants includes staying silent about what you want from someone so that your want does not impose upon them, as well as shaping talk that might impose on someone in ways that reduce the imposition: You can make requests with an apology for asking, or hint that you want something in a way that allows for hearing it as simply a statement of fact ("It's cold in here, don't you think?").

In addition to cooperating with the face wants of other people, silence and strategic uses of language allow us to protect our own interests. If I know a secret that will hurt someone's feelings, or if there is something about my wants and needs that will impose on another person if he or she knows about it, I can avoid the awkwardness for both of our sakes by staying silent on those topics. In the essay in this book called *Falling in love,* the awkwardness had to do with finding out I enjoyed reading and writing more than I did watching college football in the company of dorm mates. In *A veggie tale,* it was about the purely accidental process of becoming a vegetarian, rather than making a political or lifestyle-driven decision to do so. Fortunately for me, those identities were only temporarily awkward. Neither of them carried drastic social or legal consequences, as covering up a drug habit or involvement in a murder would have. The principle behind staying silent, and then hinting, and then, after quite some time, saying the awkward truth in direct and straightforward ways, was the same: I was saving both myself and the people now trusted or burdened with knowing such things about me some amount of trouble in particular moments of conversation.

The difference between being an intellectual or a vegetarian versus a drug addict or a murderer seems too obvious, however. Why would it be awkward to belong to the first two categories? Slightly reframed, the question highlights a particularly rich dimension of how silence means: *In what social world* would those identities be awkward? Answers to that are easy: Being an intellectual is awkward in a working class social world where people earn respect by *working hard,* which may take many forms but does not include sitting still reading and writing much of the day. Being a vegetarian is an imposition in a social world where good manners demand that you eat what is put in front of you, and in which serving meat is a measure of prosperity and hospitality.[2]

The power of social worlds to shape identities, relationships, and reality itself has been a central issue in studies of silence. An early, now classic study by anthropologist Keith Basso (1970) described six situations in which the Western Apache culture prescribed silence: the beginning stages of courtship, being with people who are sad, meeting strangers, being *cussed out* by people who are out of their minds with alcohol or rage or both, children coming home after long absences (such as being away at boarding school), and taking part in curing rituals. He pointed out that the common thread among these situations was uncertainty about identities and relationships between the participants. Rather than dealing with uneasiness—inevitable in every cultural group where people come and go—through chattering to fill the dead air, the Western Apache remain silent. This is not awkward, the way it would be among middle class white North Americans, because the group shares an understanding that it is silence, rather than talk, that makes many difficult situations somewhat easier. Imagine how much easier first dates would be if the expectation were silence, instead of self-presentation and relationship initiation through talk! Or being around someone who was grieving, or a child who has grown several inches while she has been away and may have been taught that she comes from a vastly inferior race, as was historically the case for Western Apache children sent away to boarding school. Silence in fact seems like a most sensitive and intelligent strategy for those moments.

In addition to descriptions of other Native American cultures' preferences for silence over talk under certain circumstances, other groups have been described in national terms as groups who associate silence with virtue. Japanese and Finns are two such groups, and the different meanings they attach to silence are illuminating. Finnish political scientist Markku Koivusalo has commented that "Finnish literature's most beautiful portrayals of friendship and love present the silence of being together. A firm relationship with another is not brought about by exchanged words but by way of shared unspoken gestures."[3] A valued, "natural" way for Finns to be, together as well as alone, is described as contemplative, thoughtful, and undisturbed. Unnecessary talk—'small talk,' for English speakers and others—interrupts and interferes with this way of being in the world, while silence creates the ideal space for it. The Finnish appreciation for silence has been connected to the vast, sparsely inhabited forests and countless lakes that form their natural world. It has also been described, often by Finns themselves, as a deficit, an inability to make small talk rather than a deliberate choice of silence under conditions in which talk is not really necessary for humans to coordinate their actions.

By contrast, Japanese preferences for silence (even compared to their East Asian neighbors in China and Korea) are associated with truthfulness, tact, embarrassment, and defiance. If a common American expression is "If you can't say something nice, don't say anything at all," it might be said that the Japanese have several forms of the same idea: If the truth would be awkward or disrupt the social harmony of the group, or if you're madly in love with someone, or if you do not intend to do what you're told—don't say anything at all. The historical and social roots of Finnish and Japanese silence are, of course, both deep and complicated, and some excellent accounts of those cultural patterns are listed at the end of this chapter. For now, the point is that meanings of silence extend far beyond individual personalities, relational states, or interactional moments: They are part of a system of norms, premises, and symbols that pertains to a group of people. Every group of people marks some situations as best dealt with by silence: prayer, in some religious traditions; libraries or classrooms when people are working on tasks that require concentration; tragic occasions marked by "a moment of silence" for the victims. Once a situation is socially defined as requiring silence, individuals and relational partners are no longer completely free to decide what silence—or refusing to be silent—means. Although people can choose to be silent when they are expected to talk, or choose to talk when they're expected to be silent, those choices will be interpreted and evaluated through the system(s) of meaning in place within the group.

Although this detail may seem obvious and its importance thus doubtful, differences across cultural groups regarding the meanings of silence in particular situations can become significant grounds for intercultural tension, which can turn into stereotyping and discrimination. Because silence on an interactional level can be understood as a dispreferred second—guilt when asked about innocence, "no" when the expected response is "yes" and vice versa—cultural patterns of silence can be misinterpreted as those unfavorable responses. Finnish people, as I suggested, sometimes describe themselves as socially handicapped by their inexperience—or perceived inability—with small talk. Japanese students in Western classrooms can have similar trouble with teachers' expectations that they speak up when told to, whether because they do not know the answer to a question or fear that knowing the answer will mark them as a show-off. Such issues can be just as problematic as the task of speaking English as a second (and difficult to learn) language. US Latino and Native American students in predominantly White classrooms may also be silent when their teachers expect them to talk, for different reasons but with the same effect: They are perceived as insecure, defiant, or unable to provide correct answers, rather than as belonging to a cultural group that has different assumptions about what silence means at a particular moment.

Courtrooms are another crucially important venue for communication in which, ideals about fairness and justice aside, participants are assigned to roles that strictly define when and how they may speak. Experienced participants, such as judges, attorneys, and bailiffs, control the talk of less experienced participants: plaintiffs, defendants, juries, witnesses. Under these circumstances, having less experience and less power in the situation (and often having more at stake: possible imprisonment or execution, large sums of money, ownership of land and other significant possessions) can be compounded by cultural differences between the regulars and the novices. Knowledge, experience, perspective, and opinion can all be either allowed or silenced by the rules of speaking in a courtroom. Silence when a spoken response is required can be interpreted as guilt, ignorance, or defiance, rather than as discomfort or inexperience with courtroom structures and their rules.

Silence is clearly a form of communication that is rich with meaning, as shown by the wealth of research just sketched. To move from the realm of silence as a relatively bounded, identifiable phenomenon (a pause may be timed, whether it lasts less than a second or more than a day) to consider the ineffable realm of the unsaid is an even more complicated matter. A social scientist would ask how a claim that something is unsaid, yet relevant to meaning, could be supported. There are some obvious, easy ways to make such claims: *Listen* for times when people say, "I really wish I'd told her she looked silly in that hat, but I just couldn't hurt her feelings." *Ask* people about those times: What moments do you remember in your friendship with X that you thought about saying something (critical, flirtatious, self-disclosive) and decided against it? Why did you decide not to say that, and what do you think would have happened if you had said it? *Watch* for evidence that something is left unsaid in social media texts: "Someone who shall remain nameless was spotted kissing a certain prominent member of Congress on the steps of the Capitol last night just past 11 p.m." "I am very grateful that, just this one time, I kept my mouth shut" (posted on Facebook).

However varied and intriguing the information that might be collected in those ways, they do not seem to get very far beyond what Hawthorne referred to as "those poor rags and tatters of Babel"—in other words, language itself. If there are larger, more complex, and thus more significant shapes, sizes, and meanings of that-which-is-left-unsaid, there need to be other, probably squishier, ways of finding them. I describe next some landmarks: aspects of language that allow for a wide range of information, emotion, evaluation, and other human dynamics to remain unsaid and yet, very often, be communicated clearly enough to affect people, events, and relationships. From those landmarks I propose a list of items for a scavenger hunt: As you read the essays and stories that follow, as you walk around in your own rich human life, what do you start to notice about communication by tuning in to what is left unsaid? What do you notice about how and when people leave meanings implicit, vague, or downright obscure? How often do they seem to be doing so intentionally, and what makes the implicitness seem intentional? How do people manage to continue their conversations and their relationships despite leaving so much unsaid?

Language use landmarks

A useful metaphor for pursuing the nature of the unsaid in communication comes from music, particularly jazz. In contrast to classical music, jazz is known more for musicians and their improvisations than for composers and their compositions. Jazz composers arrange chords—combinations of notes—into progressions and tunes, add rhythms and changes and repeats. Musicians work spontaneously with that basic structure: They play parts written for one instrument on a different one, make up new melodies on top of the original ones, create solos that are different every time they are played, change keys or beats, make short songs longer or long songs shorter. All of this creative spontaneity depends on what, and who, is already in place: the occasion, the audience, the other musicians and their talents, the improviser's own skills. To improvise, they have to know the original tune as well as how to work within it in ways that sound good, keep the band more or less together, and keep the audience—even when the audience is only the rest of the band—interested enough to stay with them.

Communication starts with a range of languages, media, and contextual resources at least as broad as those available to jazz musicians. Having one common language, for example, creates certain possibilities; having multiple languages, or none at all, creates others. Within every natural language there are mandatory and optional elements for a sensible utterance: In some, verbs or pronouns (I, me, you, they) may be left out of most sentences. In others, all nouns must be designated male or female. Every language provides at least a basic vocabulary for describing objects, ideas, actions, and people, as well as ways to expand or contract that original set. Languages are also structured to be flexible: words have synonyms to express different emotions, ideas, and desires. Observations may be expressed in multiple ways, and scenes and settings may be anchored to different poles of time, space, and the material world.

Language is, of course, only the beginning of resources that people use to communicate. Being able to see and hear other people, both those involved in the immediate communication event and others within range, creates some possibilities and closes off others. You may be comfortable screaming harsh rebukes at your partner or your child in private, but not in public. You may not be willing to do so in either case—a personality/communication style issue like an individual musician's personal style. If your interlocutor can see you, you may be able to wink, raise an eyebrow, or silently mouth words that would have some different effect if said aloud. Laughter, sobs, pats on the knee, facial expressions, even music—bursting into song or simply humming a few bars—are all part of the wide range of resources available to construct meaning.

I mention these variations and ranges of possibility not to suggest that anything is possible when it comes to humans' constructions of meaning. To the contrary, all of these resources for improvisation depend on a certain amount of pre-existing structure, much as jazz music is constructed out of a particular range of instruments, notes, chords, and tunes. The elements of communication that make improvisation possible are certain properties of language use that make it plastic: They make words and actions bendable, adaptable to different situations, people, and the wide variety of goals that motivate people to choose particular options from among an array of choices available to them. These plastic parts allow meaning to emerge in the spaces in between what is said, what is done, and what is in the end understood (or misunderstood).

Plastic parts: Polysemy, ambiguity, and strategic choice

I start with some quick definitions of these plastic parts, and then extend and illustrate them in examples drawn from literature.

Polysemy means many (*poly*) signs (*semy*), that is, meanings. The simple word *can* shows some of its multiple meanings here:

1. I *can* drive a car.
2. I'd like a *can* of soda.
3. He wasn't working very hard so I had to *can* him.

Polysemy applies to phrases, utterances, and sentences, as well as individual words: "Do I smell something?" might imply a request for information—do you smell it, too?—or it might be a hint that someone should take cookies out of the oven before they burn. One of the reasons Lewis Carroll's *Alice in Wonderland* is a classic in the English-speaking world is that the residents of Wonderland stretch polysemy in unexpected directions, confusing Alice, who comes from a more constrained, literal world:

> "When *I* use a word," Humpty Dumpty said in rather a scornful tone, "it means just what I choose it to mean—neither more nor less."
>
> "The question is," said Alice, "whether you *can* make words mean so many different things."
>
> "The question is," said Humpty Dumpty, "which is to be master—that's all."

> "I beg your pardon?" said Alice.
>
> "It isn't respectable to beg," said the King.

The early version of the novel[4] might have been called *Alice's Adventures in Polysemy,* to put a finger on one of the language-based reasons the story became a classic. On the other hand, the price to pay from such a title might have been too high for such precision.

Ambiguity is a more familiar idea than polysemy, and the two are related in a way useful to matters of the unsaid and unsayable. The only way people can hope to make sense of words and phrases that stretch to mean different things is that they are taught very early how to use contextual cues to know which of the possible meanings is most probable. They—we—are also taught to keep going even when we aren't completely sure what is going on in a sentence (listen for the next one, maybe it will clarify the ambiguous one), a conversation (think back to what came before, is there a clue to what this might mean?), or a relationship (we did have that fight last time we got together). At every level, people can look backwards, forwards, or to the side to clarify an ambiguous meaning. Many times, it's easier to just carry on as though we understood when in fact we do not, and we learn to do that, too. Without this tolerance for ambiguity, polysemy would be as unbearable to ordinary people in their everyday lives as Alice found it to be in Wonderland.

The final property of language use that makes it plastic is *strategy*. Sorting between possible meanings of words, searching for contextual cues that might highlight the most likely meaning of a phrase, carrying on in a conversation when you aren't sure you know what's going on, and all manner of other calculations of meaning that often need to happen in the moment clearly require more effort than a one-word-one-meaning system would. The effort is required from all participants[5] and presents a greater risk of misunderstanding than completely clear, straightforward speech would—if such a thing existed. To the extent that human beings are logical creatures, there must be a payoff for those efforts that, on average, makes them worthwhile. The payoff might simply be practical: Because no two people are exactly alike, no two conversations will ever be exactly alike, and we have to be able to combine known elements into forms that fit the situation at hand. The religious and philosophical traditions that focus on human agency raise far richer and more exciting realities: Human beings have, most of the time, at least some room to choose what they will do. Those choices all have risks and benefits, and the more sophisticated the human being, the better he or she gets at calculating what the possibilities for action are in any given situation and at using communication resources (as well as other kinds) strategically in order to minimize one and maximize the other.

To study, teach, or practice persuasion—and everyone who communicates does at least the last of those—is to experience the necessity for strategic choice. If I assume strangers on the street corner will tell me what time it is, I can simply ask them the time, without trying to persuade them to do so. If I want them to give me a dollar for a bus ride home because my purse was just stolen, I may feel a need to explain that circumstance to increase the chance that the dollar will be cheerfully given. If I want a ride to the airport an hour away, I cannot ask a stranger on a street corner; I have to ask a reasonably close friend or family member. If I want to borrow a car to drive to that same airport to pick up my illegitimate child from a premarital relationship that no one knows about, I will have to choose my target and my persuasive appeal even more carefully. In all but the first, ask-the-time instance, some degree of strategy is required for me to get what I need in the situation.

Polysemy, ambiguity and strategy underlie several communication phenomena that rely on humans' abilities to construct meaning from the unsaid. These phenomena can be noticed, in relatively concrete forms, in their natural habitats: hints and indirectness, secrets and lies, relational and cultural codes, and underneath it all the human condition of power imbalance and ideology. Rather than define and elaborate on those phenomena, this book offers narratives that show them in practice.

Plastic properties: Some concrete illustrations

Here I turn to literature to illustrate how the unsaid takes (relatively) concrete forms, before moving into the narratives I use to examine the means, meanings and consequences of leaving things unsaid. Literature offers a wider range of experiences than I can draw on or make up myself, edited into focused moments that make it easier to point out some key features of the unsaid that will be relevant later on.

Portrait 1: Sexual difficulty

Ian McEwan is a British novelist whose eye for human failings is so keen he has been nicknamed "Ian McAbre." Although *On Chesil Beach* (2007) may be the mildest, in terms of blood and death, of his *oeuvre*, it is a wrenching illustration of where unsayables come from and their power to undo the best of human intentions. The opening line previews everything the novel goes on to explore:

> They were young, educated, and both virgins on this, their wedding night, and they lived in a time when a conversation about sexual difficulties was plainly impossible. But it is never easy.

By page 2, the trouble has started—or perhaps started to become apparent:

> The couple had driven away ... and arrived in the early evening at their hotel on the Dorset coast in weather that was not perfect ... but entirely adequate: it was not raining, but nor was it quite warm enough, according to Florence, to eat outside on the terrace as they had hoped. Edward thought it was, but, polite to a fault, he would not think of contradicting her on such an evening.

It comes as no surprise when, several hours later, the couple find themselves at an impasse—not just ANY impasse, but one that will determine their futures, both individually and as a couple:

> Here was a boundless sensual freedom, theirs for the taking, even blessed by the vicar—*with my body I thee worship*—a dirty, joyous, bare-limbed freedom, which rose in his imagination like a vast airy cathedral ... It was so simple! Why weren't they up there now, instead of sitting here, bottled up with all the things they did not know how to say or dared not to do? (118–119)

Another virtue of fictional characters—or at least their creators and narrators—is that they are smarter than we are. They know in the crucial moment the answers to questions that the rest of us take lifetimes to identify, let alone get to the bottom of. Not that this cleverness always helps to solve the problem:

> And what stood in their way? Their personalities and pasts, their ignorance and fear, timidity, squeamishness, lack of entitlement or experience or easy manners, then the tail end of a religious prohibition, their Englishness and class, and history itself. Nothing much at all. (119)

Spoiler alert: In the way of fictional drama, it ends badly. The failure to consummate their marriage on the night culturally mandated for doing so overrides the couple's profound love for each other and their unusual compatibility. She goes back to her parents' home that night, and they never see or speak to each other again. They lead busy but empty lives and never love anyone again. The sexual oppression of the 1950s becomes the unfettered freedom of the 1960s, just 10 years too late for these star-crossed lovers to acquire a verbal and behavioral vocabulary that would have allowed them to connect with each other. The waste of good people's vibrant love for one another that met all but one of the cultural mandates of the day for an appropriate match, the subsequent impoverishment of their long lives, and the power of what they could not say to one another on that crucial evening come together in a melancholy ending.

The landmarks of the unsaid along the way are partly the author's, and partly the characters': "They were young, educated, and both virgins ... and they lived in a time when a conversation about sexual difficulties was plainly impossible." To join characteristics of the couple into a sentence that describes a time when a particular kind of conversation was impossible makes an implicit—unsaid—claim that the young people cannot have this conversation because of the time they live in. Or is it because they are young? Because they are educated? *Educated* in what sense, if they aren't able to have the one conversation that the future of their marriage apparently depends on? Is it because they are virgins? To the extent virginity is a physical state, why would it get in the way of a conversation, and what does the time they live in have to do with it? Polysemy and ambiguity are profoundly embedded in the opening line of the novel, as is another unspoken claim: The times (read: the cultures) people live in can make crucial conversations impossible. A loving couple blessed with the approval of their families, their religion, and their society may find out, after one evening of physical and interactional fumbling, that they cannot ever have the conversation that might have made for a much happier life together than the one they each led apart.

What is this horrible oppressive "time they live in" that made conversation about sexual difficulties "impossible" instead of merely "not easy?" Why wasn't their love and the apparent support of their society powerful enough to overcome it? The couple is British and the time is the mid-1950s, between World War II and the turbulence of the 1960s. The word "educated" hints at what is later made explicit: upper class. They couldn't talk about sex or, as we find out on page 2, simple differences of opinion like whether to sit outside for dinner, because conversations of both kinds fell outside of the rigid expectations that distinguished upper class people from everyone else. They were oppressed by their privilege, strange as it may seem; don't rich people have more power, thus more options and more fun?

Clearly not: When the moment comes that they might be soaring on the wings of sexual ecstasy, they find that they are weighed down partly by who they are as individuals and partly by "the tail end of a religious prohibition, their Englishness and class, and history itself. Nothing much at all." What they need to say to one another is unsayable due to the pressure from religion, culture (including upper-classness), and a history of leaving many things, small and large, unsaid. A personal or a national history? McEwan's story shows there is not much distance between those two levels of history, and that in the moment when the relationship goes wrong it doesn't matter which is the better explanation. Either way, the unsayable dooms their relationship.

That lack of daylight between the personal and the historical/cultural is what I would call *interpersonal ideology.*[6] Note that there are various levels of power imbalance woven together: The young couple are educated, that is, upper class, so they have economic power to be at a splendid seaside hotel being waited on hand and foot by local people working hard, and working late, to attend them on their honeymoon. The power of religion to condone some relationships and condemn others has made theirs legal, official, and good—and yet somehow is getting in the way of its sexual consummation and, thus, its survival. Their love and compatibility turns out to be far less sturdy than the weight of a culture and class position that declare most strong emotions, and all bodily matters, to be too undignified to be given voice.

Surely, there is something uplifting, positive, and happy to be gained by humans' ability to communicate without words! Louise Erdrich is an American novelist who writes as insightfully and poignantly—and often—about Native Americans as McEwan and other British writers do about class oppression. *The Last Report on the Miracles at Little No Horse* was a National Book Award finalist in 2001. It tells the story of a woman who, for complicated reasons, lives much of her adult life passing as a male Catholic priest. Halfway through the book, a young priest named Father Jude arrives to gather information from the woman-living-as-a-priest, Father Damien, about reports of miracles happening in the remote area of North Dakota where Father Damien lives. During their first conversation, Father Damien describes the community of nuns who support his work with the Lakota:

> "You know that tired old joke about hearing nuns' confessions, like getting stoned to death with popcorn? Not the case, not here. My sisters are robust women. Full of juice."
>
> "There have been scandals?" Father Jude asked (2001, 134).

Father Damien's reply is not yes or no, and several turns later Father Jude is still pressing him to be specific about what kind of nuns might be described as "robust" and "full of juice." In Father Jude's world—Fargo—

> "Certain norms of behavior are taken for granted. Right. Wrong. ... Black is black and white is white."
>
> "The mixture is gray."
>
> "There are no gray areas in my philosophy," said Father Jude.
>
> "I have never seen the truth," said Damien, "without crossing my eyes. Life is crazy."
>
> "Our job is to make it less so."

> "Our job is to understand it."
>
> "And in understanding"—Father Jude looked severely troubled—"to excuse immoral actions?"
>
> "Never those that hurt people."
>
> "Sex hurts," said Father Jude, simply.
>
> "Have you seen a doctor?" said Damien.
>
> The two paused, their breathing sharpened, surprised that they had so quickly fallen into such a pleasurable dispute. (135)

Damien's question to Father Jude relies on polysemy, specifically a play on the linguistic ambiguity of "sex hurts," and the potential for humor comes from the fact that he is asking a supposedly celibate priest. What might have sounded like a battle over the nature of right and wrong, and by extension an implication that Father Damien was not a very effective priest if he didn't know the difference, is a pleasant surprise for both of them: They are having a very nice time in this argument.

If all humans had at their disposal was literal, direct language use, communication would be all work and no fun. It would be perilous work for Father Damien if the only responses he could give to an outsider's question about scandals among the nuns were "no"—in which case it wouldn't be clear why an old joke about being "stoned to death with popcorn" didn't apply to them—or silence, likely to be taken as a guilty "yes." Instead, he gives an indirect response that hints at a range of behavior unacceptable to the Catholic church, yet, in its own cultural context, endearing and understandable. When Father Jude suggests that if the nuns are sexually active, there is no cultural context that can excuse their behavior, Damien responds with a straight-faced question about whether Father Jude is the one that is sexually active. The hints, the indirectness, polysemy in action—two somber people speaking of serious matters find they are enjoying their conversation and, in the process, building a friendship.

One final example highlights the strategic dimension of choices made about what to say, and what to leave unsaid, when a person's identity is complicated enough to make conversations dangerous, for them or for relationships that are important to them. Jeffrey Eugenides's novel, *Middlesex,* won the Pulitzer Prize in 2003. Its opening sentence, like the one that begins *On Chesil Beach,* suggests the whole story in a nutshell. For many readers, the first sentence makes them want to open up that nutshell and follow it backwards to the tree it grew on and the wind and rain and sunshine that grew the tree and the long line of trees that gave rise to the one the nut fell from—which is essentially what the novel then does.

> I was born twice: first, as a baby girl, on a remarkably smogless Detroit day in January of 1960; and then again, as a teenage boy, in an emergency room near Petoskey, Michigan, in August of 1974. (2003, 1)

The "rebirth" of the narrator, named Calliope in 1960 and later claiming the name Cal, happens at the point when the physical changes of puberty lead to his discovery of his sexual identity as a male rather than a female. Cal/liope is a hermaphrodite, born with both male and female external genitalia, although no uterus or ovaries. Raised as a treasured, cherished daughter until her teenage years, Calliope's first sexual attraction and experience are with a girl her own age. Treatment in an emergency room after an accident leads her mystified parents to take her to a specialist in psycho-hormonal disorders. Extensive physical examinations are accompanied by even more extended psychological assessments, during which Cal/liope conforms to the gender identity expected of a teenage girl despite his growing certainty that he is fundamentally a boy. He keeps his still-developing sexuality a secret by lying, saying he is attracted to boys and has even had sex with one. When the specialist observes feminine mannerisms, from how Cal sits and walks to how s/he talks, and adds this to Calliope's declarations of attraction to boys, he recommends surgery that will make the hermaphrodite genitalia unambiguously female.

This advice, which Cal's parents would presumably have welcomed as an affirmation of the lifelong understanding of their child as a girl, upsets Cal so profoundly that he leaves home to live on his own for several months. He leaves a note accusing the doctor of lying; he is not a girl but a boy. The one who lied to keep his troublesome, still somewhat unformed, identity a secret is Cal. Being unable, or not yet ready, to say how he really feels about who he is has much to do with the shock and disappointment he knows this will bring to his parents. His identity as a transgendered person also carries an enormous price in social stigma, one he is understandably hesitant to take on. Although he and his family eventually embrace his uniqueness and he works out a social identity that allows for a rich romantic and sexual life, years of concealment and a lifetime of linguistic ambiguity when he talks about his childhood are required to make that happiness possible.

Conclusion: Relational codes, cultural codes, and interpersonal ideology

All of the examples of the unsaid and unsayable I have discussed involve, most obviously, gender and sexuality. They also, more importantly for purposes of this book, revolve around identities and relationships. I focus attention in these directions to provide some central threads that I hope will tie the nonfiction essays and fiction stories that follow into at least a loosely connected package. So far, the package contains some ideas about sizes, shapes, and meanings of actual silence; some others about the ways humans make themselves understood even when much is left unsaid; and some broad strokes about the costs and payoffs of this complex set of phenomena. The British newlyweds paid dearly for their inability to speak of sexual matters; the priests had a fine, vigorous conversation with one another that avoided a possible disciplinary action against one who wasn't controlling the nuns' womanly urges; and Cal/liope left the specialist's office with his parents' happiness restored, if only for a few hours before he ran away into the New York City night.

A last scaffolding comment I feel a need to add is a substantial layer—or two layers, really—of consideration about why so much must be unsaid in human communication. Politeness theory, described earlier, focuses on the need to leave unsaid (or said indirectly, rather than clearly) that which might upset the interactional applecart of the moment: the criticism or admission of guilt that will stop tenderness in its tracks, the insistence on putting feelings into words that destroys a delicately balanced ambiguity needed for people to finish the business at hand. Politeness considerations, although specific to particular moments of communication, are grounded in systems of meaning that are partly historical sediment from past moments and also adapted, and sometimes reconstructed, in response to the moment at hand. On one level, that is the relational and interactional history of the people involved: They are newlyweds who don't talk about sensitive subjects, or ones about which they may disagree. They are recently acquainted colleagues exploring what they have in common, and how they are different, within the common framework of their role as Catholic priests. They are parents and an adolescent child, who after several harmonious years of respect and affection must deal with the child's troublesome sexuality.

On another level, no relational unit is ever quite as unique as the partners may feel. The second-generation Greek immigrants in *Middlesex* will not only need to find some way to understand and love a daughter who has declared herself a son, they will someday have to explain the matter to their extended family and tight-knit community. The newlyweds in *On Chesil Beach* have, in a real sense, been backed into an interactional/relational corner by their sexually repressive culture. Splitting up for good on their wedding night is something they will have to explain to members of their culture. Whatever we do or do not know about them as individuals, or about their culture, it should be obvious by now that the story they will tell is unlikely to reveal exactly what happened on that night.

The patterns of communication and meaning that form between relational partners can be thought of as relational codes: systems of rules, assumptions, and symbolism that evolve between people over the course of their relationship. Some elements of those codes are made explicit: "I could never marry outside my faith. I just couldn't do that to my family." Many others must be left unsaid. "I could never marry someone from a vastly different social class. My family would be so unhappy about that, and they would make sure we were unhappy, too." Speaking up versus staying silent often has significant relational consequences: Saying "I'm the one who ratted you out to the police" might end a friendship or sever family ties, and might be grounds for revenge, whereas keeping the secret—perhaps through vehement lying denials—could allow the relationship to remain intact. A child who is never told she was adopted as a baby may be spared the pain of knowing she was abandoned, or that her biological parents were killed. By not telling her, the adoptive parents also avoid questions from the child that might be uncomfortable for them to answer.

Relational codes are thus, to some extent, unique to the partners and their shared history: One family deals with an alcoholic member through an intervention followed by constant vigilance, another through working hard to pretend there is no problem with alcohol.[7] To a greater extent than is usually obvious to partners, however, relational codes are shaped by the cultural contexts in which the relationship goes on. A couple in which a US American woman is married to a Colombian man—as I describe in three of the nonfiction narratives in this book—has different options and constraints depending on whether they live in Bogotá, Houston, or, hypothetically, Dubai. Cultural codes are, similar to relational codes, historically transmitted and socially constructed systems of meaning. They involve larger groups of people and are thus less negotiable and slower to change—but change they do. The British newlyweds might well have been able to talk through their uncomfortable wedding night if they had only had that night in the mid-1960s rather than the mid-1950s. Although Cal/liope and his family might always have had some difficult conversations as his sexual orientation emerged, from the late 1990s on he could have found like-minded people on the internet to talk it through with first, before his family found out by accident.

Cultural codes constrain some aspects of personal relationships and enable many others. To some extent, the power of cultural codes depends on how much privacy a person, and thus his or her relationships, is able to have. In *The Last Report of the Miracles at Little No Horse,* Agnes DeWitt slips on the identity of a dead priest, Father Damien, as easily as his cassock because of a disastrous flood that leaves hundreds dead and, given conditions on the American frontier in the late 1800s, unaccounted for. She lives as a man for decades because as a priest she lives alone, with no one to notice that (for example) she is not actually shaving every morning. Cal/liope's unsteady sexual identity becomes an issue in an emergency room, when she is examined by a doctor who does not know her family and thus has nothing to lose from declaring openly what he sees. Identities and relational codes can only be different from the ones around them to the extent that they are either unobserved (partners in an open marriage might be careful never to go on dates in places where they might run into friends or family) or the people involved are willing to pay the social consequences of negative evaluation from the culture. Many US gays and lesbians know that coming out will mean loss of important friendships, family ties, perhaps their jobs and even their lives. They also know, however, that they will not be arrested for doing so, as would commonly happen in parts of the Arab world. Coming out may, on the other hand, strengthen many of the important ties in their lives and create new ones, as well as empower them.

I referred earlier to the enormous power of cultural codes to reward some relational actions and types and punish others as interpersonal ideology. I will not try to parse out cultural and relational codes and the power dynamics that shape them any further at this point.[8] In the narratives that follow, I encourage you to look for power and meaning in the particulars of what people do and do not say, especially with regard to their identities, their relationships, and their places in the social worlds they inhabit. I include some hints, in the form of questions and comments (reflections and expansions), at the end of each one. I hope that reading narratives with these concepts in mind can lead to being able to observe, describe, and interpret the social world around you through these lenses.

Reflections and expansions

1. A particularly useful review of literature from many areas of the social sciences that I drew on extensively for this chapter is Nakane's *Silence in Intercultural Communication* (John Benjamins, 2007). Earlier and also useful volumes include Jaworski's *Silence: Interdisciplinary Perspectives* (Mouton de Gruyter, 1997) and Tannen and Saville-Troike's *Perspectives on Silence* (Ablex, 1985).
2. What instances of language use, especially that which involves silence and the unsaid, can you collect that make the properties *polysemy, ambiguity,* and *strategy* clear and memorable tools for analysis?

Part I

Autoethnographic narratives

Transcribing the unsaid

It is not true that the person who is silent says nothing.

Apache proverb

Robert Hopper wore a navy beret stepping off the plane. We smiled across the lobby, and then he looked down, self-conscious, maybe expecting shock at his appearance. I hoped there was no sign of that, having seen his shiny bald head at a conference a few months earlier. He was tall and lanky and had thinning hair the whole time I knew him, so being completely bald and even thinner wasn't such an abrupt change as it might have been. The chemo erased even his eyebrows, though, a change I didn't get used to.

He usually did comfortable, lingering hugs, but this one was almost perfunctory. I didn't ask him "How ya doin'?"—a conventional greeting so mandatory that it goes by unnoticed most of the time. Then you notice it didn't happen, and know that not asking means, somehow, *please don't tell me how you're doing.*

We went straight from the airport to my undergraduate class at the University of Iowa for his first guest lecture, and shifted to talk about that task right away.

Transcribing Silence: Culture, Relationships, and Communication
by Kristine L. Muñoz, 47–61.

"So this is intercultural communication, and it's what, juniors and seniors?"

"Yep. We've covered the usual stuff, how cultural premises shape ideas of what's real in the world, lenses that we use to evaluate what's appropriate, bases for relationships, all of this hearable in communication practices, then shifted to specific communication practices—"

"Personal address." We grinned at each other; personal address was the starting place for much of my scholarly work. What it means about the person, and the relationship, when a teacher insists that his undergraduates call him by his first name, Robert, instead of Dr. Hopper, in a place like University of Texas where faculty are always addressed as Doctor. What it means about the person when, having been Bob all his adult life, at age 36 wants to go back to his childhood name of Robert. I never got used to calling or referring to him as Robert—Bob was hard enough, when I was 19—so after that he was always Hopper to me. Awkward enough that mostly I avoided all terms of address.

"And the commands and requests, and now of course we're on conversational practices, and that's where you come in."

"Got it. I have a video clip to start us off ..."

His voice was still so *him*, something the chemo and the surgery hadn't touched. I listened to the sounds more than the words, wanting to engrave every tone inside me where I could find and replay it whenever I needed him. The cornfields went by outside the window, still bare and brown in early April, and I wrapped his physical presence, less than an arm's length away, closely around me.

He left the beret on when we got to class; I was ashamed to be relieved.

I had been planning how to introduce him to the undergraduate class for weeks, thinking about it constantly as I swam or drove or chopped vegetables; it was a moment I had dreamed of for literally years. The students were squirmy about the papers they were writing, due the next week. The assignment was to tape record some naturally-occurring conversation, then transcribe a few minutes of it and make a claim about culture based on the transcript. Their questions about transcription tumbled on and on:

"What if I've concentrated mostly just on the first five lines or so and then skipped down past this other part that's kind of irrelevant and talked about the last maybe ten lines?"

"Put '10 lines omitted' or however many it was in brackets in between the parts that you did use."

"On the handout there's this category for downward intonation, but I don't see any symbol there; it looks like an empty box."

"Yeah, that didn't show up so well, it's supposed to be a period."

"So *all* punctuation is intonation, it isn't at the ends of sentences the way it would usually be?"

"Right."

"What are these numbers in parentheses again?"

"Pause length, measured by counting with the rhythm of the conversation, one thousand ONE, one thousand TWO ..." I hoped they couldn't hear my patience thinning in my voice; I was so eager to get to the introduction.

"I'm confused about these things to show when two people talk at the same time—"

"Brackets."

"Right, where do they go?"

"In between the lines, or you can put them in the middle of the line wherever it happens—what's up?" The students were smiling up past me. I turned around and Hopper was writing on the board, showing them where the brackets went. I finally paused to notice the moment: me impatient to say in words how important Hopper was to me and to the field of communication, when their serious questions about the assignment showed him that I was, after all, teaching them to pay careful attention to ordinary conversation. Their questions showed them struggling to get transcribing right, engaged with how hard it was to do that instead of dismissing the whole effort as silly: "What does it *matter* if someone is saying heeheehee or Hahaheeha, or how long the pause is between this utterance and that one?" Hopper was hearing in their questions his own meticulous attention to tiny details of everyday talk, hearing his passion for those details coming from students at another institution far from the one that he taught at for 27 years. I met him in 1978, his seventh year at UT.

Robert Hopper taught me to transcribe.

Conversation analysis is a discipline viewed as arcane even by many academics who make their living studying things no one else pays much attention to. Its data are often the most mundane conversations imaginable: Family dinner table conversation, dominated by talk about table manners and homework, is a huge favorite. The analysts who do it listen to audio tapes, and watch video recordings, in tiny moment-by-moment increments. They focus hours of attention, sometimes spread over weeks or months, on exchanges that took only a few seconds or a minute in real time, that almost always went by completely unnoticed by the people involved. Transcribing the words is the easy part, sometimes almost incidental to everything that follows that first step: intonation, pauses, inbreaths, overlaps between one speaker and another. Instead of asking, "What does this mean?" conversation analysts begin with questions like "What are these people doing? How are they getting it done?" The questions stay away from *why* are they doing it, on the assumption that we can never know any of those matters. All we can know is what they did, and how, and what happened next, and next.

It isn't easy to make such work sound like something you would get excited about, but everyone has experienced the power of just those tiny details of talk. We know on some level—and this is true of speakers of every known language—that silence, even micropause silence, is deeply meaningful. It isn't easy to teach people to transcribe conversations, partly because the technical details are numerous and difficult to master. The quality of the recordings you generally work from isn't what you hear on television, or even over the telephone; the symbols that show precisely on a printed page what happened in a spoken and visual world are complicated. Worse than that, when you get people to listen to what *is* said so closely (while keeping them away from ideas about what people are "feeling" or "thinking" or what they "meant to say"), they become uncomfortable and self-conscious about their own messy talk. Poring over a half-second pause for hours takes you inexorably into the biggest, most important things we ever communicate, with or without words. I became haunted by the many ways to interpret those pauses, and what they might be leaving unsaid: Did you hesitate to say you loved me because you thought it was irrelevant or perilous to say that? Because you forgot, because you knew it went without saying? Or because you never loved me?

At last the questions from my class petered out, and I launched into the introduction I had dreamed for years of giving:

"By now you folks know I love to tell stories. Twenty years ago this very semester I was a sophomore in college, and my boyfriend at the time, whose name was Jim Bob, offered to introduce me to Robert Hopper, a connection that (as you see) is still very much in place to this day. Jim Bob was out of the picture about a week later." The students giggled. "Hopper is, for better or worse, the reason I went into university teaching, so you have him to either thank or blame for your experience in this class."

"Twenty years is a long time to learn from someone. There was a group of faculty and graduate students back then who got together most Saturday mornings to play basketball on a half court in one guy's back yard. I was the only female among these weekend athletes, and I noticed, after awhile, a pattern in the humor: Every single week, at least once, when we were dividing up teams, someone would say "shirts and skins" and someone else would chime in "Kristine's on the skins." The students wince, knowing this is not entirely funny, wiser than I was at their age.

"Funny thing is I don't remember who was making these jokes, but I do remember very clearly who it wasn't. Robert Hopper has trained us all to hear the subtleties of language use that construct and reinforce gender roles, and it's very exciting to have him here to share some of that with us today."

It seemed wholly inadequate. I sat down drenched in sweat, and heard nothing he said for the first 20 minutes. It dawned on me, as the class went on and the sweat dried, that Hopper knew I loved him, and that on some level I knew he thought I was plenty smart. Planning the introduction so meticulously made me feel guilty to have gotten so fixated on explicitness—that nothing counts if it's between the lines, that you can't believe in people picking up on things without them being said. Words are, after all, just a small part of what people say when they talk to, and about, each other. There is meaning in silence, and in knowing someone for 20 years. It *is* nice to have occasions where you can put things into words, and it *is* a shame if someone drifts around or out of your life with no way of knowing that they were special to you, but you have to give people some credit for being able to pick that up some way other than in words.

Was it in learning to transcribe that I started to insist on saying things out loud?

Hopper taught me to be a feminist.

I was no good at basketball, or at any sport for that matter, but I was deeply interested in being part of that Saturday morning social scene. Graduate school was so different that way: faculty and students went out for beers, got together and played guitars and sang, played basketball. Hopper assured me it didn't matter that I wasn't any good, most of the others weren't either (which I saw for myself when I went to play). I'd never been the only woman in a group before, and I watched and listened intently to figure out how to behave. I knew some of the others weren't happy to have me there, and I finally asked Hopper if it was really OK.

"You do not need to ask permission," he said evenly, and then his eyes crinkled a little. "It's my basketball." He and Rod Hart, the faculty member whose backyard had the half court, showed me a one-handed push shot, some zone defense, an eye fake. I learned how to throw elbows, how to get in the way when someone broke for the basket, how to shove with my hip and shoulder. I learned that men talk about, for example, where to buy slacks in a very particular shade of charcoal.

There was so much for me to learn to be a graduate student, too. Hopper crossed out the word "girl" in one of my papers—a reference to myself, or a female my age—and put "woman." I never wrote *girl* again (I still struggle gently with the current undergraduates, who hang on to "girl" more fiercely). At the end of one of my term papers for his course, after corrections on style, structure of the argument, content, he commented on my "classroom presence": "Too much fooling around in class," he said. "No more rookie stuff—if you don't take yourself seriously as a scholar no one else will, either. *No more rookie stuff!*"

I was crushed; I thought I'd found my stride in these very intimidating seminar discussions surrounded by people so much older and smarter than I was. It escaped my notice (this is embarrassing) that most of my cohort were men, in class as much as on the basketball court. For years I was convinced that any success I had in academia came about because of people like Hopper who for some reason liked me. I started to notice once in awhile, though, that I had made a slam dunk, even though he was nowhere around for the assist.

Although it is almost irresistible to find poignancy in every first and last event—the first time I fixed him dinner, the last time he saw my children—the night he came to our house felt completely ordinary, something we might have done a dozen times before. The ordinariness was the best part.

"Do you remember meeting a friend of mine named Robert Hopper?" I asked them a week before he came.

"N—no." Erica was almost nine.

"We were in Austin for Phyliss's wedding; do you remember being in that wedding?"

"No." Gabe was 11, and definite in all things.

"Yes."

"Remember you wore that pretty dress Grandma made you?"

"I remember the dress, I don't remember the wedding."

"I remember I had to wear little short pants that looked really dumb."

"Yeah, well, at the time you insisted you didn't mind. Anyway we were in Austin for her wedding, and we stayed at a hotel"

"I REMEMBER THAT! There was a POOL!" They connected instantly to the real importance of the event: a hotel with a pool.

"We came out into the lobby and this very tall man sat on the floor to talk to you for just a couple of minutes, and after that Grandma came out and took charge of you while I went out to breakfast with him. That was Robert Hopper and he's a really important person in my life, and he's coming to your birthday dinner, Erica."

"YaaaaHOOOOOO!" Somehow this buildup made the birthday dinner at home an appropriate marking of the event for her. Gabe would have insisted we eat out, but this did not occur to Erica. I had toyed with the idea of all of us going out—wouldn't that be easier since we were coming straight from the graduate class?—but I wanted Hopper to come here, I wanted to have something be simple and non-public. Ordinary.

"You will notice that he has been sick, he looks like someone who's been sick. You shouldn't worry about that; it's nothing you can catch, and he loves children and is looking forward to seeing you again." Jairo, my husband, pointed out later that I never told them what he was sick with. Cancer is something they are familiar with; two of my aunts died of lung cancer. The children became vehement anti-smokers, but I didn't think it had made them afraid.

"I thought maybe you had done that on purpose," Jairo said.

"I don't know why I didn't say that; I didn't *avoid* telling them."

Sometimes the unsaid is not unsayable but just overlooked, forgotten, or deemed irrelevant.

Hopper helped Erica get a computer game up and running while I fixed dinner. I heard them giggle together in the study, a deep mysterious pleasure for me. That time in Austin, before the wedding of the short pants and Grandma-made dress, in the lobby of the Ramada Inn with the POOL, I came out to introduce them to him. They were three and five, Gabe tough and cool even then and Erica in a stage of deep shyness around strangers, particularly men. The minute Hopper saw them he sat on the floor, and within three sentences she was sitting on his lap and Gabe was draped around his shoulders. They knew right away that this was a man who loved, adored, and was fascinated by children; some of his earliest, best research was on children's speech, which he always took very seriously. My mother came out to meet him and to take charge of the kids. The two of them talked over our heads.

"You must be really proud of this daughter of yours," he said.

"Oh yes, we are, and you've been so important to her along the way."

"Well she is really something special." All the things I wanted so much to hear from both of them, the ones that neither had ever put into words to me, could somehow be said about me, to one another, complete strangers in a hotel lobby. It seemed odd and it was unforgettable, a pearl for my lifestring.

There was one more time during that visit when I tried, perhaps foolishly, to put the unsayable into words. It started when I pulled up in front of the hotel to drop Hopper off after the birthday dinner.

"So a question I've always wanted to ask you is, where in your constant practice of transcribing conversation, of finding meaning in microdetails of everyday talk, where do you locate all the stuff that words can't encompass, all of the things that in the long run may be better off left unsaid, like how much you've meant to my life?"

(3.5)

He responded to it as a real question.

"Would you like to come upstairs for awhile, or sit in the lobby and talk? I need to get out of these clothes into something more comfortable."

"I'll park the car and be up in ten minutes." I called Jairo from the pay phone in the lobby. It was past ten; he was asleep. "I'll be a little while longer."

"Are you OK?"

"I'm good. We're dealing with life and death and people being important to you."

"Gooooood. Be careful."

"I will. I'm OK; I just had a couple glasses of wine." Well, three.

"See you soon."

I went upstairs, and we talked until 3 a.m., having found at last the hours to say everything that needed saying, swapping the most secret stories we had. He told me about his family and his childhood; I had never felt we were close enough to ask about the details. I cherished the mundanity of the stories—the times he and three or four of his seven siblings went to the grocery store with their father, who bought two loaves of Wonder Bread, and one of them was eaten before they got home. How he hid out at his oldest sister June's apartment after she was married, liking the feeling of being part of the adult world. It felt like we were sitting around a campfire going back and forth between stories and singing, but for once I didn't have to share him, and I didn't interrupt—much—with stories of my own. I wanted to hear ALL of them; I loved the tiny details: His stories showed parts of what it was like to be HIM, a man, a scholar, a sixth child.

We talked about friendship, and about transitions from being someone's mentor to being someone's friend. The awe I had for him in the beginning was a very large mountain to climb, despite plentiful encouragement from him to do so. It took a lot of years and a lot of false starts and a lot of switching modes of transportation, from elephants to pack mules to, finally, a gondola. The gondola that inched me over the summit was an article he invited me to write for a special issue of a journal the year after I finished my doctorate. I was grateful for the invitation and eager, as usual, to pass muster. It would be my first publication after grad school.

I produced a draft and sent it to him. He sent it back for revision with several suggestions, most of them helpful and reasonable. We differed over the use of the word "ritual," key to the analysis in the article. I argued as sweetforceably as I could for the definition I started with. Hopper responded, arguing for his own definition of ritual and asking me to use another term—canonical sequence or something. I demurred. He remained unconvinced but agreed to disagree, and it was published as ritual. I hadn't wrangled with an editor before, to know how common such differences of opinion were, nor how much bloodier and less productive they could be. It felt like a tense struggle that left coolness in its wake, and I worried a little that we'd never be Close again. At the same time, I wanted to dance around my office with my arms in the air, humming the Rocky theme. I was a grownup! I had arm wrestled The Champ and come out on top! He let me win, of course; but something important had shifted in my opinion of him, and of me. I would always respect him, always want to please him, always think he knew more than almost anybody about certain things. But I would not ever again believe that when we disagreed, he was always right and I was always wrong.

He taught me, and others of his students, how to lose someone you can't imagine living without.

On the way back to the airport, rain.

A big truck ahead of us, swaying a little from the high speed and the wind.

Tears.

"See, all along this pastor at our church has reminded me of you, he's tall and athletic and he has a beard, and he's musically gifted, he plays the guitar and sings beautifully, and he touches so many different people. He and I can talk about inclusive language," though we hadn't, and it was a conversation I really did mean to have with him someday. "He can talk to the kids during the service and the little old ladies, and he just makes everyone feel completely welcome and special, and he reminds me of you." Were the truck, the rain, the tears making Hopper think of his mortality in more immediate terms right now?

A strong hand, gentle on my knee, made me think tears were OK even behind the wheel in the rain, though for all I know he heartily wished he were driving just then. I gripped the hand hard with my left, keeping the right one on the wheel, slowing a little to widen the distance from the truck.

"Since you've been sick I've felt like he was someone I could talk to when I needed ... when things were ...

(5.4)

"I've found him easy to talk to, and as usual he knows just the right things to say."

(6.8)

Better not try to re-create what those were, but the pastor's deep voice is in my ears: "It's hard to face losing someone that you feel has protected you from growing up," he said one wintry day as we sat in his office watching the snow fall and I used up most of the box of Kleenexes. "As long as they are there, you feel you have a light to follow, and if they're gone, then it's up to *you* to be the light, and you never feel like you're up to the task." I remembered Robert's song about his father—

Now kids look up at me and smile and lie.
I ask them can't they please go play outside.
They ask to look at pictures from back when.
They look like I look ten feet tall to them.

4 lines deleted

A father is to son as big to small.
It's hard to get to know the man at all.

"Briefcase with Initials," Robert Hopper, 1977/87

"Well, so in one of these conversations I had with this pastor I talked about
(2.0)
the difficulty of feeling there's nothing I can do, there hasn't been—"

"Kay said to tell you that the plant you sent has grown up large and lovely and it's thriving, and she's told at least five or six people you are the only one in all this time who thought to send something to *her.*"

So there *was* something I could do, and did, and it helped.

Misted smile—"Good, I'm glad she liked it" Just words again, so inadequate.

"There's been so little I could do, send you some tea or a CD once in awhile, and what this pastor said was, well, something else will come to you. He never mentioned this possibility but one day it did come to me, that the playground there at the church, they're forever doing fundraisers for it. I could make donations to that playground because kids are one of the strong associations I have of you, my kids of course, but kids more generally, so I've made contributions like that, and it's something I can keep on doing because they want it to grow and grow until it fills up that space and
(3.2)
that way you're there."

I looked for ways to have him with me always. There is a paper copy of an e-mail from him, a small ordinary one that turned out to be the last one he ever sent me. It lives in my billfold and turns up at unexpected times, when I'm searching for my driver's license or an insurance card, and I warm my hands on it. There is a picture on the desk behind me, of him with his first grandson—the only one he got to meet—reading over my shoulder as I write this. There are, maybe most vivid of all, the connections to other people whose lives he touched—the former students, the colleagues, Kay Hopper. I see them at conferences, I visit Kay in Austin, and his name always comes up; he does indeed live on in our stories and in our scholarly work. When Robert died, later that year after his visit to Iowa City, I felt a grief beyond words, but I never for a moment felt alone.

We did survive the rainy trip to the airport, and the sun came out as we sat in the glassed-in concourse. We talked about credit cards, the ones that charged fees but gave you frequent flyer miles for every purchase versus the ones that would let you shift a balance for free. He had a good story about canceling one when the terms of service changed, and I swung comfortably with the ordinariness of it. Everything Big had been said already, and this was a tiny everyday intimacy that felt lush and supple, a connection to last forever. There was no need to tell Hopper I would treasure the everydayness of that story, nor count up the poignant moments of the week. It was all right there, in the pauses and the inbreaths and the glances and the hand movements, as hearable as guitar music around a campfire, as forever as life and death. The flight was called and we hugged, almost casually; he waved over his shoulder and smiled, the beret at a jaunty angle as he walked down the jetway.

Reflections and expansions

1. One difference between a terminal illness and a sudden, unexpected death is that there is time to say things that have been left unsaid. Not everyone is able to say what they need to or might want to, of course, and there is always the risk of saying things that would have been better left unsaid. A large category of decision making in this area is when, and whether, to say out loud that the person is dying when everyone, on some level, knows they are. What makes this a particularly awkward balance between silence and talk? Can you imagine a conversational slot—a topic already under discussion, for example—that would lead more or less naturally to breaking the silence and acknowledging the fact of approaching death?

2. A question I am frequently asked when I write narratives that use peoples' real names and circumstances is whether those people read the story, and if they did, how they reacted. Robert Hopper did read an earlier version of this one and said he was fascinated to see himself from another person's perspective: "sort of like looking at pictures and saying, is that what I look like?" Kay Hopper has read various versions, and claimed to be pleased with each of them. Is there anyone else in this narrative you think I should have had read it before it was published?

Forbidden love

The moment it happened was an October Saturday, autumn in Central Texas too subtle for those raised in four seasons to appreciate, but the sky is so blue and the breeze so fresh and the smell of cedars so rich you can't believe you'll ever want to live anywhere else. The University of Texas, where I was a freshman, was playing Arkansas, a nationally-televised and hugely important arch rivalry. Those of us who couldn't drive to Little Rock for the game had popcorn and Oreos and a six pack or two of Lone Star on hand—the drinking age was 18 then and you could, as I recall, have alcohol in the dorms—and our RA had connected her TV in the lounge at the end of the hallway.

I lived in room 111 Kinsolving, first door off the lobby on the communal bath side, 50 yards from the TV and the crowd. My roommate Leslie had gone to the game with her sorority. We each had a desk, a bed that you pulled out from the wall about a foot to sleep on and shoved in during the day so it seemed like a sofa, and one side of a closet. I had a paper due on *Huckleberry Finn* the next

---

Transcribing Silence: Culture, Relationships, and Communication
by Kristine L. Muñoz, 62–72.

week and was determined to get a start on it before the game. It was my first semester in college, and the paper was assigned for a class called The American Experience, a nine credit course with 732 students enrolled (almost exactly the number of students in the high school I'd graduated from a few months earlier), three professors, and probably 20 TA's who led discussion sections. The course combined English, Government, and History classes into one big, interdependent survey of the 20th century. I loved everything about that class, starting with the cavernous room full of unfamiliar faces. For a teacher's kid from a small town, anonymity was a sparkling dose of utter freedom. The professors were among the best I ever had, smart and engaging and witty, and that class was *hard*. None of the busy work that constituted most of my high school experience, a hundred pages or more to read every week. This paper was supposed to talk about imagery or symbolism or metaphor or something like that, and as I started to outline it I had little sense of how to get anything out of *Huckleberry Finn* apart from the child abuse and the swearing.

This was long before I could compose on a keyboard, so I was writing the paper in longhand, knowing I'd need to leave time to type it on the typewriter I got for graduation. (Typing here on my laptop it seems almost impossible I ever wrote anything that way, and my writing hand hurts just thinking about it.) I had *Huck* in front of me, class notes about literary devices, an assignment sheet. Bleah. An hour till game time. I promised myself a Lone Star beer if I could just get through a thesis sentence, and sighed deeply at the injustice of being inside on such a beautiful day, in my room instead of down the hall where the first round of popcorn was already disappearing from the bowl.

The Mississippi River is often discussed as a character in that and other Mark Twain works, so whatever I wrote that day (30 years later all I can retrieve is that it was about the river) was hardly the most original word on the topic. Something shimmered that morning, though, something that wasn't Central Texas crystal clear air scented with cedars or a pile of women laughing around a TV or burnt-orange hats and Cadillacs. It wasn't even the gleaming trombones waving precisely up and down through "Texas Fight," a sight and sound that to this day brings me to my emotional knees. It was seeing something in a story that wasn't there the first time I read it. I was an avid reader, almost always novels, that before that day had only been stories to me—good ones, mediocre ones, all of them precious to some degree just because they were stories.

This time, though, the story had a character that *wasn't a person*. Figuring that out, wrapping my mind around this weird and somehow completely sensible idea, was a transformational moment. The crystal blue day disappeared, the voices and laughter and music that had been pulling me down the hall became a distant murmur, there was nothing but me and *Huck* and a pencil and some loose-leaf lined paper. I could feel my heart beating hard, my eyes focusing so intently on the page they seemed locked into place. Some part of me stood aside and pointed at the person hunched over the desk and snickered: Look at what a NERD she is, stoned on an idea, a series of thoughts, a string of words.

Being stoned was a state I was more than familiar with, there in 1970s Austin, and this was delightfully like the best of those times. *Zooming* is how it feels, when your mind and your body melt together, though you didn't notice until then they were separate, and noticing that you DID think they were separate becomes an absorbing thought all on its own. You can feel very smart when you're stoned. Sitting there in my dorm room that day I'm sure I didn't feel smart; the territory was too unfamiliar, I was deeply uncertain that anything I was saying actually made any sense. But I couldn't take my eyes off the page my hand was moving across, except to grab up *Huckleberry Finn* and gulp down page after page, looking for pieces related to the picture I was drawing.

When the girls yelled down the hall that the game was starting, I all but groaned. Couldn't it wait till I ran out of this very heady and unexpected steam? I trudged down to sing "The Eyes of Texas" and the fight song and watched the kickoff, my hand itchy to have the pencil in it again. A sentence started to form in my mind—a better way to phrase the thesis statement, a third item for the preview—

"I'll be right back." I meant to just write down that sentence and come back to watching the game. I had more than earned that Lone Star and had all of the next afternoon blocked out to finish writing the paper. I sat down, scratched out a few words, wrote in the ones that had cut through the hazy inattention at the end of the hallway.

That's when it happened, and I could not have been more stunned if the Virgin Mary had appeared sitting on a lawn chair outside my window: I was much more interested in writing my paper on *Huck Finn* than I was in watching *Texas play Arkansas*. Imagine that a man goes to his closet to pick out a tie and realizes he's a woman; imagine a horse looks into her trough and realizes she is a swan. The idea that an intellectual task could be more appealing than the orgy of identity that is a college football game was exactly that strange and impossible to me, but somehow it was happening.

The murmur from down the hall grew to a roar when Texas scored to tie the game (it had been very quiet while Arkansas was in the lead). I tossed the pencil aside but literally caressed the page I was writing, and ran down to see the instant replay.

"Tina,[1] what are you *doing* down there?" My hallmates were dumbfounded to notice I'd been gone almost the entire first half. "Damned paper I have to write," I said and didn't look at them. It was very weird to be working during the football game, somehow shameful. I was not ready to be weird, or shamed.

Five minutes later I was back at my desk, looking up a word in the thesaurus. I cared about sentences in a brand new way: For the first time, they were carrying precious cargo. I heard the fight song as the half ended, the buzz of excited voices. I got up and all but tiptoed to the door, and very softly, surreptitiously, as though I were about to shoot up heroin or have sex, locked it shut.

Two months later, the multicolored fall turned to brown and gray winter, I took the final exam for that class. It was a long, exhausting essay test, as difficult as the whole course had been. Once again, it was as exhilarating as it was tiring: There was so much to say, the questions were open doors beckoning me inside a fabulous castle. After the exam all 732 of us crowded around the TA's in charge of our discussion sections and waited to get back our graded papers. The weary elation of finishing the exam, and with it my first semester as a college student, turned to terror as I stood with my group. What if all that fun during the football game was an illusion? What if the horse was really a bedbug instead of a swan?

My TA's name was Art Miller, and he had the lugubrious face appropriate for a graduate student in English. He called out names in his humorless voice—"Jenkins. Watson. Diehl. Robertson." My palms dampened as my peers looked at their grades, some of them grunting at what they saw, and a few of them blinking back tears. Oh, God, this could be bad. This could be very bad. Ron Diehl was the star in that class, and I could see a C- over Art's shoulder.

"Fitch." Art gave me a long look as he held out my paper, and I thought I saw pity in his gaze. "This is." He paused, and the world really did stop turning. "The best paper on Mark Twain. I have ever read from an undergraduate. Nice work." The A+ on the front page seemed to glow, fluorescent, neon, somehow projected on the ceiling. I felt my classmates' heads turn toward me, and Art's words were both the loveliest I'd ever heard and the most embarrassing. I took my paper and stuffed it in my notebook like it didn't matter, mumbling Thanks, and turned to walk away, practically holding my cheeks with my hands to stop from beaming until I got outside.

I fell in love that semester, and obviously I would like to describe the object of my adoration as Learning: I fell in love with Learning. The hours that went by before I stopped smiling—and the fact that I can repeat Art's words verbatim 35 years after they were uttered —points to a different possibility, which is that some part of falling in love with Learning was in fact a deep love for public praise attendant upon those efforts. No matter. I could not possibly have said, after one semester at Texas, that I had found my life's work in academia, specifically at large state institutions where the football team is more important to most students than Mark Twain or metaphors will ever be. When someone asks how I got into university teaching as a profession, though, I answer that I loved college so much I never left. They laugh as though I must be kidding, and I remember that football game I didn't watch and Art Miller's long, somber face as he held out my paper to me, and I know it's true.

That flip answer, and the easy laugh that it draws, were hard to get to. When adults asked me what I wanted to be when I grew up, my answer was "a cowboy." Later I read a biography of Louisa May Alcott, and said "an author" a few times. I could never muster the voice of authority for that one as I did for a cowboy, which was so easy when I loved Roy Rogers and lived for *Bonanza*. I said "an author" more timidly and waited for the humor-her patronizing looks, which probably came from the fact that no one who asked me recognized that as a profession. You might just as well say "I will be someone who counts flowers on wallpaper." Soon I quit saying I wanted to be an author, and looked for a response that would be easier for people to understand.

Journalism was the only writing my high school offered, and I liked it well enough, and then I had an answer that was easy for people to understand. The truth is I knew I was not going to be a journalist, not after Careers Day when a working journalist came to talk to us and said he earned $7,000 a year, even then a salary well below the poverty line. Not after the segment on the evening news when an eight year old girl who had seen her best friend gunned down in a completely random drive-by shooting as they walked home together from school had cameras shoved in her face, and *a journalist* held out a microphone and asked her how it felt to see her best friend bleeding to death on the sidewalk. The people with the mikes and cameras were surely bringing home more than any $7,000 a year, but I knew at that moment that asking people questions at the absolute worst moments of their lives was not work I would do for any price.

When I fell in love with learning at UT, it was a secret lover for a very long time. I had no experience being good at school or even interested in it, so the identity was completely foreign to me. I was not in the category of *the smart people*, a group that starred my older brother and included my three best friends but did not come any closer to me. Another barrier was the disdain for intellectuals—nerds in high school, brainiacs in college, geeks on television, ivory tower eccentrics in adult life—that permeates American culture. That disdain and the incomprehension that goes with it may have been more pronounced in South Texas small towns in the 60s and 70s than they were even 30 miles away in Houston, where my cousins grew up and one of them went to Yale. Was it because I was a girl? A second child?

All I knew was that staying in college forever was a wild idea, at best. I am intrigued by how academics take that particular road; I have only met one who said his only career ambition was to be a university professor. Not at all coincidentally, his father and grandfather were both academic superstars, and his son is now an ace graduate student at Harvard. Everyone else I have asked had quite different plans, or no particular plan aside from avoiding the draft during the Vietnam era, and can describe a process of drifting into it. I doubt very much that I was the only one who fell secretly in love, but that isn't something you can *say*.

Robert Hopper, as I explained in the previous narrative, played a key role in showing me there might be a road into academia I could hope to get on. Saying it out loud to my friends and family, particularly those who did not go to college, "I am going to graduate school, and I plan to get a PhD," sounds like avoiding work, not preparing for it. If you're sitting still, how can it be work? If you come in to the office at noon and leave at four, and some weekdays you don't go in at all, how can that be something people will pay you to do?

Both of my parents had college degrees, and my father was a junior high school teacher, so this should have been easier to explain to them. It wasn't. When I told them, during my last semester of senior year, that I was staying at Texas for a master's degree, my father looked away in embarrassment, and my mother's face sagged, somewhere between despair and anger. "Why don't you get a *job*?"

she hissed. "What are you *afraid* of?" Why couldn't I say to her, "Mom, I'm not afraid, I'm in love?"

By then there was another side to this. Two years after falling in love with learning on that magical day in Austin in October of 1976, I fell in love with teaching, an even more profound and lasting epiphanal moment.

It was an accident. I associated teaching with the suffering my father did in a junior high school, facing defiant students that made fun of him and enduring a complete lack of support from the school administration. After my year abroad in Spain, I came back to Austin with a year to go to finish my undergraduate degree. I registered for a class called International Communication, reasoning that I was interested in all things international and needed several more hours in communication. On the first day, the professor called the roll, and all the names but mine were Rodriguez, Al-Hassan, Wu Jingha, Cleochon Numtip ... I shrank down further in my seat with each passing letter of the alphabet. When he called "Kristine Fitch," I said, "I think I'm in the wrong class," and started to gather myself to leave. "No, stay here, talk to me after class," he said.

He was Joe Neal, director of the international office at Texas for many years and, by the time I met him, at least a hundred years old. He was a Lyndon Johnson good-ol'-boy kind of guy who played a more pivotal role in my life than he ever knew. After calling roll he described the course, a combination of public speaking and intercultural communication required of international teaching assistants. Although the international TA's had passed all the English language tests to be allowed in the classroom, the State of Texas believed they needed further instruction in college teaching (why they didn't realize that we American TA's needed more instruction in teaching than we got was not explained). The class was primarily discussion sections, where American TA's met with groups of 12–15 international students for practice presentations and some information about the expectations of US undergraduates. When I met with Joe Neal after class, deeply sheepish about having signed up for a class aimed at international graduate students, he said that he was short a TA. "You can't *take* this class for credit but you could *teach* it," he told me. He introduced me to the other TA's, both master's students (one of whom looked distinctly irritated that some *undergraduate* was taking on part of her job) and said they would tell me what to do. No sweat. I thought he was crazy to put a 21-year-old girl—as I described myself then—in charge of a group of much older international graduate students, but I needed an upper division communication course, and this one fit my schedule. I wasn't about to say no.

That first week of class, we went through the syllabus, explained the first speaking assignment, introduced ourselves. The students were fascinating and came from—in my limited understanding of the world—absolutely everywhere. "Everywhere" was mostly South America and Western Europe in those days, with a few Middle Easterners, but I was agog to be meeting such interesting and varied people. At the end of class that week three or four came up to ask me questions: Where's the library? Is the plural of syllabus sylla*buses*? Is it OK if my first speech is about an internal combustion engine? To my amazement, I knew the answers to every single question. As the last one walked out the door, a thought came to me with the clarity of a neon sign: *I LOVE THIS.* I loved people asking me questions and knowing the answers. I loved feeling that I could lead people through an experience—in this case, practice presentations—that might make their lives better. I loved that the people in that class were so different from me and seemed to believe I could teach them something.

I did not stand there in that classroom and say, *this is it, I'm going to teach college the rest of my life.* I couldn't imagine that, wouldn't have believed it. From where I stood, college teaching seemed as unimaginable (and every bit as complicated) as brain surgery or space travel. I did feel, for the second time in four years, that I had fallen deeply and irrevocably in love.

Why couldn't I say that to my family, then, when they asked *what are you afraid of?* When I ran into people from high school and told them that I was going to graduate school, why did I shrug and say *beats looking for a job,* thus confirming the idea that that's why people go into academia?

Maybe confessing that I was deeply in love was too intimate and private. Maybe it seemed presumptuous: Don't you have to be Smart to be a college professor? Are you claiming you ARE smart, or do you think you can fake your way through this? Wasn't this like an actor saying after a bit part in the school play that her career ambition was to win an Oscar?

Decades later, I know that college teaching has much less in common with being an astronaut or an Oscar winner than with being, say, a plumber. The world will always need plumbers, and some people take up plumbing and find out they're no good at it, and some people find out they have a knack for it and enjoy doing it. Success, and the pretty good money you can make, keeps them in the plumbing business. I know my family and friends would have looked at me just as oddly if I'd said to them back then that I was going to be a plumber. The difference, judging from my failures in anything that requires hand/eye coordination, is that I would not have fallen in love with plumbing and would not have been any good at it, and thus would not have stuck with it.

I am conscious just about every day of my life (OK, a little less so during finals week) that I am unspeakably fortunate to earn a living doing what I love. The sense that not everyone is that fortunate may be another reason I don't say things like *I fell in love with learning.* The closest I have come to saying that was during an honors ceremony for undergraduate students in my department that included induction into a national communication honor society. I was chairing the department, and the program organizer asked me to say a few words.

"So I'm here to say a few words," I started. "First word: Congratulations." (Pause; chuckles.) "Second word: Thanks. Thanks to you parents for raising smart, responsible kids, and for entrusting them to the University of Iowa."

"And thank you, students," I continued, "for making college teaching the absolute best job in the world. Those of you sitting here are the ones who come to class," I pointed out. "You're the ones who *read*, who think, who ask good questions that challenge us on what we think we know about communication. You are ..." I paused, close to choking up, "the reason none of us can believe how good we've got it to have this work to do every day, the reason none of us can imagine doing anything else." I wanted to tell them they are the reason I'm still deeply in love with this life I fell into by accident when I was their age. Once again, they are not words I can say out loud.

Reflections and expansions

1. What holds people back from saying out loud positive things to others who love them, like "I'm in love with learning"? Are they different from the reasons not to say negative things out loud, like "I hate spending time with my family because they bore me stupid"?
2. There were two audiences that demanded silence about my plans to go to graduate school: family on one side, worried that this meant I was hiding from real work, and friends on the other, ready to say *well la-ti-DA, who do you think you are*? My interpretation is that both of these are grounded in a lower middle class position (Alfred Lubrano's *Limbo: Blue-collar Roots, White-collar Dreams* describes all talk of college as similarly perilous, and more so, among the working class). Apart from weird career ambitions, what else would have to go unsaid in class-based speech communities (working, middle, upper class)?

The lady DEO

For a few years before I became department chair,[1] people talked to me as though I were the heiress apparent. Sometimes that took the form of "You would be good at it and you're well-positioned in the department to take it on." The less flattering version was "Who else *is* there?" One image of those years stayed with me: Sometimes when I rode my bike, my mind wandered toward the possibility of being chair, and occasionally the idea turned into a fantasy. Part of me wanted so badly for that to happen I could hardly keep the tires on the road.

Other parts of me weren't so sure. Chairing an academic department is not like being promoted in a corporation, a promotion that signals your arrival at a higher, further point in your profession than those around you. To the extent the reward system in your institution revolves around research, chairing can force you to put that aside, which feels like falling behind. Although some faculty do just as much research while they chair the department, for most mortals there aren't enough hours in the day for that to happen. Admitting that you want to chair your department can thus be heard as giving

---

Transcribing Silence: Culture, Relationships, and Communication
by Kristine L. Muñoz, 73–85.

up on the work that presumably you got into—research and teaching—to do something else. Administration can look, particularly to people who haven't done it, as less difficult and competitive than producing research, an easy way out of the rat race.

Besides that there are complicated relational dynamics: The colleagues who elect you chair are often senior to you. Some will have chaired the department themselves or will have turned down chances to do so, something that can affect their reactions to your assigning them to jobs they don't want to do. Sometimes chairing leads to more administration, in the same institution or a different one. Other times it is a term with a limit to it, usually three or five years, after which you go back to being a faculty member like you were before, on the salary rung of faculty rather than administration. There is often suspicion of why you're doing it: Are you after power or money, the only reasons most faculty can think of for doing administration? Have you run out of theoretical things to say? Are your articles getting rejected at journals so you know you've lost your touch for scholarship? One of my colleagues said that anyone who *wanted* to chair our department deserved whatever suffering he or she came into.

Still, I plugged up the gentle hills of Iowa City and whizzed down them, smelling flowers in yards or cooking from the houses I passed, thinking with a clarity that surprised and sometimes alarmed me: I wanted to chair my department. Specifically, I wanted to be the first woman to do it.

Two months into the job I had dinner with a friend from graduate school, our first real conversation in a decade. She was also chairing her department, and we marveled over starting out together and, after following paths that crossed only occasionally, finding ourselves in the same place professionally. She told me that becoming chair of her department meant standing up to senior men who had "run the show for years from behind the scenes." The lesson she learned from that was that "academic men are just not ready to deal with strong women."

The story made complete sense, a quite understandable adjustment of male dominant norms to a competent woman. It also left me almost wistful: Even early in my time as chair, I knew my colleagues were not going to behave in ways that could be easily tied to gender, and I knew that the inevitable criticisms of my handling the job would never be framed as "She's a strong woman and we're not used to that" (not that criticism of my graduate school friend was put into those words, either).

No one outright accused me of being bossy while I was chair, a word singled out in Tina Fey's *Bossypants* and Sheryl Sandberg's *Lean In* as code for "a woman who dominates in ways reserved for men." Instead I heard criticisms of my making decisions without proper consultation of my colleagues. In some cases I HAD in fact consulted them, but had done something other than what they advised. There were times when I was chair that the department made no forward progress on issues I thought it could, and should, have done. Was this because I was an ineffective leader, or because there were people invested in me not leading, and thus putting a stop to things I proposed? If those two reasons amount to the same thing, is there any way to parse what role, if any, my being a woman (as opposed to being someone who was simply wrong most of the time) played in the stalemates?

I did not walk around wondering about this. I focused on how to get done that which needed doing, because walking into the departmental office often felt like walking into a hospital emergency room: I never knew what critically wounded soul might come bursting through the door. I tried to avoid, as much as I possibly could, taking criticism and opposition personally. That was most difficult when I was accused, both directly and indirectly, of duplicity. I heard people say that I had flat-out lied about something I had done, either to get my way or to protect myself from more criticism. Lying happens both in the said and the unsaid, of course, and when I heard this, I tried to see if it was true. There were obviously times when there was information I could not share and had to construct explanations around that which I *could* share. In many cases (although this is obviously my own recollection, which will never be the only version of events), I was protecting someone else. In retrospect, I probably should have said more often "There are details here I'm not at liberty to share," but at the time that just seemed to call attention to situations that were already tense with suspicion. I do know what it feels like to flat-out lie, to invent something that bears little or no relationship to the truth, and that I did not ever do. The accusations that I had done so stung deeply, and in writing this I find the wounds have not healed.

On the other side were things I heard praise for. Morale was higher, there was more team spirit, less territoriality. I was a good listener, an able speaker on ceremonial occasions. Trains ran on time. I got some resources from the dean that my colleagues were grateful for. There was agreement that I was damned good in a crisis.

There is no question that I learned more from chairing my department than from almost any other experience I've had in my life. I found out that leadership made me more dependent than ever on getting people to be team players: chair committees, write reports, teach the classes in most demand instead of what they wanted to teach, hold extra office hours during preregistration. Those were things I could not do myself, nor could I force any individual to do them. Given that academia rewards originality and independence above all else, teamwork involves an unselfish temperament that can look, in extreme cases, like masochism. The individual successes of my colleagues benefited the department when I talked about them to the dean, the press, and to prospective graduate students and faculty. The rewards of teamwork were harder to describe and report: satisfied and well-educated undergraduates, reports done well and turned in on time, thoughtful adjustments to curriculum, an evenly balanced load of committee responsibilities. Gender stereotypes would predict that men would focus on their individual successes most diligently and trumpet them most loudly, while women took up the slack with teamwork. In my department, there were no such clear lines, in that or in any of the interpersonal dimensions of organizational life

That made being the first woman to head my department a confusing business. Did it matter that I was a woman, or didn't it? Or how did it matter, when did it matter, why did it matter? Many of my struggles as chair involved figuring out how to match the demands of the role as I understood it—most of the rules were unwritten, of course, and unspoken except behind my back (funny how often those tales came to me third or fourth hand)—with the person I believed I was. Did being a woman make all those questions more complicated? As a colleague put it: Was there more emotional labor expected of me, more policing when I stepped over the lines of gendered expectations? Or did my beliefs about who I was, and my anxiety over what people thought of me, cause the trouble?

There was little mention of my being the first woman, and I didn't delude myself that I was any Sally Ride, Sandra Day O'Connor, Hillary Clinton, Danica Patrick. People voiced their reactions to what I did as chair based on whether they agreed or disagreed, whether they saw what I was doing as good, bad, efficient, inappropriate, productive or not. Their evaluations, at least the ones I heard, never invoked gender in any way, probably because of the absolute taboo against saying something that might be taken to mean "isn't that just like a woman?" When something is never talked about, you can't know whether it's true and unspoken (or said only out of your hearing), or untrue, or irrelevant. So when questions about gender whirled through my head, answers remained stubbornly unclear: How did male department chairs respond when people complained, claiming the chair was responsible for a bad situation, when in fact it was someone else's doing and the chair covered for him or her? Did that even happen? Did it happen to them as often as it did to me? To what extent did men let such complaints upset them? What did people expect of me in this moment, this situation, this role? Did they expect something different of me than they did of the men? There were questions that started off being about something else and turned into gendered questions:

Am I doing this task competently? Am I making the best decision, or making the decision based on who it will or won't piss off? *Did men ask themselves these kinds of questions?*

Equally difficult was the fact that there were very few people I could really talk to, fully and completely, about those questions and the events that raised them. I had trusted colleagues in my department that were both male and female, and I could talk about some of the problems and some of my interpretations with them. The unbearably clichéd observation that it's lonely at the top perched on my shoulder from early on, however, and after a few sideways glances I realized I was telling too much to people who were part of the system that was giving me heartburn. The male confidants always had a different interpretation to offer when I attributed something to sexism. The female ones were generally ready to believe in sexism, with the exception, of course, being their own behavior. When I talked to close friends in other departments, I worried—no matter how fervent their vows of both confidentiality and never holding what I said against my department—that I was being disloyal. Jairo listened sympathetically, but gave advice based on his experience in industry: dock this person's pay, put a written warning in the file, get that one FIRED. I grew more and more silent about the swirling mass of emotion the job was bringing with it.

The less I talked through my fears and anger, the more I worried that I had gone over to the dark side: I'd been sucked into the male dominant view that denies or overlooks the very big but usually hidden ways gender shapes, often in unfair ways, institutional life. I was swallowing my point of view along with my anxiety, and having a woman DEO was not going to matter in any of the ways people like to think it will. In fact, it wasn't going to matter at all.

I especially struggled with showing emotion. Teary-eyed women often come to mind right away when people talk about gender roles, and as soon as I became chair I was hyper-attentive to any expressions of emotion, mine in particular, but also those of the people I admired. At a meeting I once watched one of my favorite people, an administrator, get visibly angry. He is famously efficient and professional, which can come across as cold and machinelike, but I always sensed a deeply feeling, caring person under the clockwork. I noticed how he made his feelings known. He said quietly, but in a tone of voice that left no doubt that he was as hurt as he was angry, "Ron, you either trust me or you don't." For all its openness, his emotion didn't disrupt the business we had to get done. It was a glimpse of a human being—an odd thing to say, because if you're in a room full of people what else *is* there? I noticed at that moment that the focus on the numbers and words in front of you usually takes up all the airspace, and you can be led to believe that no one but you, maybe, is still a breathing, perhaps suffering in some way or another, human body. Knowing how and when to show emotion in the workplace is tricky, and the rules that encode gender roles are numerous and byzantine.

Partly for that reason, a few months into the job I noticed that being chair was the most emotionally demanding thing I had ever done. At first I could only notice that I was really *emotional*—filled with emotion, then drained of it, depending on the hour of the day and the day of the week. For the first time I could remember, word labels for the feelings I had were elusive. I could only notice I was feeling something more strongly than I thought you were allowed to feel about work, at work, and I worried about showing any of this affect. Could a department chair scream in anger? Dance for joy? Shake in her boots with terror? Pound a desk in frustration? Most frightening of all, of course: *What if I cried?*

The enormity of the role, feeling uncertain about what would be appropriate emotions to show and how and when it would be alright to show them, and having no one to really talk to about it all, took away the words for emotions I'd always used without much thought. It got easier as time went on, and the words came back: I'm angry, I'm sad, I'm afraid, I'm happy and excited, I feel guilty, I'm frustrated. I learned I was far more able to control my expressions of emotion than I thought I was. What I never figured out was: Was that control a *good* thing, or did I add more bricks and mortar to the edifice of masculine communication styles that dominates academia?

There was also the idea that women should be able to notice when other women are getting the short end of a work-related stick. During a review of several junior faculty, a woman noted that two of the reports—one of a male, the other of a female—were quite different in tone. Both were capable and valued colleagues; the man was described as "much in demand with graduate students," his work "cited by (household name famous person) as being extremely important to the field." The woman was described as "doing yeoman-like work in the department," and as "unselfish in giving her time and energy to the important task of revising the curriculum." All of us knew the two people well, and it was easy to see the differences in the reports as reflecting differences in temperament rather than ability and importance. The woman was self-effacing to a fault, the man a tireless self-promoter. We had written reports that described him as more valued and accomplished than her, and I had missed that as completely as anyone. The reports were rewritten to be more equivalent, reflecting the fact that both faculty members had contributed differently but equally to the department and university.

I suffered for weeks over the fact that I had not caught the discrepancy myself. The limits of our narratives are the limits of our understanding, and the story we told ourselves about these junior people was that we had described them as *objectively* as we could. In this instance that means we thought we described what we saw, not how we felt about them personally or how their efforts to create a particular impression of themselves might have filtered our evaluation of their work. There's a strand of feminism that says objectivity is just another fable, and a male-dominated one at that. I generally haven't agreed with that idea, but now I wondered: What else have I missed? Does it really do any good to have women in positions of responsibility if they don't pick up on these inequalities any more reliably than men do?

Simply hiding fear was, of course, not the only—or even the biggest—challenge of emotional display. I found out that people expected confidence from a department chair, which—because this is unsaid in the job description—I found especially poignant. I do not believe myself to have come to this earth blessed with the natural, easy self-confidence some people seem to have, but I have wondered: Do those people really feel as confident as they look? Was my lack of self-confidence due to being a woman because women are discouraged from showing confidence, even when it's justified? Was it because I'm the second child and my brother was the smart one? (Someday I should ask him if he knew he was "the smart one" all along.) Or does everyone feel that way, and some men learn to hide it better?

I was shocked by evidence that I did seem to create the appearance of someone quite confident in her right to chair that department. Several times I had that out-of-body experience where you feel like you're standing aside and watching someone else do the job. I watched from a distance while a stranger that people called by my name did just fine, time after time, in situations I knew would make the real me crumple to the floor in a fetal position. I watched that person compose letters and e-mails that juggled complicated interpersonal dynamics around crucial departmental needs, often effectively. Slowly, occasionally, I noticed it was me who was doing those things. I noticed that I could, in fact, handle the job.

Confidence issues took shape in another question that I wonder how often men ever ask themselves, and with what degree of concern: *What on earth will I wear*? It's one of the places where administration and college teaching rub most severely against each other. Among the faculty in my department, ties and high heels are rare. Some of the women grad students are more fashion-conscious and outdo the faculty, with dresses and carefully done hair and significant makeup. Some of the men don't seem to understand they're going to *work*, for which I promise you they get paid. They show up to teach class in Tshirts and baggy shorts and, my personal peeve, unshaven. My own code is that I dress up a little to teach—corduroys or khakis rather than jeans—particularly the first month of class, in an old habit of trying to establish credibility through appropriate dress. When I'm not teaching, I often wear jeans, though I draw the line, with some regret, at wearing sweats to work. Teaching classes of 200 students requires me to think of myself as Madonna on stage, in terms of confidence, and has spawned its own category: comfortable dresses in bright colors, turtlenecks, the occasional blazer.

All this came from teaching; the role of chair weighed more heavily in choices of dress. For important meetings, my goal (because I read this in a book somewhere and it rang true) was to show the other people there that I took the job seriously and expected them to take me seriously. This meant buying some button-down shirts, a new blazer, and God forbid some high heels (the other line I draw is styling my hair or putting on makeup). The days I dressed to be chair, I felt a little intimidating—and thus self-conscious—when I was teaching. The days I wore blue jeans because I wasn't teaching but needed to be in the office all day I felt self-conscious to be doing the role of chair that way. I enjoyed most the days when I felt like I hit it just right: a blouse, blazer, and heels on a meeting day, or a soft shirt and blue jeans on a day when I was mostly trying to solve problems, make people feel safe, and get a lot done in a compressed, frequently-interrupted period of time.

But I noticed what I was wearing, and orchestrated clothing carefully with daily agenda items. I wondered: Are my colleagues thinking the chair thing has all gone to my head when they see me in a blazer? Are the women graduate students learning something about being a woman in academia when they see me as chair coming to work in jeans and soft shirts? *Is there any legal way to insist that men have to shave and comb their hair before they teach?*

I became more conscious of being a role model to young women. It went from being an incidental, mostly unconscious thing that I either snorted or started at, when I was reminded by others that I was supposed to be one or that by default I *was* one, to being something I did intentionally. I wanted women students to see that it was possible for a very ordinary mortal—one whose kindly, supportive master's thesis advisor once described as "usually not the smartest kid in the class, but one who *thinks* a great deal"—to be a full professor and a department chair at the same time she was a wife of two decades and a mother of successful, well-adjusted children. I wanted them to see that they didn't have to fit some mythical masculine standard to be successful. Then I wondered all too often whether my clothing told them that when I was more casually dressed than they were. What if they—and the rest of the world—didn't even notice what I wore? How would I know if they did or didn't? How would I go about being a role model if clothing were declared permanently irrelevant?

An example: A meeting was set that involved me, another full professor, and two deans. I knew I would be the only woman there, apart from a staff person taking notes on the decisions made by the four of us, and that I was also many years younger than any of the men. Okay, I said to my daughter Erica, I am intimidated, even though I know I shouldn't be. The situation was one I had definite ideas about how to handle, and I was reasonably sure that my approach would be seen as workable and productive by the other three. Another irrational (but not all that surprising) part of me had an instinctive cower response in the face of years, sex, and the length of time the deans had been in their positions relative to how long I had been in mine. I didn't try to analyze where that irrational response came from, or try to shame myself out of having it. Instead, I found a stereotypical way to manage it: I fretted over what to wear. Once I had settled on very tall heels (if you're the only woman in the room you often have to do that, I've found, to be looking people in the eye) and a dress, I knew the meeting would go fine and that, once again, I would carry off being department chair without breaking a sweat.

The best part of this was talking it through with Erica, then 16 years old, and being more conscious than usual of being a role model for the professional woman she plans to be. I told her about feeling intimidated, I told her about solving that through careful attention to what I wore, and I made sure to tell her afterward that it had gone very well. It seemed a collateral benefit to the job that none of my male predecessors could have told me about—would they have noticed themselves being role models for their sons? Would they have admitted to their sons—or to themselves—that they were intimidated? Would they have experienced this everyday moment as triumph?

I wonder what I learned from my mother, and how and when. She had a career from the early 1950s on, and she was the only mom I knew who worked outside the home. She was a medical technologist, a woman in a woman's field, though most of her bosses were men (go figure). She did not take a promotion offered that would have made her middle management, and the reason she gave me several times was that she was a mother first and work was a distant second. I grew up knowing I would work, then, but never expected I'd be a boss. Is there something she said that I don't remember, or something she *didn't* say, that made (for example) confidence—true, inner self-confidence—so elusive?

Long after I finished chairing the department, I remain mystified about whether being the first woman to do it made any difference. Holding that role for a few years raised a lot of questions for me about when and how gender makes a difference in the particular professional world I live in. It also gave me a chance to watch myself do things I never thought I could do. Very little of what I've learned could be put into declarative sentences, though I'm grateful I have words for emotions again. I look back at my teenager, far more confident at 16 than I was at any point before age 40, and I wonder: How will she look back and remember this time in both our lives? What did she learn from me?

Reflections and expansions

1. What part of being (or having) a role model needs to happen in verbal action, like telling stories of triumph or giving advice? What parts cannot be done in words? What must be left unsaid *to* the role model, and *by* one, and why?
2. Racism, sexism, and other forms of discrimination are often described now as having been "driven underground" by political correctness. The same attitudes and preferences are there, but left unsaid, making them more difficult to identify and confront. The opposing view is that US American society has genuinely become more open and equal, so that discrimination and bias occur more rarely. What are your thoughts?
3. Affect, emotion, and feelings are different things, at least in the world of affect studies. Here are some places to read more about affect, especially as it relates to the academic world:

Berlant, L. (Ed.). (2004). *Compassion: The culture and politics of an emotion.* New York: Routledge.

Cvetkovich, A. (2012). *Depression: A public feeling.* Durham, NC: Duke University Press.

Gregg, M., & Seigworth, G. J. (Eds.). (2010). *The affect theory reader.* Durham, NC: Duke University Press.

Lutz, C. (1988). *Unnatural emotions: Everyday sentiments on a Micronesia atoll and their challenge to Western theory.* Chicago: University of Chicago Press.

Mirror, mirror

2008

There's a black spider the size of a pumpkin seed that's taken up residence in my bathroom. My first impulse when I saw her was to wipe the web, and the creature, off the bottom of the ceramic toothbrush holder, and to finish the purge with disinfectant spray and a scrubbing sponge on the counter.

When I watched the spider scuttle underneath the pottery, though, I noticed the toothbrush holder was tilted up slightly, resting on the lip of the sink instead of flat on the counter. That tilt gave something for the spider to hide under when she sensed motion, whether to trap a gnat or to escape a scrub brush. Then I saw the gnats in her web, and realized again that spiders are allies. Gnats are the scourge of summertime, with windows open, lights on inside, screens sagging after 40 years of damp heat, and this spider was doing her best to help. She's staying, for now, despite the cringe: What if my mother saw a spider web full of gnat carcasses so close to the toothbrushes?

Transcribing Silence: Culture, Relationships, and Communication
by Kristine L. Muñoz, 86–99.

The irony is that, after 50 years of life, I should be free of my mother's opinions and judgments, real or imagined, because she died a few weeks ago. I look at those words—*she died a few weeks ago*—and I don't believe them. Her being dead seems as improbable as the sun burning out. The world on TV is caught up in its own disbelief: a flood, of proportions no one dreamed possible, is drowning Iowa City. Houses and businesses have disappeared forever, people are sobbing, a colleague e-mailed a YouTube video showing the Iowa River lapping at the second floor of her home. We gawk at the mudplains that were once downtown Cedar Rapids. I-80 is closed. The superhighway that starts at the George Washington Bridge in New Jersey and ends in San Francisco is *under water* three miles from my house.

My mother is dead, and the flood barely registers. I am learning about life and death and myself now, and it's like being three years old, when there's so much you don't know about the world that you learn a hundred new things a day: Dandelions are not animals. The cat means business when she swipes at your hand, even if you're just petting her. Ice cream comes in flavors besides vanilla.

I have learned that people actually do read the obituaries in the paper, and match the names there to people they know. People you would never call to say *my mom died* know it happened and will say, next time they see you, *so sorry to hear about your mom.* They say that because you are supposed to say something when you run into someone who's had a death in the family. They seem not to know that you have pulled yourself together with great effort in order to face the world, and that their well-intentioned *sorry* threatens that composure like a brick hurled at a window.

I've learned that although no one says that it's natural to lose a parent—you are, after all, meant to outlive them—you imagine that's what they're thinking. It's not like losing a parent when you are a child, or God forbid losing a child, but it is so much harder than anyone tells you it will be.

I have learned that she was the center of my life in ways I spent my whole life resisting and denying, so now there's a bigger hole there than I dreamed there could be. I have learned that I'm not yet running out of tears, though surely someday I will.

With all this that I'm learning, what can the spider teach me? Something about life going on, for better or worse? If I kill the spider, there will be a few more gnats buzzing around my eyes and nose instead of caught in her invisible web.

Or something about looking very closely before you wipe up what looks like disorder, because it could be helpful and healthy instead of poor cleaning habits.

Or maybe this: With my mom dead, I will finally decide whether the spider and her web are a good or a bad thing. I will choose on my own whether to clean her away or welcome her help with the summertime gnat population.

I think I'll keep that thought.

2010

I have mostly stopped crying.

Like other animals, my primal experiences of my mother are anchored in her smell. It had notes of cigarette smoke, coffee, and Estee Lauder. Only in adulthood did I realize that none of those smells, unfiltered, was necessarily pleasant. When alchemized through a human body that had given me birth, when each was barely detectable, when the angle of smell was from the rarified pleasure of my head on her lap, the mixture had unparalleled power to soothe. They were faint traces because somehow, in defiance of all logic, she had a painfully acute sense of smell despite her lifelong habit of smoking. She worked endlessly to keep cigarette smells out of the house, the car, and her clothes, and was so successful that I only much later learned to identify smokers by their smell. My mother was so successful at defeating the smell that you would never know she smoked unless you were literally on her lap, and then it was so faint that I didn't know for years that the smell I associated so much with comfort and safety was, in fact, L&M Full Flavor 100's. I tried to take up smoking in my teens, to her outrage; fortunately, I developed asthma before I could acquire a taste for it. Her smoking was one part of who she was that she was determined I would not be.

Coffee has been, as much as a morning imperative, a recreational possibility all of my adult life. My mother did not, as I do, "meet friends for coffee." The only times she sat down to drink from a cup were first thing in the morning and after the dinner dishes were washed at night. She worked from 7 a.m. to 4 p.m. in Houston, an hour's drive from home, and my father did not consider cooking or cleaning his responsibility. I can barely imagine the length of her days, nor how she found energy on top of work to be a den mother for the Cub Scouts, a troop leader for the Girl Scouts, a crafter, and one of the public library's best customers. She would not have known how to sit still and talk over a cup of coffee, even with the time to do it. The semi-rural town I grew up in had none of the cozy coffee shops that dot Iowa City, nor did she have the disposable income for five dollar lattes. Morning and evening coffee were moments of solitude for her, a loner in a world that expected women to carry conversations and relationships in their already-busy hands.

Her acute sense of smell extended to distaste for anything frivolous or artificial: Despite our gas dryer, she dried her sheets on the line to enjoy the fresh air, both in the hanging and, later, in sleeping between them. Between that sensibility and her being the oldest of five children born to a mechanic and his hypochondriac wife just before the Depression, I don't know how or when my mother developed a taste for Estee Lauder. Maybe it was the allure of "free gifts" that came with the purchase of perfume, elegant makeup kits with lotions, eye shadows, and fingernail polishes she had no use for. When I was a preteen and fascinated with all things of grownup women, she passed them along to me, but I knew not to ask her for instruction. Eyebrow pencil and face powder were the extent of her makeup use, applied faithfully every day with the unvarying white polyester uniforms she wore to work in the hospital. Maybe that faintest whisper of Estee kept the antiseptic smell of the hospital at bay, even if only she could tell it was there.

Lingering over coffee and a cigarette, dabbing on a whiff of Estee Lauder—they seem to have been her only personal luxuries. In a life spent organizing the lives of others, working, cooking, cleaning up, she took little time or money to indulge herself. My life was more privileged than hers in every way: I could read and ride my bike and sleep late and spend my allowance on candy, watch *Beverly Hillbillies* and *Bonanza* while she cooked dinner, cleaned the kitchen, did all the laundry. As a child, though, the greatest luxury was to doze with my head on her lap, inhaling her smell, having her sitting still, and having her all to myself. Surely I prized it all the more because, like her own moments of luxury, I got so little of it.

There's a framed embroidery piece on the wall of my study at home, where I get to love my work in ways I know she never loved hers. It's a rough brown background, like a burlap bag, and the lettering is plain black stitching, dotted lines like someone just learning to sew. There are red X's in each corner around the legend, which says:

> *Mirror, mirror on the wall*
> *I am my mother after all.*

We were in a gift shop in Central Texas several years ago, the kind of place that tries to look like a country store but sells fancy soap, handmade candles, dishtowels with bluebonnets on them, quilt squares meant to hang on a wall rather than lie on a bed.

"Here, Mom, I'll let you buy this for me," I told her, and she smiled and dug for her wallet. She looked closely enough to read what it said and looked confused. "Really?"

"Really." I thought it over a little more when I saw the price—$25. Was it something I would actually find a place for? Or was it wanting to hold on to the moment, the fact of being able to point at something and say "Buy this for me," knowing she would do it to make up for all the times she said *no* when I was growing up? No to a Coke at the swimming pool (there was a water fountain), no to a comic book to read in the car (your father will take you to the library), no to a long dress I wanted for the senior prom (you have that bridesmaid's dress from last year). Mom lamented many times not buying me that dress. It wasn't about not having the money; it was about not paying full price. She bought it when it went on sale, and it hung in my closet until it was stained gray with dust, proms being a phase of my life long over by the time the dress showed up as a Christmas present. She did not let my father buy brand new cars because they depreciated so quickly, and as long as there was sturdy air conditioning for her long freeway drives in the Gulf Coast heat, who cared what color they were?

"I am my mother after all," said the embroidery, and that was surely what made her shake her head. She couldn't imagine anyone wanting to be like her, and we both believed we were complete opposites. I was emotional and sentimental like my father, instead of quiet and resolute. I had boyfriends who flaunted our intimacy; she rarely dated, focusing on working her way through college and then saving everything left after living expenses to travel to Mexico, California, Hawaii. I embraced beer and marijuana all the way through high school, dicing with jail and death driving home. I saw her frightened eyes when I came home at 4 a.m.; she was such a stranger to substance abuse she never found words to talk to me about the chances I was taking. I wanted her to *talk* to me; I wanted her to *listen* to me. Instead, she took on a second job three evenings a week, and I drank more, inhaled more deeply, drove further.

I took going to college for granted, then slid into graduate school on the momentum of never having worried where the next month's rent would come from. Mom was the first in her family to finish high school and the only one for many years to go to college, but when I told her I was staying at University of Texas for a master's degree, she snapped at me: "Why don't you look for a *job*? What are you *afraid* of?" I remember her tone, somewhere between rage and terror. I just shook my head, feeling slapped.

None of my extended family understood graduate school, and seemed to assume like she did that it was an attempt to avoid actual work. I gutted out the all-night paper writing and exam grading and lived on $350 a month for the next nine years. Her words stung for the entire decade, and holiday dinners were grim attempts to explain how I could be nearly 30 and still—*still*—be in school. That, yes, there were people out there who would hire someone like me to study and teach … whatever it was I was doing. She could never remember: Communication.

When I defended my dissertation, although I had a tenure-track job, a husband everyone liked, and two small children, she still had never said, "Well, OK—I guess this *is* a real job." I tried to play it cool about graduation, thinking the costumed ritual might be an ordeal for my family; or worse, look silly. No, of course they were coming, she said. She could stay and take care of the children if there weren't enough tickets—"NO, Mom, if you're coming a thousand miles to graduation I will FIND you a ticket." I wondered, as the time came closer, whether it was a mistake to have urged my parents to come—I talked them into it, didn't I? And my brother and his wife, and my mother's closest sister—I was putting so many people to so much trouble. I grew irritated, imagining she was privately rolling her eyes over my demanding to be the center of attention. Like I always did. Like this was some big damn deal.

We had a video camera by then, one of the early ones with huge tapes that filled up quickly, and batteries that seemed to last only minutes. Jairo filmed bits and pieces of the ceremony, zooming in on me waving from the tenth row, my doctoral hood matching everyone's around me. We came home in several cars, and I wanted to watch the video right away. "Let's open presents first," Jairo suggested, "and that way they can all go back to the hotel if they don't want to watch it."

The drapes were closed in the living room; I assumed the babies had taken naps just before we got there. The video of that day shows me opening the first present, the watch I'd asked my aunt for. Then an empty, gift-wrapped box from my brother and sister-in-law: They had given me the doctoral hood, to keep rather than rent it, and we all laughed at the empty box. I still had on the hood and the gown, too exhilarated to take them off. Let them think I was demanding attention. The camera panned to the side and caught a smile on my sister-in-law's face; she grinned and shook her head a little, knowing what was coming next.

The last present was a small box with a card from Jairo, saying he was proud of me and how hard I had worked for this day. He had suggested getting me something monogrammed with my name and *PhD*—a picture frame, a name plate for the door, maybe a key ring. I opened it casually, determined not to make a big deal of the initials. PhD, so what. It was a key ring. "Oh how pretty," I said, and held the key ring up to show the others. "Isn't this ..." In the video, I stop and stare at the key ring. "This key does not go to any vehicle we own," I say slowly, and there is laughter around the room. The drapes swing open behind me with a whoosh, and two-year-old Gabe says "New car! New car!"

"No, sweetie, those are rental ..." I stop again and look out the window, and the camera goes from my dumbfounded face to a gleaming maroon Dodge Grand Caravan parked in front of the house. There are shouts: "Go outside!" I walk, dazed, into crisp Seattle sunshine. The sky is impossibly blue, there is not a cloud, the air smells like cedars. "I don't believe it," is all I can say, again and again. "I don't believe it." Everyone piles outside and crowds around the van, which has a banner across the windshield—"CONGRATULATIONS!" and, I find out, 25 miles on the odometer. "Jairo?" I turn to him, thinking of the $535 in our savings account and how on earth he thinks we'll pay for this vehicle. "Your mother," he mouths at me around the camera, before I can start scowling.

My father was the last one out the door, his face pink and his eyes red. "We're so proud of you," he whispered when I hugged him. "Thank you, Dad." He shook his head a little—"Your mother did this all on her own." I looked around for her, the key clutched in my hand. "Where's Mom?" I asked Jairo, the camera still running. It swept the excited people clambering into the van. Still a novelty in 1989, none of us had been in a minivan before. She was nowhere to be seen. "*Where is my mother?*" I was holding tightly onto the tears, determined not to embarrass us all with emotion. My brother yelled for her from the front yard—"LOIS!"

She came to the door, barely stopping to glance outside. "Getting lunch on the table," she said, and turned to walk back in. "I know everyone's hungry ..."

"MOM!" I went over to her and hugged her fiercely, silently.

"*So.*" She pulled away. "I think everything's ready, I just need to cut up some watermelon." She walked briskly toward the kitchen, and Gabe toddled after her, calling her—"Grandma! New car! New car!" She reached down and took his hand: "Let's have lunch first, and then go for a ride," I heard her say. I watched them walk away together, my arms hanging at my sides.

I realize I can't actually see the spider's web under that toothbrush holder. I can see her moving in purposeful ways, I can see the gnats stuck here and there, but the web itself is invisible. Spider silk is not only several times stronger than high-grade steel, it is stronger than Kevlar, which is five times stronger than high grade steel and is used to make, among other things, body armor. Thus can this spider, only slightly larger than the gnats, trap them and take her time eating them—or drinking them, as *Charlotte's Web* taught us.

There was so much we didn't talk about in my house—my drinking and drug abuse, how late the boyfriends stayed at our house, how we pretended my father was in charge. There was a center of what couldn't be said, something so taboo it was five times stronger than high grade steel. It provided body armor, it provided food, it was invisible. Perhaps ten times in my life, a stranger broke the silence.

"What happened to your mother's face?" It wasn't always a child, asking with the innocence of childhood. Sometimes it was an adult. Once, in fact, it was a sallow boyfriend, who asked my mother instead of me: "What happened to your face?"

"It's a birthmark," she answered and then changed the subject, as we had all learned to do. I hated the people who tore the hole in that silence. It wasn't a small birthmark, like Mikhail Gorbachev's on the top of his head (how I loved that man for his smaller, but quite visible, connection to my mother!). It covered almost exactly half of her face, from her collarbone to the crown of her head, and it was a deep, sometimes purplish red.

The minor forms of this kind of birthmark are called port wine stains, and today many can be reduced or removed by laser treatment. Those treatments weren't dreamed of in the 1920s when she was born in dusty Kingfisher, Oklahoma, and in fact hers wasn't just a port wine stain. After she died, I found an article printed from the internet in a file with her paid bills, receipts, Christmas cards. Her kind of birthmark had a name: Sturge-Weber Syndrome. This kind produces raised bumps on the skin, and can also produce growths that extend inside the skull. These growths can happen early in life and be large enough to cause mental retardation and seizures, or they can be fine silky spider-web tendrils that, late in life, caused my mother to go deaf in one ear and lose part of her vision on her birthmark side.

I try to remember what side of her face the birthmark was on. How can there be any doubt, a moment's hesitation? That disfigurement made her who she was—tough, resilient, able to tune out any conversation, reticent, unemotional. It shaped who we were to one another: I was the mysterious girl child, born (thank God!) without any birthmarks but thus going through life on a journey she had never taken. She lived every day knowing people were staring at her, and developed a protective ability to withdraw, a spider who scuttles underneath the pottery at the slightest hint of motion, as deeply embedded in her nature as the birthmark was on her face. I was the child chasing after her attention, into substance abuse, coming home at 5 a.m., showing up with boyfriends who couldn't read or who screamed at me in her presence, pouring energy into creative writing and then into graduate school. None of them were things she could imagine doing or wanting. The harder I ran after her, the further away she got. *I am my mother after all*—How? When? Why, for God's sake?

How can I not remember which side of her face the birthmark was on? It was the right side, I conclude. Definitely the right side. I am so sure I don't get up to look at the family pictures in my hallway, just the way they were in her hallways. It was on the right side.

Here was *her* mother: When her oldest daughter, the one with the birthmark, finished high school and said she was going to college to be a nurse, the mother responded: "They'll never let you be a nurse, your birthmark will scare the patients." Mom said she was a "fat, lazy slob always pretending she was sick." Yet my mother wanted to be a nurse, just as her own talky child studied communication.

When I was an undergraduate, I wrote in a paper that my mother was beautiful. The beauty I described was mostly that lovely smell when my head was on her lap, but I also tried to capture some of her strength, and occasional warmth. I told of how some seventh-grade girls laughed at a new outfit I'd bought, with my own money, thinking it very stylish. Instead of pointing out that this was the peril of paying full price for clothes, Mom let me cry and may even have hugged me. She was kind to her mother-in-law, whose sweet personality must have healed some of the wounds of her own childhood. She arranged to remodel the house for that grandmother to live with them for the years between living in her own home and the Alzheimer's floor. Being a den mother and a scout leader were not things my mother had any desire to do; they involved phone calls to parents asking them to drive, and being the center of attention of children other than her own. They needed to be done, so she did them. In my paper I did not, of course, mention the birthmark. I have never, until now, mentioned her birthmark. I gave her the paper to read, my heart gasping, and she beamed when she handed it back to me. Wordless, as usual, but—she *beamed.*

She and my father moved to Iowa City for what turned out to be the last year of her life. My children were grown and gone to college, and Jairo and I went to my parents' apartment for dinner every night of the week. She had learned to cook vegetarian casseroles, and I had learned to ask her small questions, instead of Big Ones: "Do you Comet the sink every night, or just when it's grungy?" "Have you ever used fabric softener?" "Did you have a Victory Garden during the war?" "Is there any food you just really can't stand?" "Which catalogue do you like better, Lands' End or Travelsmith?" She had heart trouble and bone cancer, and she said over and over, *if I could just figure out how to die I would.* It was so unlike her to want something and not be able to make it happen. I went all the way through that year pushing aside the reality that she was dying, hugging her every time I got there and every time I left and every time I made her laugh. Somehow, mysteriously, I often made her laugh, and the sound filled the world with stars.

I had a hysterectomy—scheduled long before, not quite optional but also not urgent—on the day she died. As she got sicker that summer, I wondered if I should put it off, but she was beyond the point when I could have asked her. She would want us to get on with our lives, I decided, not try to plan them around her and the uncertainty of her lifespan. The surgery roared closer as she declined, and Hancher Auditorium, the Pearl on the River, in Iowa City drowned in the flood.

On the Saturday before she died, she perked up from the haze of morphine and brain metastasis and sat at the table while the rest of us had dinner. Her brother, the one surviving sibling, had been there for three weeks by then, staying with her around the clock, and my brother had been there for several days. She hadn't eaten in a week, but she tasted a tiny spot of mashed potatoes I had made. "Mine are better," she mumbled, and we laughed. The evening turned festive: we put Willie Nelson, my favorite, and Tennessee Ernie Ford, Mom's favorite, on the CD player. "*Tell me a story,*" she sang loudly and tunelessly several times, something she sang when we asked for stories when we were little. I told about a time she'd plopped down on a new folding bed, to show its sturdiness to houseguests, and it collapsed beneath her. She smiled. "Should have bought you that prom dress," she mumbled. "But you bought me a minivan," I told her. She looked blank. "Don't you remember that, Mom?" She shook her head no.

We knew, from what the hospice nurse had told us, that this was probably a last surge of consciousness before the end. On Tuesday I stopped by to see her on my way to the hospital for surgery, and kissed her forehead; she had been asleep or unconscious for 24 hours by then. I couldn't get a word out of my mouth.

I came out of surgery at two o'clock and Erica called to tell my brother, who—on instruction—told Mom. At six, Jairo came into the hospital room where I was learning that I was one of the rare people who gets no pain relief from morphine. Erica was with him, and a taut-faced nurse with wide eyes. "At five oh five this afternoon," he said, "your mother died."

Even tears rolling silently down my face made my abdominal muscles tense, and they were excruciating. "That stinker," I whispered—a word she would have used, instead of something vulgar like I would; but what bad name do you call your dead mother? "That *stinker,* she did this on purpose!" She died on the day she was most sure I would have other things to think about besides the hole that had opened up in my life. She was right: It was all I could do not to scream out loud with the exquisite pain in my belly, and her long-awaited, much-desired, deeply dreaded passing was the least of my worries.

I let the spider stay; I admire her. One just like her comes back every summer, to the same spot underneath the toothbrush holder.

Erica refused to let me pay full price for her prom dress, but did—and does—let me cook all day to fill her freezer at the university with food.

I paused in front of a family picture in the hallway one morning and noticed: Mom's birthmark was on her *left* side. So always on the right when I looked at her.

I sit quietly in the morning, smelling the coffee as it brews, and I hang my sheets outside on the line. I do not smoke.

I feel my strength—or is it hers?—when I pass the embroidered wall hanging. *I am my mother after all.*

Reflections and expansions

1. Why would it seem important to tell someone in a coma that her daughter came through surgery OK?
2. How does this family, as a relational unit, use silence? What do they achieve through silence, and what do they lose? How do other families you know of use silence: (a) your own; (b) fictional ones created in literature, films, television; and (c) semi-fictional ones created in "unscripted" media—documentaries, Real Wives series, Kardashians? How similar are uses of silence between the real, the fictional, and the semi-fictional families?
3. How can you live closely with someone for most of your life and still find out there's much you don't know about them?
4. How do patterns of silence pass from generation to generation, and under what circumstances can they change?
5. What plastic parts of language—polysemy, ambiguity, strategic choice—do metaphors (like spiderwebs and mirrors, in this narrative) rely on to make sense?
6. What kinds of narratives are most likely to be told over and over again, in families and friendship groups? What kinds are likely to be told either once in a lifetime, or never?

A death foretold

I came home from choir practice that night humming and glowing and at peace with a world filled with music.[1] *It was the first week in November, the leaves were gone from the trees, not many Christmas lights up yet. A time of gathering darkness, made brighter by the people, the harmonies, the song. Three year old Gabe was at the door by the time I was halfway through it. His words mixed in with Jairo's, who was talking loudly into the phone on the other side of the living room.*

"They killed Anto—

"Pero donde fue es—

"Auro—

"Y que pa—

"What?" Was this a TV show they'd been watching, that Gabe was trying to tell me about? Who the hell was Jairo screaming into the phone to?

"Mataron a—a—Auxilio " Gabe's Spanish was not foolproof, but this message was not getting across in either language. I hung my purse on the doorknob, unwound my muffler, took off my coat. "What, sweetie? What happened? What were you watching?" He couldn't really *be telling*

Transcribing Silence: Culture, Relationships, and Communication
by Kristine L. Muñoz, 100–121. © 2014 Left Coast Press, Inc. All rights reserved.

me about someone who was killed. *This was a translation problem, or a report on a movie presented as real life.*

Jairo turned to look at me, his eyes large in a still, shocked face. Something was *wrong, maybe somebody died—he had many elderly or sickly relatives in Colombia. He told the person on the phone that we would be here, they should call back, he would try to get hold of someone—a family member, I guessed—in New York. "Chao"*—bye—*as he hung up the phone. Gabe was still trying to string the right syllables together.*

"They killed Absten—mataron a Arber—Aure—Artemio—"

Finally, Jairo finished the sentence. "Mataron a Aurelio." They killed Aurelio.

The carpet was rubbery where I stood, in the middle of the room, Gabe hanging onto me, Jairo in a foggy bubble ten feet further. The sofa registered behind me, and I wished I were sitting on it.

"Aurelio—" There was something in that sequence of words I couldn't understand, my Spanish wasn't foolproof either. That couldn't mean—

"Aurelio Muñoz. Lo mataron." They killed him. *A strange choice of words—they killed him. "They?" If something killed Aurelio, it was a heart attack, predictable from a lifetime of heavy smoking, heavy eating, heavy drinking ... "They who?"*

"Todavía no saben quién fue." They don't know yet who it was.

"What? Who *it was? Somebody ..." I was really confused now. Was it a car accident? crazy drivers being the norm all over Colombia—but sadness started seeping in. Aurelio was dead; that much I was pretty sure of.*

"Cinco balazos en la cabeza. Alguien lo mató." Five gunshots to the head. Someone *murdered* him.

The whole room turned gray and cold. The only light came from Jairo's eyes, wider and more still than I had ever seen them.

I thought seriously: I'm going to turn around and go back outside the door, come back in, and start this moment over, and it will happen entirely differently.

I found my way to the couch and sat down.

My first trip to Colombia, in 1983, was a spin through a never-ending crowded room—endless friends and relatives to meet, endless repetitions of the same conversation.

"Where in the States are you from?"

"From Houston."

"Oh, you met Jairo there, of course." I perfected a shy smile, one befitting a celebrity greeting the press. Maybe the Best Actress winner the morning after the Academy Awards. It felt like that much of an accomplishment to be there, the fiancé-elect (since we hadn't really said yet that we were engaged) of the Local Boy Who Made Good.

"Your Spanish is very good."

"Oh, thank you. Jairo is an excellent teacher." The fact was that I understood a third to a half of what was going on. Enough to know I was similar to Jairo's mother in ways that would make Freud proud, and to know that she and I would have to work hard to like each other. Not enough to follow the story of how Dioselina came to know his mother for 20 years and "help out in the house." But I saw her cooking, cleaning, washing clothes by hand, ironing my blouses before we went out on our numerous shopping trips and visits. I didn't know yet where his father and brother disappeared to in the evenings, greeted by icy stares yet smooth tones from his mother when they came back, ebullient, an hour or so later.

"You're very tall." Until I went to Colombia, I was a woman of medium height. Jairo was a shade taller than I was, so it was a surprise to suddenly have people looking up at me and commenting on my immensity. There were stares on the street, remarks about my blue eyes. I had never seen so many combinations of lush black hair and rich dark eyes, and I stared right back.

Nobody who marries into a large family can really keep the members and connections straight in the early days (or years). Asking questions—who was on whose side, who was married to whom, what connection made it imperative that a visit be arranged—made for many conversational opportunities. I did know when we ran into women Jairo had dated; the hushed attentiveness around the room when we were introduced, the brief civilities we exchanged, the intense interest in what we wore, how our hair was fixed, how sweet we could make our voices. I learned to act well-acquainted, even affectionate, with my future mother-in-law, Ruby. She was an excellent teacher without a word of instruction. She may have had romantic ideas about forging motherly/daughterly bonds with me, unaware of my struggles to come to terms with my own mother. We enacted connection, and hoped the acting would make it so.

From Bogotá we went to Cali, and I met Jairo's grandmother. She had steely blue eyes and a voice used to commanding, and was five feet tall on her tiptoes. Leaning down to shake her hand felt like a Japanese bow, and quite appropriate for her stiff dignity. Her children and grandchildren fussed over her and teased her, ignored her commands, and I was glad to be offstage. Cali was a sweating inferno, and I suffered in every direction: intestinal distress, away from home on Christmas for the second time in my life, between the heat and the nerves never feeling quite dry or clean. I found a few things to say that seemed to work in many circumstances:

"Oh my, this is *delicious*, I really must take some back with me."

"The palm trees are lovely; we don't have those in Texas." A lie, but everyone beamed.

"What a nice place for a swimming pool!" Nothing was too inane to try to be a part of the conversation.

Most of the real questions went unasked, of course—

"Do you people *always* drink this much, or only around the holidays?"

"Don't you think that dress is a little revealing for a family Christmas party?"

"Why do you keep parading Jairo's old girlfriends in front of me?"

"Why do we have to go have lunch at these peoples' house when you said yourself you don't like them? and they're the loudest, pushiest ones?"

After several days in Cali we drove further south, to cool, foggy Pasto. I sighed with relief to be away from the crowds and the heat and the rivers of *aguardiente*—firewater—they pickled themselves in day and night. When I told Jairo of my relief, he looked at me sideways. "You thought these people drank a lot?" Did I hear a little more emphasis on *these*?

"Don't they?"

"At least they put it in a glass first."

Aurelio was a very successful sales manager for Bavaria, a national brewery. He was so good at it that they moved him to a bigger market: Duitama, in Boyacá. The transfer was later described as the beginning of a road that led to his death. His irrepressible humor would not go over well with the dour boyacenses *(people from Boyaca); appointment of a* pastuso *(person from Pasto) to such a visible post would gall them. Aurelio complained that they had no sense of humor; there was no way to connect with people who took things so deadly seriously. He pined to be back in Pasto—"There I was* somebody,*" he lamented.*

There was a vendor who paid Bavaria with a bad check. It was up to Aurelio to tell him that the rest of his contract would not be honored. The vendor took him to dinner to try to convince him to give him another week to cover the check. Aurelio said no: He had no connection to this person, no way of knowing if he really was good for the debt or would string him along for months. He tried smoothing the man's feelings with his silky charm, to change the subject to something they could laugh about, but the answer was still no. "I'll kill that sonofabitch pastuso,*" the man said loudly as he left the restaurant. A dozen people must have heard him, but they were* boyacenses, *too: tough, clannish, silent. Even by Colombian standards they are quick to anger and violence.*

We got to Pasto on December 28, *Día de los Inocentes*—the equivalent of April Fool's Day. The ride was punctuated with stories of tricks and mayhem from other years: the kitten imprisoned in an air duct so it screamed in terror until located and retrieved hours later; the alarm clocks set for 3 a.m.; the group of amateur actors who dressed up as guerrillas and burst into a crowded cafeteria, brandishing all-too-real-looking machine guns. The country-wide tradition had expanded to a week of revelry in Pasto, in keeping (I was told) with the natives' simplemindedness. Much of it sounded too close to the bone for me. On *Día de los Aguas,* the trick was to throw water on people, whether strangers, friends, enemies, or family members. You had to be on guard as you walked under a balcony, or rounded the corner of a building, or drove down the street, watching out for people with buckets, hoses, Dixie Cups. The temperature hovered damply in the mid-40s, a bone-chilling ambience as unchanging as Cali's muggy heat.

The biggest prankster of them all, I was warned, was our host Aurelio. He was my father-in-law's cousin, they grew up together somewhere near Pasto, they were as close as brothers. He was *terrible.* "In what way?" I kept asking, a phrase I came to use a lot doing ethnography. Shaking heads, "You'll have to see for yourself," were the only answers. I wondered how bad a businessman, a father of teenaged sons, could be? and wished they would stop telling me so much about people before I met them.

The family's house was spacious and airy. Instead of a garage separated from the house, there was a kind of well adjacent to the living room. A very garage-like door slid up into the ceiling, the car was driven into the house, and the door slid back down. I knew by then that because of the risks of both theft and vandalism, cars couldn't be parked on the street overnight in most parts of Colombia. I focused on the logic of keeping your cars—there was room for two—inside the house, the safest possible place, rather than adding on a room that would have to be secured as elaborately as the house was. Still, it took a real effort not to be distracted by the sight of cars parked a few yards from the crystal figurines on the marble-topped coffee table.

We got there in late afternoon and met his wife first, before Aurelio got home from the office. Small and round and sweet-voiced, Libia was the calmest person I'd laid eyes on since we landed in Colombia.

"So, you've been taking the whirlwind tour?" she asked. I liked how she took my hand instead of kissing my cheek when we were introduced. "Lots of relatives to keep straight?"

"Oh, and such wonderful people," I started my litany of praise.

"Oh, and haven't they all loved giving you the once-over," she laughed, and something in the way she said it made me want to sit on the sofa all evening and tell her about the past two weeks, ask her to explain it all to me.

Someone said Aurelio and Libia had overcome strong resistance from both families to get married. Although she wasn't quite sure what the reasons for this opposition were, their fathers had the same last name, not unusual with a common name like Muñoz. Someone else insisted they were cousins, perhaps distant ones but surely related more closely than kinship ideals would allow. Years later I asked Libia if that were the case, and she laughed out loud. No, they were no relation; both families insisted that Aurelio finish college before they got married, a command they ignored. They were married for 30 years, and Libia was beside him in the passenger seat of the car when Aurelio was shot.

By the time she told me about the night he was murdered, I had heard several versions of the events. She was teaching me how to make a stuffed roasting hen, an elaborate dish that involved deboning the chicken while keeping nearly all the meat and skin intact.

I was chopping onions more finely than I'd ever done, to prolong the task she'd found for me. A good cook like Libia is hard to "help"—at best you do the minor tasks, stay out of the way, enjoy the excuse to be there in the kitchen.

"Aurelio always said he felt sorry for the chicken when I made this," she said, sliding the knife inside a drumstick and wiggling the bone from side to side. "He used to say, what if her friends saw her like this? all limp and discouraged and then filled up with nuts and onions like a Christmas cake." She laughed, warmed with the memory.

I diced more slowly, retrieving every sliver, subdividing it into precise pungent cubes. "The guy who did it is in prison now?" No need to spell out what guy, who did what.

"Well yes, the one who pulled the trigger. Poor man, he's not the one they should be punishing of course."

I knew it was obvious from the beginning that it was a hired killer. "How did they catch him?"

"Oh someone saw him drinking at a bar across the street just before it happened. It wasn't hard to find him, really."

"This was very near your apartment wasn't it, that it happened?"—my voice got more elaborately casual with every question, I was down to trimming edges on the onion pieces to make them symmetrical in size and shape.

*Libia nodded, never looking up. The knife flashed along one side of the breast bone as she neatly separated away the ribs. "We were just pulling up to the gate, and Aurelio honked for the doorman to come and open it. Instead of Tomás though, out comes this guy in a ruana, his hands underneath like this, and he came over to the side. Aurelio rolled down the window and said, ¿Qué pasa maestro?—*what's up buddy?*—those were his last words ever, qué pasa maestro." I sneaked a look at her eyes, but they were focused on the knife, the task. The delicate sawing and separating never slowed. "The guy just stood there, white as this countertop, stuck his hand through the window and started firing. Five shots. Aurelio slumped over on my side, on top of me, in my lap, and the guy leaned in and pointed the gun at him, to shoot him some more. I said "¡Ya no más! Ya lo mató, ¡ya no más!"* No more, you've already killed him, no more! *"and he pointed the gun at me. I thought, well, he's going to kill me, too, so I can't identify him." I had heard more emotion in her telling about the misadventures of their string of household help. "But he just kind of looked at me, and at Aurelio, and ran away."*

"Did he—live for awhile?" Kitchens make questions possible that would hurt too much anywhere else, as long as you don't run out of onions.

"No, not really. There was blood everywhere, you can imagine, and I screamed for the neighbors to come. They came out right away and helped me get him into a taxi, but really he was dead before we ever got in. I knew he was dead, five bullets from two feet away? Four in his head, one in his chest." Finally the knife was still. "He never had a chance, but we went

to the hospital as though maybe—" Her voice thinned. Wordlessly, she handed me a bowl. I slid the macerated onions in slowly.

"The killer finally told who hired him?"

"No." A firm shake of her head, the knife moving again, trimming away some fat. "That kind never do. He knows he won't be in prison for long, someone will take care of his family while he's there. If he ever told who was responsible, he would be dead." Matter of fact. "Really, I'm not sure he should be in prison at all. All he did was pull the trigger, he had no reason to be killing Aurelio. We all knew that from the start."

"So they could never prove who was behind it."

A sigh. "No. The police said they could investigate further, try to get more evidence, but then we had that bomb outside our house New Year's Eve—" Two months after the murder, a trash can exploded 25 feet from their front door, minutes after Libia's sons and several nephews and nieces came in from running an errand. They understood it as a warning against further efforts to prove who was responsible. "What's the point, really? We know who did it, the man who arranged it has that to live with all his life. Prison wouldn't change anything."

She sounded so resigned, so calm. I tried to imagine what it must have been like for her. At seven o'clock she met Aurelio at his office, and waited while he called their sons in Bogotá. He called them, or they called him, at least once a day, just to say hello, how's it going, what are you doing? The webs of their daily routines intersected at dozens of points, even from hundreds of miles apart. Around 7:30 they left in the company car, a Mazda, and Aurelio drove slowly through the congested streets of Duitama toward their apartment. Did they hold hands? He always had stories of the day to make Libia laugh. After 30 years, they had less than 15 minutes left together.

He came home from the office that first day in Pasto and stepped out of the car, already shouting. "What's this about a *gringa*, Jairo? What will Teresita say?"

We all stood up from where we'd been chatting in the living room as the door rattled down behind the car. "Aurelio, *respetico*, she's company." I stared at Ruby; I'd never heard her giggle.

I always think of Aurelio and his sons as tall, but the pictures in our album show them to be my height. He had a way of filling a room, though, with a luxuriant black mustache and a voice that boomed. He was barrel-chested and elegantly dressed, and my father-in-law-to-be beamed at him like I'd never seen him do.

"Luis Alfonso, how's life treating you? Ruby, what a delight to have all of you with us. Beloved Libia, the hours have been endless. Don Jairo, always an honor." He passed out hugs and greetings and I waited my turn.

"So you are the *gringa*." He paused and looked me up and down, and everyone snickered at his frank appraising gaze. I stared at him coolly and stuck out my hand; no hugs from me for this loudmouth. He grabbed my hand and kissed it with an elaborate courtly flourish, and the others roared as though this were fine humor. "Kristine, do sit down. Let me get you a whisky and tell you alllllllll about this guy you think you want to marry."

"Aurelio," Ruby cautioned him.

"There's a lot you should know about him while there's time to back out," he began. I glared at the floor, wondering why his obvious jokes got such huge laughs, wishing he would center his attention on someone else.

The evening passed slowly, and I was glad to go to bed. Jairo and his father stayed downstairs talking to Aurelio, their laughter loud and frequent well after midnight. I huddled under the rough wool blankets that weighed several pounds but didn't quite keep me warm, and wondered how often we would have to visit Pasto. For that matter, who knew whether we would end up living in Colombia permanently someday? Jairo was in graduate school, studying engineering. If he had trouble finding work in the States and got a great offer in Colombia, I couldn't very well refuse to go. Could I deal with all of this on a permanent basis? I wondered. Could I learn to laugh at the jokes, could I live with being stared at (or would people someday stop staring), could I learn to enjoy Aurelio's sense of humor as much as everyone else apparently did? Was it always this way when people became a couple and intertwined their lives, or were cultural differences making this harder than it would otherwise be?

A few days later was New Year's Eve, full of action and, as always, full of sound. Ruby had us up early to drive all over town collecting a mysterious array of ingredients: several dozen red roses, a particular brand of men's aftershave that was almost unknown, molasses, eucalyptus branches, saffron. I couldn't quite understand what all this was for, except that the recipe had come from a *curandero*—a faith healer—in Cali, and Ruby was ever so pleased to have gotten hold of it. After lunch she flew between the kitchen and an upstairs bathroom to mix and chop and boil and strain things, humming.

Meanwhile the sons, Oscar and Ivan, and their friends were putting together an *año viejo*—an "old year"—which turned out to be a lifesized doll made of newspaper, dressed in old clothes. All week as we drove around town there had been groups of children and teenagers rattling cans at us as we stopped at stoplights, collecting donations for these often elaborately constructed scarecrows. I wasn't sure what the money was for—the secondhand clothes? the small pieces of felt sewn on for eyes and mouths? All of them wore hats of some kind; maybe it was the hats that cost money?

Late that afternoon I found out. Eleven of us wedged into Aurelio's jeep (he and my father-in-law were just beginning to toast the sunset) and careened around congested streets to a fireworks stand in the center of town. Oscar got out and waited in line while the rest of us waited in the jeep, a few smoking cigarettes. There were giggles and excitement and a flirtation going on between Ivan and one of the girls, a chorus of commentary and encouragement from the rest of the group. I watched this, puzzled; earlier in the week we had met Ivan's girlfriend, and this wasn't her. Why all this egging him on to *cuadrarse* (square off) with her (evidently this meant romance, not a fight) when he was in a relationship with someone else in the same small town?

Finally, Oscar came back with several brown paper bundles. "Careful with this, it's kind of spilling," he pointed out as he handed it back. “What is it?” I asked out of habit. “Gunpowder—Hey! Put out the cigarettes!” They were hastily snuffed out amid guffaws, as I gulped and looked over at Jairo, who smiled and shook his head.

Back at home, the teenagers laced the newspaper-stuffed doll with the gunpowder. Ruby had an evil looking mixture in several large plastic bottles lined up near the bathroom door. Libia had taken over the kitchen, and along with the maid, a narrow-eyed girl who looked to be around 12, was bustling around enough food for half of Pasto. I shuddered to think what the evening might hold. My offer to help in the kitchen was greeted with polite, somewhat embarrassed confusion, as though a child had suddenly asked where babies came from in the middle of a conversation about politics.

“Kristine, your bath is ready. You can go first.” Ruby beamed at me and pointed at one of the plastic bottles near the bathroom. “This one is yours, see? You pour it over your head and rub it in all over your body real well. It’s important not to rinse any of it off, just kind of rub it in and let it stay.”

I stared at Jairo, waiting for him to save me from this. The stuff in the bottle was brown and lumpy, it was 50 degrees outside and permanently chilly inside the house, I was supposed to pour this over myself and not rinse it off? This couldn’t be happening. “What’s this all about?” I murmured to him in English.

“Just a good luck thing you do on New Year’s Eve.”

“I think I’ve had all the luck I need, thanks.” Ruby pressed the bottle at me; there was no way to refuse. I hunched miserably in the bathroom, making whatever would sound like appropriate splashing noises and fighting tears. Maybe this intercultural marriage thing wasn’t such a good idea. Maybe Ruby was just odd, and maybe I would get used to her, and maybe we would live in the US and only come to Colombia once in awhile. Libia was so pleasant, sweet, and normal. But those sons of hers, apart from being mere teenagers, were just like their father. There was no connection between me and these people, there never would be. I wanted to get on a plane and fly home to Texas.

Downstairs Aurelio had dance music blasting on the stereo. As I came into the living room I heard an explosion down the street. This was not firecrackers; it sounded like a shotgun. I gripped the railing and fought cold terror.

"They're after you, *gringa*!" Aurelio shouted, and grabbed my hand. "C'mon, dance with me so they'll think you're Colombian!" My father-in-law grinned fuzzily from the sofa—haha, they'll think she's Colombian—instead of telling him to leave me alone. Where the hell was Jairo? Why wasn't he here to tell me what to do? Was there a polite way to tell your host to bug off in this culture? I hated how close Aurelio held me, hated the cigarette and *aguardiente* smell of his breath, hated feeling so helpless and clueless.

The doorbell rang and Aurelio let me go so he could answer it. "We'll have another dance later, OK, *gringa*?" I shrank upstairs.

The evening lasted for weeks. People came and went, all dressed in satin and soft wool and emeralds, all of them brothers or sisters or cousins or aunt's husbands (who were not uncles, nor were uncle's wives aunts), all of them laughing and hugging and talking loudly over the music. The explosions outside got more frequent and some seemed to be right outside the window. I looked out through the lace curtain at the street and saw small fires here and there on the street, consuming remains of *año viejos* sprawled on the pavement. After awhile it was too cold to stay in my room, and I went down hoping I could hang on the fringes of the merriment and watch, listen, learn what to do before somebody thrust me onstage again. I would have loved to get drunk on *aguardiente,* drunkenness being a proven strategy for blending into any number of tense situations, but the bitter licorice taste gave me a headache and didn't blur the uneasiness at all. Were women even allowed to get drunk in this culture? Who could I ask, and how?

I went to the kitchen, hoping to find a beer. The thin child maid sat hunched on a tall stool and stared at me. "Is there beer in here?" I stood near the refrigerator, wondering whether it was polite to help myself. She didn't understand me. "Beer?" I couldn't decipher the look in her dull black eyes—amusement? fear? curiosity? Yes, she said, there's beer in there. So .... what do I do? I wanted to ask her. In your culture, am I expected to tell you to get it for me, or do I get it myself, or should I go through the hostess? How do you ask a twelve-year-old about how to do something *in your culture*?

Finally, I opened the refrigerator and grabbed a beer, trying to ignore her and the nervous feeling that I might be committing some horrible faux pas. The opener was carefully hidden in a drawer, of course, instead of being stuck with a magnet to the refrigerator as it would have been at my house, and I had to rummage through several of them before I found it. Yes, in the States it's perfectly acceptable to ransack the host's kitchen at a party. I started out with the beer bottle in my hand and at that point, the child came to life. *"No no no señora,"* she waved her hands and hopped off the stool. I stood in the doorway, blushing—what did I do wrong? She scrambled to the freezer and took out a thick, frosty mug, muttering something I couldn't understand, took the beer from my hand and sloshed it in. Way too much foam—I nearly groaned—and a frozen mug was the last thing I needed in this frigid climate. I silently took the beer from her and left the room.

The party was in full swing, people dancing, laughing, shouting, and I had never felt so alone and so tired. Another explosion went off outside—would this ever end? It sounded like a war zone.

The explosion in the trash can outside their house, that New Year's after Aurelio was killed, was a real bomb, not an año viejo. I wondered how they could tell the difference: pretend violence, real violence. Stuffed scarecrows in the street, dead husbands and fathers in taxis on the way to the hospital. Too much a part of life to be surprised, if you're Colombian.

Aurelio, standing between Jairo and his father, caught sight of me.

"C'mon, *gringa*, time for us to dance again! Let's go, it's nearly midnight!" I cringed against the wall and tried not to grimace. Why didn't Jairo step in and do something about this? Why didn't Libia?

Why did no one realize that being pressed up against this big-bellied man with his flowing mustache and his bitter-licorice breath had as much appeal as embracing an alligator fresh from the swamp?

The nightmare went on and on. The crowd was a whirling mass of elegant birds, fluttering and lighting and chattering incomprehensibly in the brightly lit room. As it got later their tongues got fuzzier , their steps unsteadier, and I wanted badly to join them. Something, anything to connect me to them. The beer I'd worked so hard for was the only one in the house. A man who worked his whole life for the largest brewery in Colombia could only serve Chivas, Coca-Cola and *aguardiente* on New Year's Eve; beer was for lower class people.

At midnight someone turned off the lights and Jairo hugged me. For once we could focus on each other, instead of him attending to his mother, his father, the gallery of unknown faces swirling just beyond my reach. The explosions outside paused, then a wave of cracking, booming sound began, a mad crescendo of violent noise to celebrate a moment designated by humans (arbitrarily, I mused, in this land of human-constructed meanings—you can get drunk on ideas if you don't like *aguardiente*) to be the end of one year and the beginning of another.

When the lights came on I looked around. Jairo's father was semi-conscious in an armchair and his mother was stroking his hair, looking straight ahead of her, enduring the moment and waiting sternly for it to pass. One of the younger cousins was weeping quietly in a corner, her brother (was it her brother? was she a cousin?) with a languid arm around her. Apparently she was yet another of Jairo's earlier conquests, her heart forever broken to see him lost to this pale blue-eyed stranger who danced so badly. Maybe he really would be better off with her than with me.

In the middle of the room were Aurelio, Libia, and their two sons. The four of them stood with their arms around each other, heads down, a tight silent circle. They were still there, motionless, long after others had moved on to distribute more casual hugs around the room. I looked at Aurelio, the loud playful bear, at how closely he gathered his family to him, holding them in fiercely loving embrace, for once not shouting or laughing or hoisting a bottle. All four of them dabbed at their eyes when they moved apart, and a tiny crack formed in the wall of disapproval and dislike I'd built against him.

The party died down around 3 a.m., with explosions still happening now and then. Jairo was putting his father to bed when I shut the door behind me and crawled gratefully under the covers. It was over; I had survived; I was alone.

I was deep in a dream about exploding clowns when, after loud knocking and unintelligible shouts, the door burst open. Aurelio lumbered in, my father-in-law behind him, both of them in bathrobes. "Wake up, *gringa,* time for the grapes!" He plopped onto the side of the bed, and I could tell he was still drunk. I recoiled inside and tried to pretend I could sleep through this maniacal scene. Aurelio held a bunch of grapes under my nose. "You have to eat these, quick! It's good luck! If you don't eat the grapes who knows what will happen this year!" I tried harder to ignore him, my stomach churning. "Here!! Eat them, twelve of them!" He started stuffing grapes into my mouth one at a time. Helplessly, I loosened my clenched jaws and chewed listlessly at the grapes, wondering if he would stop if I choked on them. Ruby came in then, yelling as loudly as he was: "Aurelio *qué grosero! Cómo se le occurre entrar a la pieza de uno, escándaloso! Déjela en paz!"* (How dare you come barging into someone's bedroom, you bad-mannered thing! Leave her alone!) Her scolding was lost in chuckles from the door, the rest of the family gathered around to enjoy the spectacle of Aurelio being his hilarious *terrible* self. When they finally dragged him away and shut the door, I huddled under the covers, sobbing and screaming how much I hated this horrible Colombian boor, how much I hated Colombia and all Colombians. The whole idea of joining my life to these people was insane.

It was easier to avoid Aurelio during the rest of the visit. He and Luis Alfonso alternated between drinking and sleeping it off, while the sons took Jairo and me around Pasto. We rode to the top of the volcanic mountain that dominated the landscape, crawling over boulders and through ruts in the road as big as the Jeep. Along with the respective girlfriends we went dancing one night, at a discotheque that got so dark during the slow songs that you bumped into other couples on the dance floor and had to feel your way along the booths to find where you'd been sitting. One day the sun came out, a glorious relief from endless drizzle and fog, and we drove in several cars to a jewel of a lake that sparkled under a velvet blue sky. There were motorboats there with drivers that you paid a dollar for a ride out around an emerald island in the middle of the lake. I wished they would let me off there, let me stay all alone among the evergreens where it was quiet and smelled good and no one had a bottle in their hand.

On the last day Aurelio emerged from his festive semi-coma, and we went to what he described as the best place in Colombia to eat *cuy*. I refused to ask what this delicacy was, so I wouldn't have to see his eyes twinkle as he teased me. He'd say it was tiger, or elephant, or human flesh, and think I was gullible enough to believe him; no thanks. I'd figure out what it was when I saw it.

The "restaurant" was a long drive out into the still, lush countryside. It was one of a group of small houses made of mud and straw, leaning against the years, more dirt than rustic charm. We parked in the dusty yard near a pen made of sticks and corrugated metal.

"Here we go." Aurelio peered into the pen, rubbing his hands in anticipation. "Here, Kristine, I'll pick you out a nice tasty one."

These must be the *cuy*. I looked down, my face carefully set in a smile, ready to voice enthusiasm over whatever local custom was about to be revealed. Inside were a dozen guinea pigs, coated with the same dust of the yard, some running in circles and others lounging on the ground. I stared at them, telling myself I was much too culturally sophisticated to be horrified. I listened to Aurelio negotiating with the proprietor; we needed four *cuy* for the seven of us, "with all the fixings." Whole or cut up? I heard the owner/cook ask. Cut up they cost twice as much as having them whole.

We went to an inner patio of the house to wait, passing through dim rooms with a sagging bed, some carefully hung clothes, a faded couch. The patio had a wooden table and some chairs, and here the cold beer was plentiful. Soon we could smell the roasting *cuy*—I was pleased we hadn't heard the slaughter. For once, the sunshine was bright and the air was dry; for once, the chatting seemed easy.

"Jairo, we need to run that errand after lunch," Aurelio said.

Errand? Jairo just grinned at him.

"YOU know Jairo, the ERRAND." There was no wink, the tone seemed completely serious, but I heard something in his voice that made me smile.

"C'mon, Jairo, they'll be waiting for you at Teresita's house."

Understanding was dawning on me. The name Teresita had come up at odd moments, everyone laughing but me. Now a grin tugged at my mouth. Jairo was someone I could tease.

"Is that the phone I hear? Yes, Tere, we're on our way, don't you worry." Aurelio mimed hanging up a telephone. If there was one in this village at all, it was at the police station. He widened his eyes meaningfully at Jairo. "The ERRAND, Jairo."

"The *errand,* Jairo," I mimicked, and was rewarded with a chuckle from the group.

"What can we get you from the supermarket, Kristine? Come on, we'll be back before the *cuy* is done, or if we're not you all just start without us."

"The closest supermarket is an hour from here," I intoned, my face serious.

"Ohhhhhhhhh but we'll hurry. We won't take long will we, Jairo? Look at poor Jairo, how pale he is."

"Aren't you feeling well, dear?" Visions of the parade of old girlfriends. This was worth needling him about. There were more chuckles around the table. I couldn't believe it; this was suddenly easy.

Aurelio directed himself to my mother-in-law. "Ruby. How are you going to manage two daughter-in-laws?" I giggled. "Ask Luis Alfonso, he knows what it's like to try to keep two women happy."

"He'll tell you *all* about it," I chimed in. I could needle her, too.

"Kristine, you have your list ready for the supermarket? Jairo you go put on some smell-good, quick they'll close up on us. Is that the phone again?"

"I'll bet they're calling from the supermarket."

"Teresita's there, and, boy, is she mad at Jairo."

"Here he is late *again*."

"See you later, Kristine; now don't take it into your head to go for a stroll in El Saladito"—a small town near Pasto, whether fictional or real I never knew, but the home of any number of Teresitas.

The conversation moved on after awhile, and I glowed. The first time you get someone's jokes, a person or a culture's, you're on your way to connecting. Aurelio had been giving me chances all along, with the shouts of *gringa* and the dancing and the grapes. What I needed was time to watch, listen, see how it was done: a slow-paced cloudless day, a wooden table with beer bottles glinting in the sun (apparently it was OK to drink beer in the middle of nowhere on a warm, sunny afternoon), and the savory smell of roasting meat and wood smoke to soften the edges. The *cuy* was delicious, and in fact it tasted quite a bit like chicken.

We left Pasto the next day to drive back to Bogotá. Oscar and Ivan got up to see us off; Aurelio held off going into the office. Libia had made us some *empanadas* for the road, and they smelled rich and inviting from the brown paper bag. "Here, Kristine, you might get thirsty"—Aurelio handed a six pack of *Costeñita,* the lighter, less foamy beer I'd come to enjoy, in through the window. Nothing was ever said about that New Year's Eve, but every time I went to his house after that there was plenty of beer. I learned which drawer they kept the opener in, and Libia sometimes let me help in the kitchen.

"Take care."

"Thanks so much for everything."

"It's been great to meet you."

"Come back anytime, *esta es su casa* (this is your house)."

"Bring us back your *gringuitos*!" yelled Aurelio as we backed down the driveway, and I saw Libia playfully slap his arm. This was the most direct reference yet to the idea that Jairo and I were getting married. For all the jokes and introducing around to the family, the subject had been carefully avoided. Naturally, Aurelio was the one to break the ice. He specialized in outrageous behavior, just beyond the boundaries of the expected, and he was the one most able to extend the web of family around a partner for Jairo they never envisioned.

The day after we stuffed the hen, Libia offered to trim my daughter's hair. She'd done it before, in Bogotá, in the backyard. "I have the hair scissors with me," she said.

"Always prepared."

"You never know when you'll find someone needing a haircut." We laughed together.

We put newspapers on the floor and I went to get a chair, while Erica dragged herself away from the Saturday morning cartoons. Libia pulled out a pair of scissors smaller than my hand.

"That's all you need? I thought you had bigger ones."

"At home I do. These are easier to take on a trip." As she clipped away at the hair over Erica's ear, meticulously evening out the ends, she had a faraway look. "These are the scissors Aurelio used to trim his mustache."

"Really?" I remembered the flowing black walrus, how over the years I got used to him scratching it along my cheek when he said hello. "Did you ever trim it for him? I trim Jairo's." I brushed the hair off of Erica's neck, feeling shy.

"No, he did it himself, every Sunday. He'd stand there in the living room where the light was best and put on good music, of course, and trim that mustache. You know that first year you came to Pasto?" She stopped and looked over at me. "You all left on a Friday. Well that Sunday he was trimming his mustache, and I was keeping him company, and he said he thought you and Jairo were a good match."

"Really?" I couldn't look at her, the woman who loved that man for 30 years and then held him while he died a senseless death.

"Sure. He thought you were just what Jairo needed." She clipped on for awhile in silence, then we talked of other, lighter things. When the haircut was over and Erica scampered away, she touched my arm. "Here. You keep the scissors to trim Jairo's mustache." She said it simply, a smile in her eyes.

I hugged her, fighting a grip in my stomach. "I'll do it on Sundays, and I'll put on good music."

She hugged me back, hard. "That sounds like the best possible use for those scissors."

When I wrote this narrative, I wished less of it were true. I wished I hadn't seen so much loveliness in Aurelio's marriage, his dedication (despite all the Teresita jokes and hangovers and holding women tight when he danced with them) to his family. I wished it had been a heart attack or cirrhosis that got him instead of a hired killer. Sad as that would have been, I could have understood better, a familiar cause and effect. You smoke, you drink, you die; it fit more easily into my head than "you move someplace where the people are different from you and you don't have any connection to them except business, and they get mad at you and hire a man with no way to support his family except to shoot you." I wished Libia had been spared seeing it, that her sons hadn't been three hours away when it happened so that she waited alone in a hospital for them to get there. *I wish I'd made all this up*—but it's all too true, all too real, and in the Colombia of today, it is all too common.

The day after Aurelio was murdered I had to teach my graduate seminar in ethnography. It was brutal to drag myself into the office, clench my teeth against the screams of rage that I wanted to bounce off the walls, and look around the conference room table at bland unknowing faces that had no way to sense that anything was wrong. The whole project of ethnography seemed ironic, even ridiculous, that day: I had spent most of a decade explaining what I called "Colombian culture" to mostly middle class, mostly US American (like me) audiences. To explain and describe a culture not my own was to claim to have made sense of it. Maybe not the sense the natives would make of it, but *my* sense, that at that moment seemed all nonsense. The neat patterns I'd seen in the data and called "premises," "norms," "symbols" suddenly seemed meaningless fictions. "Colombian culture" was nothing but pain and blood and darkness now, a widow, a hired gun, a vendor with a bad check and a worse temper. There was no "sense" to be made of that, and I didn't want to look for any. I didn't want to find *sense* in what was senseless. To find *a cultural explanation* for something so tragic would be obscene and dehumanizing, a set of lies that would tell nothing of Aurelio's life or his family or his wicked sense of humor. I knew I would write about it someday, but I hope never to *make sense* of it.

Reflections and expansions

1. Ethnographic methods courses and books often focus on participant observation and interviewing as the primary means of collecting data. Much of what is most difficult for a cultural outsider to understand, however, involves questions that cannot be asked. Questions that amount to "Why are you doing that?" or "What does that mean?" create two problems. One is the face threat that comes from the implication that the questions are beings asked because the words or actions they relate to are deficient in some way. You don't ask "What does that mean?" if the utterance or conversation makes sense, so by asking you imply that it doesn't. To see why this is so, try asking a few times at everyday moments:

   "Why are you laughing?" when the laughter is clearly not amusement.

   "Why did you do that?" when someone trips, drops, or spills something.

   "What were you *thinking*?" a parental favorite when a bad choice is made public.

Scenes from an intercultural marriage

In the spring semester of 1999, I lived a dream come true: I had a research leave in England for eight months, with both my salary and a research grant. I lived in a place remarkably similar to Iowa City called Loughborough, quieter and more cerebral than London, 90 miles south. Erica, then 10 years old, came with me and wore a uniform to school, and we both rode bicycles everywhere. I had an office at the university, colleagues to talk about research with, freedom from the structure of teaching and the stress of committee work. In almost every way, it was the happiest time of my life.

In one very significant way, though, I was miserable from the first lovely day to the last. Living for several months without Jairo showed me just how dependent on him I had become in the 16 years we had been married. I was so out of the habit of paying bills that our electricity was briefly shut off. A clock fell off of a wall and its second hand dislodged; I fretted over having to buy a new one (where do they sell wall clocks in England? Or anywhere, for that matter?) until Erica pointed out that we could simply take the face off and put the hand back on

Transcribing Silence: Culture, Relationships, and Communication
by Kristine L. Muñoz, 122–139.

its pin. When my bike had a flat tire, I sat beside the road and sobbed, convinced I would now have to walk everywhere. I was forced to face the fact, especially humbling for any woman who thinks of herself as a feminist, that I had learned many ways to be helpless.

As winter eased into spring, yard work became symbolic of all the things I had no excuse for not knowing how to do. There were sliding glass doors from the living room out to the backyard (*garden,* as the English called it) so that it filled the view from the sofa, looking every bit the rental house garden: overgrown, unkempt, unloved. I gazed out the doors day after day, wishing I would do something about the mess: pull some of the weeds that covered the rockery, trim the bushes, poison a dandelion or two before they spread more thickly across the grass.

But I couldn't get myself to go outside. I hated looking at the mess of a garden that could be beautiful with some time and energy. I hated even worse the physical sense of vacancy, like an arm missing, the sense that if Jairo were there we would spend whole days outside, enjoying the sunshine and weeding and trimming together. We'd have lunch in the slender shade of a fir tree, and at the end of the day we'd toast our progress with martinis. If he were there it wouldn't be *yardwork,* it would be *gardening.* It would be time together, working on something I could enjoy because he enjoys it so much it's contagious. We would coordinate our actions in the well-worn ways that spending years of your life with someone makes possible. When we work in the yard at home, he directs, and I do as I am told: "Trim this back like this, try to make it even all the way around. It's OK to chop it off short, it'll grow back in no time." "These are the weeds, see? and these are something nice, leave them there." Without him to lead the way in England, I felt more incompetent than ever. I fumed at the disarray, and at myself.

Part of the fuming was feminist guilt: How did I allow myself to get so dependent on a man? Surely I could get out there with clippers and a trowel and take a stab at figuring it out; lots of people do. Being in England without him made me realize that I had not fixed things or balanced a checkbook or paid bills for so long I didn't immediately know how. My only comfort was what Jairo told me of his own moments of helplessness: Twelve year old Gabe had his first girlfriend, and wanted to talk endlessly about her and his feelings and all the new experiences he was having. Jairo knew he was supposed to listen and be supportive, but the talk about the feelings and the meanings and how crazy wonderful it felt to hold hands in the dark was driving him nuts. He moaned about trading places with me—he would gladly do all the yard work if I would listen to Gabe's nightly explorations of adolescent love. I realized we had become the cliché I swore to avoid: a conventional male/female relationship.

Part of my disappointment was clearly garden-variety ideological shortcoming (pun intended): My generation of women was supposed to be immunized against depending on men by the strident debates of the 1960s and 1970s. More specifically, I was chagrined that a child of Lois Fitch could be so inadequate in everyday tasks like bill paying, checkbooks, and weeding. My mother worked as a medical technologist, first part time and then full time, from the time my brother and I were babies. Although she did most of the second shift—cooking and housework were still up to her, however many hours she was working—my father quite cheerfully devoted himself to child care in ways that most men of his generation scorned.

I thought I had escaped the bondage of tradition when I kept my last name when I got married. Jairo and I walked down the aisle together at our wedding—none of this Dad giving me away ("I really hoped I could sell you," he quipped. I never knew if somewhere inside, he was sad to have been denied that role). I kept my own bank account with the savings I had before we were married. By 1999 I was living several thousand miles away for career reasons, leaving Jairo to cook and clean and scowl at our son's confidences. How much further from conventional could I get? (The obvious point that getting married was itself a deep, reverential bow to convention was not one I was confronted with until—coincidentally?—that dreamlike semester in England.)

Facing my incompetence with numbers and fixing things brought the more profound experience of feeling incomplete without Jairo. I saw what had been invisible to me until then: specific details of what it means to be half of a couple with this individual for most of my adult life. A question I sometimes get, when people know I am married to a Colombian, is what impact cultural differences have had on our relationship. Sitting there staring gloomily out at the unkempt garden in Loughborough, I wondered what answer I could possibly give to that question. The weedy backyard is an English garden by virtue of being located in England, and our marriage is intercultural because he is Colombian and I am American. Beyond the accidents of geography and dialect—less meaningful to me than ever, looking at the dandelions and the crumbling rockery outside the house, and the unpaid bills and the broken clock and my borderline depression on the inside—what did any of it mean? Jairo and I, coming from cultures that presumably differed in their gender roles as much as any other dimension, had clearly absorbed many of the same male/female role expectations. We even absorbed those we tried hard to resist, the ones that made me sob over a bicycle tire and Jairo bellow with rage when the phone rang for the fourteenth time in one evening.

Identifying what makes ours an *intercultural marriage* involves looking back over a mosaic of events, experiences, decisions, emotions, and actions that make up the life we have led together. Some of those moments are memorable enough to tell stories about, like Jairo driving my car home after our first date (we were lucky to survive). Many more are just what happens next when you wake up beside the same person day after day, things that could happen to any couple sharing a life together. The problem is trying to say with any certainty which of the moments that define me and Jairo as a couple are about cultural issues. I look back, of course, for the conversations: What did we—and other people—say? What went unsaid?

1. Houston, January 29, 1983. I was teaching in an English as a second language program at the University of Houston. I co-taught with a woman named Carol, who had taught in this program for decades and had created the class she called Cross Cultural Communication. After the first day's session we looked through the class list.

Me. So a good mix in this one—Korean, Japanese, Greek, South Americans, the odd Arab.

Carol. Arab?

Me. That one (pointing at the roster): Jairo. HY-ro? Or JAY-ro? Looks Arab, but this says Colombia. Must have Arab parents.

Carol. Immigrants maybe. Do you remember which one he is?

Me. Nah. Maybe the one in the black sweatshirt—

Carol. Yeah, had to be. It said St. Tropez on it.

2. The same day, in an apartment in Houston. Jairo was living with his cousin Diego, who had been in the US for five years. Jairo came to the US to work on a master's degree in engineering, starting in Houston because he could live with his cousin.

Diego. So how was the first day?

Jairo. Seemed OK. Probably good for me to do this semester of English first and retake the TOEFL.

Diego. Any nice looking teachers?

Jairo. Hah! no such thing as a nice looking *gringa*—all of them so cold and arrogant. One was OK, though, aside from her skinny legs.

Aside from her skinny legs became the phrase that lingers between us still, that we use to refer to those early days of first impressions. There were no angels trumpeting from the heavens, no mystical premonition that we would look back on that January day from decades later as the beginning of a long story. Where we started, in fact, was with stereotypes: this looks like an Arab name, maybe he's from an immigrant family (when in fact Jairo is a very common name in Colombia); *gringas* are cold and arrogant.

3. Two days later, after class, in a hallway outside the classroom:

Me. (eager to practice my Spanish) Me gusta tu ... ¿cómo llamas esto?

I like your—what do you call this?

Jairo. Una bufanda. (smiling) La tienes a la vista.

A muffler. Look at it all you want. (The conventional response to a compliment in Colombia is 'la tienes a la orden'—*use it all you want*—so this was a play on words that of course I did not catch.)

Me. Y ¿cómo llamas esto?

And what do you call this? (a small gold pin on his lapel)

Jairo. Se llama un tunjo—es un espíritu de los indios, representa la fertilidad.

It's called a tunjo*—it's an indigenous spirit that represents fertility.*

Me. (blushing) Ahh, ni voy a mirarlo!

Ahh, I'm not even going to look at that one!

4. Near Houston, a month later, February 1983, in the living room of a rented house. Me and Tom, a man I've lived with for 18 months. He is rolling a joint, and notes that there isn't much left of the stash.

Tom. Don't you have any Colombians in your class? (snickers)

Me. Matter of fact I do.

Tom. Couldn't you get them to ask Uncle Pedro (mispronounced with exaggerated English-speaker ignorance of the real sound, PEE-droe) to send them a little something?

Me. Mmm. (silence while we smoke the joint) Tom, do you envision someday giving this up?

Tom. What, getting high? (I nod; he giggles) Nope, not really.

Me. You plan to be 50 years old and getting high every day of your life?

Tom. Yeah, I do. (giggles again, looking pleased) Something to look forward to.

(TV is on; we watch in silence for awhile)

Me. What would you say (I rub his chest softly, sweetly) if when we got married I hyphenated my name? if I wanted to be Carson-Fitch? (I feel him stiffen. He pulls away to light a cigarette and puffs hard on it, staring at me.)

Tom. I'd say we were finished, that's what. (Another long puff, hard stare) If you aren't even willing to take my name I don't know why we're getting married.

Me. I just wondered; I'm not really thinking of *doing* that.

Tom. So why'd you ask? *Jesus.*

Me. Come on, it was just a question.

Tom. Well I would still like to know what the hell kind of question that is, what kind of a wimp you think I am. (The conversation became an argument, which lasted for two hours and ended up with me in repentant tears and feeling like the most emasculating bitch who ever lived. I vowed never to bring it up again; I would take his name, whatever would keep the peace.)

5. Houston, April 6, 1983. After class, in a hallway dappled with springtime sunlight, the excellent student Jairo has stayed to ask a question about an assignment. We chat awhile in Spanish, and I notice the hallways have emptied.

Me. Would you, uh, (digging my toe into the floor) I mean probably you don't want to, I know you need to catch your bus and all.

J. There's lots of buses.

Me. Would you like to—I mean—uh—maybe—would you—do you want to—maybe—uh—(I am sweating profusely and looking everywhere but at him) wanna go for a cup of coffee?

J. Let's go!

I had never asked a man out before, but thought that South American attitudes toward hierarchy and respect for teachers meant he would never make the first move. He confirmed this in our later conversations about that magical moment, and said he was floored when I suggested coffee—but maybe that's how they did things in the US? He was also pleased when I amended the suggestion to "or maybe a beer"—an opening to a different kind of relational event than coffee, in, as it happened, both of our cultures.

6. Three hours later, outside Nanny's, a bar where we have each had three beers and a great many chips with salsa.

Me. I can give you a ride home, or—would you like to drive? (*thinking: I know it's important to Latin men to be in charge, I'll show him I'm not the controlling type, that's caused so much conflict with Tom)*

J. No, that's OK, I'm not used to the traffic here or anything.

Me. No, really, I don't mind, here, you drive.

The 15 minute ride to his apartment is terrifying for both of us: He has never driven anything larger than a VW Beetle, and my car is an aging Oldsmobile Cutlass Supreme. It is his first experience of power steering or power brakes, and he drives in the middle of two lanes on the freeway. I grit my teeth to keep from screaming. When we get to his cousin's apartment, we both sigh with relief as he turns the car off.

Me. You'll forgive me if I drive from now on.

J. From now on sounds *very* promising. (His head hits the rearview mirror as he reaches across to kiss me. We both laugh.)

7. June 2, 1983, a warm, muggy Houston day in Hermann Park. Because Jairo has three male roommates and I live with my parents 30 miles away, we spend a lot of time in parks. As a very junior teacher in the ESL program, I have just found out that there are not enough students for me to be employed there for the summer. There are no guarantees for the fall, either. I am devastated, though not surprised; he is sympathetic.

Jairo. So job security isn't a primary characteristic of this line of work.

Me. Nope. Layoffs like this are typical. I never planned for this to be forever anyway. I'm just doing this until I'm ready to go back to graduate school.

Jairo. And get a doctorate?

Me. That's right. *(wondering: will he think this is too much ambition? By this time Tom and I have broken up, over the name change, my plans for a doctorate, and so many other reasons.)*

J. Wow, that's really neat. My uncle has a PhD; I've always thought that would be an amazing accomplishment. Good for you.

Me. I'm thinking about the University of Washington, in Seattle.

J. (playfully) And what's there for me to do in Seattle?

Me. There's Boeing, you could build airplanes.

J. Let's go! (*lots of grins, hugs, laughter. What a wild idea, I thought, a Colombian willing to move across the country for* my *career—something Tom, a middle class US American, had indignantly refused to consider.*)

8. July, 1983. Hermann Park Outdoor Theater, Houston; before a performance of *Madame Butterfly*. My parents, about to meet Jairo for the first time, locate us across the crowd and wave to get our attention.

Dad. (hissed) Is he *black*?

Mom. I don't *think* so; he's South American or something.

We didn't hear this conversation, of course, because my parents were committed to teaching my brother and me—unlike most of our peers in south Texas at the time—that racism was evil and stupid. Mom told me about it much later, stunned at what had escaped my father in an unguarded moment.

9a. August 15, 1983, in the living room of Jairo's apartment.

Me. What's that?

J. My letter of acceptance from the University of Houston. *(He tears open the envelope and begins to read)* Dear Mr. MUNzo—geez, I have to get used to seeing my name misspelled—we are sorry to tell you...

(long pause; he keeps reading silently)

Me. What is it? Come on, they only gave you half a scholarship? *(surely he was kidding?)*

J. *(looking up at last)* They've turned me down. They say my grades aren't high enough. There has to be some mistake, I was third in my class, how can that be not good enough for the University of Houston?

Me. That's crazy. We'll go talk to them. *(My mind raced. Jairo stopped applying to other master's programs once we were dating, saying he wanted to stay in Houston. If he wasn't enrolled in a degree program, he'd have no visa to stay in the US.)* We'll get them to see reason. If they don't—

J. *(firmly)* They have to; they have to see they've made a mistake.

Me. If they don't, we'll get married so you can keep your visa.

J. *(a long, slow look)* I don't want to go about it *that* way, but after we straighten this out, let's talk about that again.

9b. August, 1983, a sweltering day beginning to cool off. Outside Butera's, a yuppie deli in Houston. Jairo has talked to the graduate director in industrial engineering, who saw they had figured his GPA incorrectly. The graduate director apologized profusely and said of course he would be admitted to the program, of course he would have a teaching assistantship. We are sitting outside at a table with a single rose in a vase, and it seems utterly romantic, despite the humidity and traffic fumes. We toast his success and our shared relief with a bottle of chardonnay.

Me. He was really so embarrassed, wasn't he? as he should be, making that kind of mistake. Dummies.

J. *(wryly)* South Americans may not be at the top of their list.

Me. Well, more fools they. Here's to you! *(glasses clink)*

J. OK, back to where we were the other day.

Me. Where were we?

J. You mentioned us getting married. What do you think of that idea?

Me. You mean, like, for real?

J. For real for real.

(a long silence; did I look at him? Did he have my hand in his?)

Me. I dunno. What do *you* think?

J. I think we make a very good team. *(A montage of the summer floats through my head—my unemployment, talking about plans for the future, all the hours in parks with talking the only intimacy available to us.)*

Me. I guess we do. What will your family say?

J. My mother said before I left that she knew I was never coming back.

Me. *Really?*

J. Yeah. I was packing and she said, I'm going to get rid of this bunk bed in here because you're going to stay in the US forever. I said, oh don't be silly, I'm just going for a year or two, I'll be back. Who wants one of those cold unfriendly *gringas? (he grinned, squeezed my hand)*

Me. Where do you think we will—would—live, here or in Colombia?

J. Hard to say, but I think here's more likely. You'll get your PhD here, and there won't be very many professional opportunities for you in Colombia.

Me. Hmf. Assuming I actually do make it through a doctorate.

J. You will, and you'll go into university teaching. You don't want to stay in ESL, there's no money, no job security ...

Me. ... cheeky students who don't do their homework ...

J. So we're agreed.

Me. We're agreed. *(glasses clinked)* To Colombian American relations.

J. Let freedom ring.

So where was culture in this process of getting into an intercultural marriage? It started long before I met Jairo. Growing up in Texas in the 1960s and 1970s meant that many men, like Tom, could not imagine moving across the country for a woman's career plans. By the early 1980s they couldn't say that out loud so freely, but they could be openly incensed at the idea that their wives would keep their own last names. In that world, for a woman to be ambitious and well-educated was dangerous, often fatal for romantic relationships. Like many women, I struggled with how much I needed to go along with Tom's interpretations of my actions: If I wanted to drive because he'd been smoking dope, I was emasculating him. If I considered keeping my name when we got married, I was casting him as a wimp. I don't know, of course, how typical Tom was of men at that time, how many of the troubles we had were about a mismatch of personalities and goals. I certainly saw our problems as *ours*, as a matter of who we were as a couple.

Now I see it as at least partly a cultural issue: Tom's resistance to my career plans were not something he came up with on his own. His drug habits were not unique to him, though it does seem in retrospect he was more attached to those practices than many people who outgrow them sooner than he did. The extremes of his temper tantrums when I tried out the idea of hyphenating my name are a mystery: Was this his personality, a mismatch with my own, or was he unprepared, by virtue of having grown up in a conservative, working-class family, to accept a wife who didn't take his family name?

The biggest question of all: How is it Tom and I grew up in the same culture and were so far apart on the most significant issues of the life we thought we wanted together, when Jairo and I grew up speaking different languages, in different religions, on different continents, and were apparently so well-matched?

To have no answer for that shows how hard it is to say anything sensible about what makes a marriage intercultural. Jairo and I are, somehow, well-matched on the important issues. He and I both grew up with mothers whose careers were significant and important, not just a way to keep them entertained when they finished with housework and bridge parties (not that either housework or bridge parties are part of the lives of middle-class Colombian women). We both grew up watching what happened when someone in the household spent more money than the family income really allowed for, and acquired the same deep shudder about that habit. By the time I was staring glumly out at the English garden, I had spent 16 years becoming less certain about what counted as a cultural difference, rather than what counted as a difference in personalities or families of origin, when it came to two people sharing a life.

I figured out a few things, though: There's cultural difference, and then there's race and class. A marriage defined as intercultural can be seen as exotic rather than inappropriate and, thus, troublesome for the social network. I'm convinced Jairo and I had an easier time with friends and relatives in the US than a more obviously interracial couple would have.[1] "Is he *black*?" my dad hissed the first time he saw Jairo, and Mom hurried to assure him he was not. The fact that the question was asked, that it was directed to her rather than to me or Jairo, and that my mother said *no no of course not, he's South American,* rather than *what kind of a question is that?* suggest that it was a delicate and important issue. In addition to being well matched as individuals, we had to be well enough matched not to create problems for our friends and families. An interracial relationship might have been a problem; it might not have, or might have resolved itself quickly once they got to know him. All unsaid, and unknowable.

In much the same way, my not being Catholic never came up on the Colombian side. What mattered was that I had a college degree and a career underway (in a word, I was *una profesional*). This is not usually the deal maker-or-breaker assumed by North Americans for South Americans. All four of our parents were the first in their families to get past eighth grade, and all four had college degrees. Yet their orientations to education one generation away from the working class were quite different: When Jairo's parents told friends and family about me, the first description (after *gringa*) was that I was *una profesional*. When my family described him to others, the fact of his being South American was so exotic it took precedence over everything else. I asked my mother once if she ever added, "Oh yes, he has a college degree" and got a mystified look. "Why would that matter?" she asked. Did she not say that because everyone assumed he did, or because it really didn't matter if he did or did not?

Beyond the need for compatibility of race and class, rather than religion or nationality, a term I have learned to apply to intercultural relationships is that there are cultural differences with teeth and without them. The ones without teeth are the ones that are easy to understand, accommodate, and even enjoy: food and holidays, what you say when someone sneezes or when you want them to smile for a picture or when you clink your wine glasses in a toast, whether you shake hands or hug or kiss on the cheek when you say hello. The ones with teeth are the ones that bite you: the expectation among Colombians that you show loving affection and respect for relatives even after you watch them get drunk and behave abominably, night after night, year after year. The expectation—really an imperative—among middle class Americans that children must leave home at age 18, whether or not they or their parents are ready for them to leave and regardless of whether they could pursue a job or education while living at home, saving everybody money and energy. Understanding that animals that shed and ruin carpets and run up vet bills on a par with orthodontists may nonetheless be considered a fundamental necessity of a healthy childhood.

Two final scenes:

10. September, 1984, still in Houston; Jairo and I have been married for three months. We attend the funeral of a family member, and join my parents outside the church to greet the guests. A middle aged woman approaches and hugs them, and my mother turns to introduce us.

"You remember Kristine, my daughter? And this is Jairo, the new member of our family..." The woman barely glanced at Jairo, and gave me something of a steely stare. "Keep your eye on him, honey, Latin men can't be trusted out of your sight." All of our jaws dropped as she moved along to greet someone else.

Although that was the only time that particular stereotype was brought up explicitly, both Jairo and my children have told me that Colombian drug lord jokes are almost inevitable when they mention their connection to Colombia. I fume: Can people possibly think this passes for polite conversation with someone you just met?

11. 2009, Bogota. Our 25th anniversary, in a room filled with tables with white tablecloths and silver bows, yellow and peach colored roses—a color combination I have never seen, more roses than I have ever seen in one place (Colombia exports more roses than any other country in the world. If you have bought or received roses in the US, they probably came from Colombia. Why don't people think of that, instead of cocaine?), waiters in tuxedos and white gloves, and dozens of people I truly love. My in-laws, of course, and their widely extended family, most of whom I can now at least vaguely place on the family tree. Friends I made during the year I spent doing my dissertation in Bogotá, in 1987, among the dearest connections I have. Libia, Oscar, Ivan, their wives and children. A man in his late 20s whom we hosted as an exchange student in Iowa City when he was a teenager, with his wife and children. Before the dinner, the dancing, and the champagne—I no longer have to search for a lone beer in a stranger's refrigerator—there are speeches and a blessing from the uncle who is a priest.

Although ceremonial speaking is largely a man's role on big occasions, I have been part of the family long enough to feel confident I can add my voice directly to the occasion. I wanted to speak to the people assembled there, to put something into words about those 25 years that had passed, the connections that had formed with the people in the room.

I started with the story of how we met, and his line—"Look at it all you want"—drew a laugh. *"Así fue que empezaron, Papá y Mamá"*—that's how they got started, Papa and Mama—the chorus of a popular dance song from the 1950's, a bigger laugh.

"All of us in here who are married know that you don't marry a person, you marry a family. In my case, I married a culture." I said how proud I was that my children had learned Colombian respect for their elders and devotion to their family; that Spanish is so important to them that both had sworn not to marry anyone who didn't speak Spanish (it's true that they said that; we'll see.) I pointed out that a long marriage always brings with it a great deal that you never expect when you say *I do*: "Jairo didn't expect to spend so much time looking for my glasses and my car keys"—a chuckle—"nor did he expect to be with my mother in the hour that she died." They knew that was recent, and there was a hush.

"None of us knew, or maybe all of us did, that marrying me meant Jairo spending most of his life a long way from all of you." Complete silence. "More than anything tonight, I want to thank you all for the sacrifice that's meant for you. Jairo has been a life companion for me like no one else could have been, and I owe that to Luis Alfonso and Ruby" (his parents) "and José Gabriel and Dora Lilia" (his brother and sister-and-law, both dabbing vigorously at their eyes) "and all of the Muñozes" (half the people in the room) "and the Correas" (Ruby's brother, the priest, now sobbing into a table napkin) "and all of Colombia. I love you all, and I love Colombia." I held up my glass in a toast, the applause was warm and people stood up with glasses in their hands, and in that instant I knew: These people and the relationships I have with them, their culture that has formed both my marriage and my children, not to mention most of my scholarly life, have also formed *me* in profound ways that I want everyone to know, all the time, about me.

So it was that, a few months later, I changed my name to Muñoz. I like it; it fits. I don't feel like I'm property or that my identity has changed, except in the sense that I have gotten to live a bicultural life I could not even dream of as a child. The name puts all of those complex moments of learning to be myself and be a part of a Colombian family into one simple word, a family name.

People ask me whether I plan someday to do research on intercultural couples, assuming it's a natural direction for my work to go since it is also the reality I live. The longer I live as one, the less sure I am about where I would start, what questions I would ask, how I would go about looking for answers. What even counts as an intercultural couple, and is there a time when they each absorb enough of the other's culture that they stop being intercultural?

Reflections and expansions

1. A metaphor for long-term intercultural contact is that it creates a "third culture," that is, a system of meaning that is not predominantly one or the other, but a unique blend of both (or all) of them. Although the term is usually applied either to an interdependent connection of science and humanities scholars or to a child who has grown up with strong influences from two or more cultures to become a "third culture kid" (TCK), it could readily be applied to an intercultural marriage. Do you see evidence in this narrative that the Colombian/American couple became a third culture, or do you think the fact of living in the US for their entire marriage made them essentially a US American couple with relatives abroad?
2. How would you define the difference between an intercultural marriage and an interracial one? Could an interracial marriage ever NOT be an intercultural one? To whom, and when, and why would it matter?
3. Do you observe intercultural or interracial marriages in your everyday life? How do you react to them? How do others react to them?
4. What impact does social class difference have on a romantic couple? Does it matter in a heterosexual couple whether the man or the woman comes from the higher social class? Is it a different situation when the relational partners are close friends rather than romantic partners?

Alone again, naturally

I come to find a refuge in the easy silence that you make for me, it's OK when there's nothing left to say to me...

Dixie Chicks, "Easy Silence"

What does it take to have a marriage last forever? Our 30th wedding anniversary happened in 2014, and I got many versions of that question. I had a list of flip answers: "If this one does, I'll let you know." "It's a series of one-year contracts, up for renewal every May." "Marrying the right person helps." "Being lucky is HUGE." The truth seems impossible, elusive, though the flip answers all have elements of my lived experience. I would love to adopt the tone of a sage and proclaim something I know to be true, as I do many times a day in my professional life. As I look for the unsaid and unsayable, I search through moments of our life as a couple, then a family, and now back to a couple, attentive to times of silence.[1]

When we dropped our son off in front of his dorm one Sunday night in October of his first year in college, it was noticeably easier than his leave-taking just a few months earlier. In August, he was Leaving Home, a moment fraught with so much emotion there was no way to pretend it was just another week away at camp. His two suitcases held

---

Transcribing Silence: Culture, Relationships, and Communication
by Kristine L. Muñoz, 140–150.

most of the clothes he owned, a few pictures of family and friends, new extra-long sheets we'd been persuaded to buy. He was getting on a plane to go a thousand miles away until at least November. I had been sobbing off and on all summer. It felt like extended labor pains that came closer and closer together, for the last week just a few hours apart. The goodbye hug in our driveway was agony, a struggle not to break down in front of him.

By October, when we went for Family Weekend, our goodbyes were downright casual. "We had a great time," we said. "So did I, thanks for coming!" he answered. "See you at Thanksgiving," we all said together. He shouldered his backpack and sauntered to the door. Before he got his key out, it opened and a crowd of laughing teenagers spilled onto the sidewalk. Gabe high-fived some of them, and I heard him say he'd put his stuff down and catch up with them. He disappeared through the door they held open for him without a backward glance.

Jairo and I got into the rental car to drive back to the hotel, and despite the music from the satellite radio the silence between us was deafening. I looked across the front seat at my husband of 22 years and felt something sitting between us I could not bear to look too closely at. It wasn't that he suddenly looked like a stranger. In fact, he was so familiar he was almost invisible, like looking down at my own hand. But there was something about being alone together that felt like barbed wire. I looked out the windshield at the soft Tucson night and focused on what I needed to do back at the hotel: finish packing, brush my teeth, set two alarms to make my 7 a.m. flight. After the early flight and a tight connection in Dallas, I had an afternoon of meetings in Iowa City. The rhythm of our lives, centered on the hectic pace of mid-career that had been disrupted for three heavenly days to focus on our college boy, would settle back into the usual whirlwind.

Days later, I caught my breath and thought back to the moment in the car, the space between me and Jairo across the front seat, and this time looked at it more closely. We were alone in that moment, the kind of alone that you notice because it's suddenly so quiet. When Gabe showed us around the University of Arizona, we saw a new version of him: very much at home, familiar with the places, lots of people to say hello to and introduce us to. For an outgoing person like our son, freshman year of college was the most people-filled time of life. He shared a room for the first time since he was three; his dorm had communal baths; he met people everywhere he went, all of them friendly and mostly available to hang out with. Although he clearly enjoyed our visit, he was excited to get back into the social whirl that swept him up before he was even inside the door.

I remembered feeling just that way when my parents dropped me off in front of my dorm at the University of Texas 30 years earlier. I felt sorry for them as they drove away, though I wasn't sure why. I couldn't imagine that going back to work could be *fun,* in the way that going back to being in college was the most fun I ever had. Adulthood in general, the fully responsible version that was still some way off when I was 18, looked so dreary. I think I also knew enough about their relationship by then to see it as a cold, lonely place to be without me and my brother.

My parents were a post-war couple, married in 1955. My mother said many times that they didn't necessarily expect happiness out of marriage. Much more important, she said, was that they made a good team: They worked together to build a house, raise my brother and me and put us through college, with hardly a cross word between them. As rarely as they showed anger with each other, though, they even less often showed affection or respect. A friend of mine, after spending a weekend at my house, pointed out that my parents had perfected the art of never being in the same room together. That included sleeping in separate rooms as soon as I moved out. To my knowledge, they never considered divorce, even as active displays of anger and dislike became more common. I don't know that either of them could have wished the other one dead, either; but they clearly did not seek out or enjoy one another's company. They lived in the same house, but to the greatest extent possible they lived separate lives.

The reason I saw the space between me and Jairo in the car that night as huge, dark, dangerous, and painful might have been that I grew up resigned to the idea that my parents' relationship was what marriage *was*. Either you split up along the way—as a fair number of my friends' parents and some of my aunts and uncles did—or you were more or less miserable together. Statistically, one of the most common times for divorce is just after the children leave home, and the inference is that the couple has held on despite their unhappiness until their breakup will have less impact on the children. An only slightly different version is that when the kids are gone, many couples find out they have nothing in common any more. They have drifted apart without noticing, and they can't find their way back together. Knowing that, and wondering if we were about to find out something about ourselves we never suspected, sat silently between us in the darkness of the rental car.

The historical aspect of this sudden feeling of being alone was that I met and got to know Jairo in a very public way. Because he was a student in my class, being alone with him was both impossible to arrange casually and profoundly taboo to even wish for. Besides that, I was living with my boyfriend.

Before we got together I found myself thinking of all the questions I would ask Jairo if we were ever alone, things I wanted to tell him about me. We didn't exactly sneak out of the building that first time, but I was desperately aware of how untoward it would look for us to be leaving together, alone.

For the first several months of our courtship, being alone was still hard to arrange. After my boyfriend and I split up I lived at home with my parents, while Jairo lived 30 miles away with three gay men. Our romance had to be kept hidden from my colleagues, because teachers dating their students was both shameful and grounds for dismissal. The difficulties made it that much sweeter when we did manage to be alone, largely in parks or sidewalk cafés. Being alone with him was Treasure Island then, the place where all worries and frustrations fell away into sheer delight, and always tinged with that little shiver of fear that we'd be found out.

Less than a year later we were married and living in our first apartment with his mother. It is a long and culturally complicated story of how that happened, but being alone together stayed almost as difficult, and therefore every bit as precious, as ever. She was as considerate and respectful of our privacy as any human being in a two-bedroom apartment with one shared bath could have been. In-law jokes aside, it was not as bad as it may sound. At least we had a door we could shut behind us, and the ecstatic freedom of choosing each other's company over anything else we might be doing. That delight may have lingered more than it might with newlyweds who live together or know each other longer, under less peopled circumstances, than we did before we got married.

Six months after the wedding we moved from Houston to Seattle, which created an entirely new way of being alone together. It was the first time either of us had been so completely and permanently away from our families, and the first time either of us had been to the Northwest. We had one part-time job between us, which was my teaching assistantship in the doctoral program that was the reason for us moving. I remember vividly that I brought home $705 a month. Even in 1985, that was a slender shoestring for two people and a dog to live on. To get to Seattle we drove some 1,200 miles in a U-Haul, with every stick of used furniture that constituted our worldly belongings behind us. It was equal parts exhilaration and terror. We drove slowly out of Houston in a downpour the day after Christmas, hoping it was just weather and not an omen.

When I look back at that very long drive, we seem so young and inexperienced, the future so uncertain. But I didn't get migraines then, and Jairo didn't get up at 5:30 to go to work, and we didn't ever stay at the office till 6 or 7 and then go separately to exercise. Any minute we had free we spent with each other, and savored every one of them, and they never seemed like enough.

When Jairo started working at Boeing after our first year in Seattle, I was in graduate school, and we had our first taste of what a consuming focus on careers does to being a couple. We made time to go on dates and tried—believers in the self-help, take-care-of your-marriage school of thought—to make it a point to regularly focus on each other and on our relationship. We were supported in doing all this by a culture that warned of the dangers of taking each other for granted, growing apart, being married to our work instead of to each other. Having time alone wasn't a problem anymore. The struggle was to focus on each other during our time together, instead of each of us reading our own book, or one person sleeping while the other one cleaned house.

Predictably, we then had children. It is a famously difficult time in marriage, statistically a time when marital satisfaction plummets. There is nothing so all-consuming of time and energy as a baby, unless it's one who comes along at a period of intense career pressure. I gave birth one month after I passed my doctoral comprehensive exam, and the nightmare scenarios of what would have happened if Gabe had come early are still with me. The second time cut even closer: Erica was born two days after I turned in my dissertation. We moved from Seattle to Boulder, Colorado, with a four-month-old and a three-year-old, and I still feel the exhaustion and stress as I write that down.

For the next 10 years, Jairo and I being alone together meant managing the children's needs: When would they both sleep in their own beds *all night*? Would they both nap at the same time (I don't remember that ever happening, but maybe it did)? If they went outside to play, how long would they stay there? Could we find a babysitter and what time did she need to be home and how far away did one of us have to drive her? Could my parents handle them for a weekend? Any shortage makes you appreciate something more; any hard-won prize is treasured more fully for the effort it took to get it. Time alone took on, for awhile, that magical feel it had in the early days in parks and behind the closed doors of our shared apartment. There were times when we literally ran from waving goodbye at the front door back to our bedroom, shedding clothes as we went.

Then a funny thing happened: The children were old enough to fly by themselves to my parents' house in Tennessee, and we had a much-anticipated Week Alone glowing in front of us. We squeezed them and kissed them goodbye and started to walk back down the concourse, glorious Colorado sunshine coming through the windows all around us like a halo. I looked over at Jairo, and there was something about suddenly being alone with him that was not bright, shiny, or magical. I don't know what I said, or whether he said something first, but before we were out of the airport we were snarling at each other. This level of conflict was rare enough to be unsettling, and I wondered if it was permanent. Had we grown apart, despite all our efforts to take care of our marriage and focus on each other? Did we no longer have anything to talk about or do together that didn't involve the children?

That was Memorial Day weekend, and the only three-day weekend I have ever thought was too long by at least a day. We ran the Bolder Boulder together, a 6.2 mile walk/run involving thousands of people, bands and costumes, merriment and revelry that we would never have attempted with children in tow. To be able to go home and collapse for the rest of the day, never getting up from the sofa to tend to any needs but our own, was supposed to be the greatest of luxuries. All I remember is that we kept fighting, and it was scary and depressing. Suddenly, I could be alone with Jairo and feel lonely, instead of grateful to have him to myself. For that weekend, being alone together was misery, and I fervently looked forward to going back to work on Tuesday morning.

This whole kaleidoscope was flooding back to me when I looked across the front seat of the rented LeSabre that Sunday night. As we pulled away from our son's dorm, I had to look away from Jairo. We went back to a lovely, quiet, *empty* hotel room; Gabe had slept on the floor the night before, taking up much of the space and snoring as loudly as his father did. If only I could say we ripped each other's clothes off as we came through the door and made wild passionate love in the king sized bed. The reality is that it was 11 p.m. and we had to be up at 5 a.m. to catch separate planes (I couldn't put us on the same plane, if the children weren't with us, until both were grown). We brushed our teeth in silence, called Gabe to tell him he had left a French assignment behind. He answered his cell phone from the grocery store across the street from his dorm, where he went to buy milk "and got distracted," he said, and I heard a girl laughing behind him. We set the two alarms, crawled into bed and went quickly to sleep.

Maybe I couldn't look at Jairo because I didn't know what would come next. I couldn't see him on the other side of the LeSabre because I didn't know who we would be to each other now that we would be alone together more or less permanently. Would we be the sweet commercial selling diamonds on TV, with the elderly couple walking hand in hand through Central Park, adoring each other while the autumn leaves swirl around them? Or would we become our parents, his as well as mine, married but sleeping in separate rooms and leading separate lives?

It gets worse. My parents, in their 80s, were together on an airport concourse (is there something about airports that brings out the worst in people)? Either my father's arthritis prevented him from walking, or his lifetime of sheer laziness made him reluctant to do so, depending on whether you asked him or my mother. He had gotten a wheelchair from the airline, but no employee appeared to push it. My mother reluctantly pushed his wheelchair to the connecting gate and then demanded five dollars from him for doing so, since she had her laziness theory to uphold. Although we laughed at this when we heard—this was so her, so *them*—it was scary. Would we turn into them, if we in fact had 30 more years together? I couldn't just say *no way—this is how they have always been with each other and it's just gotten worse. We have never been this way and we never will be.* There was, after all, that endless Memorial Day weekend when being alone together was not a good place to be.

There are two alternatives to being alone with your life partner as you age: divorce and widowhood. I look around at my friends and see envy on all three sides of that triangle. My parents could never have divorced, but might have been happier if one of them had died earlier (they were married almost 53 years when Mom died at 82). All of the widows I know talk about their deceased mates in ways that make it clear they were cheated by widowhood out of a just reward for lives of sacrifice and devotion. I don't know any middle aged divorcees who wish they were still married, though some may wish their exes were dead. Jairo and I talk about many things we want to do together one day when we have time and money: astronomy cruises, ballroom dancing lessons, camping trips to Door County in Wisconsin, endless hours on the sun porch reading to each other. Trips to visit grandchildren, or having them coming to stay with us so their parents can either make love in every corner of the house or start yelling at each other before they get out of the airport—all foamy abstractions, dreams of a future that we have learned too well is unpredictable.

Marriage as a private arrangement is, more than ever, a public issue in these United States. As a culture we believe more passionately in marriage than ever before, celebrating marriages that endure until death do them part ever more fervently. As we neared our 30th anniversary, the incredulous looks I got from people when I told them of the approaching milestone made me think there might be a medal ceremony somewhere along the way. In the US, as we wrangle over gay marriage, we also argue more passionately over what *marriage* means. But when I looked across the front seat of that rental car in Arizona, the public side of marriage wasn't there at all. I couldn't see it as a conventional arrangement of middle class opportunities and the payoffs attendant on it (financial stability, social recognition and legitimacy, an easy social arrangement that is all but invisible to me because it came about without any sacrifice or struggle). I saw only the private side of it, the specific history of Jairo and me before, during, and after the children; the messages from our social networks about marriage, and its alternatives, in middle and old age.

My mother had a ready answer to the question of what it took to make a marriage last a lifetime: You had to be a good team, able to buy a house and raise children that could take care of themselves someday. (She surely did not envision the times when Jairo and I would be taking care of her and my father, a process that called for almost as much teamwork as raising the children did with a quite different endpoint in sight.) You had to be able to live more or less together for that whole process without making each other miserable, or failing that, without making other people uncomfortable with your misery. Happiness could come from friends, family, good books, travel. It didn't necessarily come from the partner/teammate, and most of the time it wouldn't. I am from a generation that expects far more from marriage, that in many ways expects too much. I cringe when I hear someone say that their spouse is their "best friend." If I combine what I need from my life partner, Jairo, with what I need from my best friend, Daena, that is clearly a *lot* to ask from one person. Maybe what the scary night in Arizona was meant to teach me was that a key element of a lasting relationship is figuring out what to do when the world around you goes quiet. When the job pressure eases, when the children grow up and leave, when there's nowhere you need to be at 5 a.m., can you be alone together comfortably? Are you OK with the silence that suddenly descends? If you work out ways of feeling connected and safe whether you're talking or quiet, in bed together or on separate airplanes, irritable and snippy or silly and laughing, maybe that bodes well for a future together—alone.

Reflections and expansions

1. Think of all the popular songs that celebrate romantic love (that's most of them). How many of them celebrate silence in some way, whether actual quiet as in the Dixie Chicks song that started this narrative or the ability to know what someone is thinking and feeling without him or her having to say so? By contrast, which ones celebrate something put into words or action: "I just called to say I love you" (Paul McCartney and Wings, 1980s); marriage proposals (abundant examples); Pink's "Please don't leave me"—etc.? What impact do musical images of romantic love have on people's expectations of their own relationships?
2. What kinds of talk and silence constitute "making a good team"? How are those similar to, and different from, the ones that live up to other ideals of long-term committed relationships?
3. Does "easy silence" sound or look any different from tense or bored silence? Could an outside observer tell the difference, or is it purely an internal state?
4. Being able to laugh together is a relational evaluation mentioned at least as often as feeling comfortable with silence; the connecting factor is clearly that it feels easy, not like work. What does it take for people to make their relational partners laugh? How is it different from what makes someone a successful comedian?

A book by Alain de Botton called *On Love,* although cast as a novel, is a philosophical exploration of the cultural and personal dimensions of what US Americans and the British, at least, consider to be romantic love. It is lively, funny, and poignant, as far from a traditional philosophical treatise as can be, and various forms and functions of silence play significant roles in the narrative. It could be a useful follow-up to the themes explored in this story.

A veggie tale

When I was growing up in Texas, we had steak every Sunday. It was never my favorite, and there came a point when I probably groaned: "Not steak *again!*" This brought a laugh at my family's dinner table, though my mother may have gritted her teeth as well. I think her putting steak on the table once a week went beyond feeding her family to being a symbolic act. She grew up in a working class family with five children and was a teenager during the Depression. Although she says her family did not suffer, I'm confident they didn't have steak nearly often enough for her to dream that "Not steak *again!*" would be a meaningful thing to say.

Still, I never meant to become a vegetarian. Unlike other vegetarians I know, I wasn't so repelled by the idea of killing innocent animals, nor so convinced by the health benefits of not eating meat, nor so deeply invested in the arguments of ecological efficiency, as to stop eating meat for any of those very good reasons. I believed all of them, I just didn't *feel* any of them deeply enough to have a conviction based in any of them. My progression to becoming a vegetarian came by

---

Transcribing Silence: Culture, Relationships, and Communication
by Kristine L. Muñoz, 151–162.

way of a sequence of relationships, each of which nudged me further down a path I'm not sure I would have committed to on my own.

Before I explain why I became a vegetarian, let me say why I sound defensive. It may not be immediately obvious why anyone would ever feel defensive about taking on a dietary habit that, whatever his or her own personal lack of conviction might be, is shared by millions of people in the world and has excellent reasons to justify it. I feel (and thus talk) this way about being vegetarian for reasons similar to those that lead people to talk defensively about being gay, Democrat, left-handed, or fat: It means not fitting in with people around you. I live in Iowa, a state where there are *more than five* pigs for every human resident, making the economic dependence on pork a matter of unspoken reverence. Although Iowa City, like most college towns, is more diverse and liberal than other parts of the state, vegetarianism is not the norm even there. It is often treated as a mystery, a curiosity, an annoyance, a problem. Becoming vegetarian for relational rather than political or health reasons has, paradoxically, made for some painful times of being at odds with the community I live in.

Here's how it happened: At age 22 I took up with a young man who had spent his college years in Kent, Ohio, when that community still very much identified itself with the Kent State shootings of 1972. Liberals, ecologically minded, whatever. He didn't eat red meat, out of a deep conviction that it was healthier not to and that it was important to eat healthy (I'm embarrassed to say this was literally my first exposure to the ideologies attached to health food). He was the first boyfriend I ever went grocery shopping with and planned meals and cooked with, and it was easy and natural not to eat red meat, particularly since we earned $700 a month between us. I did miss having sausage for breakfast, and for a long time hung on to that as the only exception to the red meat avoidance principle. I also ate whatever was served at home, which included the usual round of ham, steak, pork chops, brisket. I assumed the no-red-meat idea would wear off when the romance hit the wall, and I'd go back to being happily omnivorous.

The romance wore off in due time, and Jairo, my eventual life partner, came on the scene. By that time I was used to chicken and fish and tended to cook that most often, though I still sank blissfully into a Big Mac from time to time. One year I lived in Colombia with my mother-in-law, who hadn't eaten any red meat in decades, and suddenly I found hamburgers at a place called Wimpy's the height of comfort food. I ate red meat then as resistance: anything not to be identified with HER and her countless fussy, picky eating habits, each of them backed by some claim to physical ailment or need.

Somewhere between 1988 and 1997, I gradually lost all taste for red meat. I learned lots of new ways to do chicken, fish, and pasta, and also learned the role that food and feeding play in motherhood. The first phase of that was naturally the most powerful. Breastfeeding was more than a phase in my children's lives, more than a temporary role for me to inhabit. It was an identity I took on—the food provider—and I have never let go of it, even when I hear obsession in it.

The obsessive part of that identity took on a life of its own that my family refers to, affectionately I hope, as the Nutrition Nazi. Having been the sole source of nourishment that kept two tiny beings alive for several months, having watched them grow from completely helpless, fragile looking things into small but far less helpless and fragile neo-humans *on a diet composed and controlled entirely by me* made me vigilant and protective beyond any logic about what they consumed. I grew more devoted to fruits and vegetables, to avoiding sweets and fat and salt and sugar—setting a good example and making sure they knew there was strong moral weight attached to following it—than I ever thought I would, or even thought I should. I still had nothing against meat, but I was getting out of the habit of eating or cooking it. I had also begun to attach ever stronger emotions to food, and eating, and the powerful rejection attached to refusing to eat what someone has cooked for you.

When my own were small I was, understandably enough, around a great many other children, and I developed a profound dislike for Picky Eaters. One of my friends complained—cheerfully, it seemed—that she felt like a short-order cook in her own house: "Johnny won't eat anything green or red, and Max won't eat anything white or gooey, so that leaves almost no common ground. I make peanut butter and jelly for this one, mac and cheese for that one, Tim's got to have his steak and potato, and *it just never ends!*"

I'd never heard such willing self-enslavement. There was no polite way to ask "What do you mean *he won't eat* ... What do you mean *Tim has to have* ... Are you the only person allowed near the refrigerator or oven? Is it some coincidence that you are the only female in a house full of males, each of whom expects you to meet his whims as well as his legitimate needs?" It dawned on me that as clearly as food is love, it just as clearly is *work*. When someone is willing to cook for you and feed you, insisting that you can't (won't) eat what they fixed is turning the key on the leg shackles.

Whatever my children were going to grow up to be, then, astronauts or dishwashers or cowboys or lesbians or, most unthinkably, Republicans, they WOULD NOT be picky eaters. They would eat what was served, or they would fix their own alternative, or they would go hungry. I had read the *Parents Magazine* assurances that there was no known case of a child starving to death because the mother insisted on serving green peas and tomatoes. I did try to accommodate the bland tastes children are famous for, and to minimize the times I fixed something that I knew they wouldn't like. I looked upon this as a healthy compromise, and tried not to resent the limitations on the menu this imposed. I also let each of them choose one food they didn't ever have to eat at home, even if the rest of us were having it (one chose green peas, the other, tomatoes, both easy enough to pick out of something that was otherwise acceptable), although they had to eat even those if we were invited to someone else's house.

Jairo was a crucial ally in enforcing this policy, being far more comfortable with insisting that *the rule's the rule* when the objections became too piteous for me to resist on my own. He also ate everything I fixed, always complimented and thanked me, and—most important of all—never assumed that food was my job. Not once has he asked me, as though it's up to me to figure it out, "What's for lunch (breakfast, dinner)?" We ask each other, *is there anything to eat in this house?* and he has a repertoire of dishes that he routinely cooks.

I am definitely more concerned than he is about when and what we will eat, so I am more often the person planning and cooking. I have a wider repertoire of standard dishes, a more confident imagination to improvise, and a range of favorite dog-eared cookbooks. I cook about 80 percent of the time; he does about 80 percent of the grocery shopping from lists that all of us construct as we go along. I enjoy cooking, particularly when I have time and energy to do it creatively. A significant part of that enjoyment is that (a) I don't have to do it every day, (b) it's not the case that if I don't do it, it won't get done, and (c) I know my family will not refuse to eat anything I do or don't cook. It remains the fact that cooking is women's work in my house. That still seemed unfair sometimes, even when I was able to negotiate more of a balance by delegating the shopping and cleaning and pull ahead in the calculation by insisting I enjoy doing the actual cooking, the creative part. I am the *chef* here, not the cook.

That emerging balance in the early years of our marriage made it easier to drift into vegetarianism. If Jairo had insisted that he had to have steak and potatoes, or if either he or I thought it was my job to produce dinner every night, I don't know that this ever would have happened.

The journey toward this place I never meant to go went further when I went to two places where, completely by coincidence, I was surrounded by vegetarians. Finland is more famous for its sausage, England for its Yorkshire pudding, than either of them is for its tofu variations. Yet somehow the people I knew best in those places, the ones who invited me to dinner and took me to their favorite restaurants and guided me around the university cafeterias, were vegetarians. Most of them ate fish willingly, though one commented that he knew it wasn't any different morally to eat fish than to eat beef.

I can't remember a single instance of anyone in either place urging me to give up chicken or hamburgers, any more than they would have scolded me for eating dessert (and most of them are eager dessert consumers). When I asked them about their meat avoidance, the answers were couched in individual terms: *I* think it's ecologically unsound to feed cows and pigs the amount of food it takes to produce a pork chop or a veal cutlet ... *I* don't like what they have to do to chickens to get them to the supermarket at a price people will pay for them. They owned those ideas, the beliefs were part of their authentic selves, and no one imposed them on me. Maybe there were unspoken persuasive attempts there and I just liked the people too much to pick up on them, but I do after all study communication for a living. I interpret many speech actions as subtle persuasion even when the actors swear they had no such thing in mind. I was simply surrounded by delicious, appealing vegetarian alternatives, and it wasn't hard at all to complete my slide in that direction. Chicken went the way of pork and beef: I looked at a lovely roasted chicken breast one day and said, ugh, I don't think I want that.

Maybe their talk, constructed and interpreted purely as information rather than persuasion, nonetheless created the aversion I began to experience toward meat. The only thing I could tell was that, somewhat suddenly, it didn't look or taste good. For a much longer time the smell of cooking meat stayed wonderfully tempting. Then for awhile, it was like any other smell: a little aroma was pleasant, but it was quickly too strong to be enjoyable. Now, I literally have to leave the room, or the building, when someone is frying bacon. In the absence of ideological conviction, however, I was just another Picky Eater.

Naturally, being veggie among veggies doesn't make you a picky eater because it isn't an issue. It's when you go back to the way most of the world operates, which is to say, if there's no meat it isn't dinner (and it may not be lunch or breakfast, either). Once someone has planned a meal around meat, it becomes very difficult for them to believe any person's hunger could be satisfied without it—even if there are hefty vegetables, salad, pasta, and dinner rolls around.

It was years, in fact, before I could bring myself to say out loud *I'm a vegetarian*. It felt like a valuable identity I couldn't legitimately claim, as though I were saying I was a PhD before finishing my dissertation. It also felt like I was Being Difficult, Putting People Out, Demanding Special Treatment—all cardinal sins in the Southern way of life. For a long time I kept eating chicken, if that's what people served at their house—by this time I couldn't face red meat at all, rude or not. It got harder to do chicken either, and eventually became impossible.

Let me explain what "impossible" means, because I've had queries from non-vegetarians about this, usually in tones more irritated than curious. If I were starving in the desert, and I came upon a perfectly grilled pork chop or chicken breast, would I turn it down? I've never been starving in the desert, so I don't know what I'd do. I do know that I've been pretty hungry at social gatherings where everything was meat and decided that, between that quite lovely looking chicken and staying hungry another hour or two, I'd stay hungry. When I am in a situation where it's just too awkward not to have anything at all, I nibble at chicken the way most of us would nibble at monkey innards or dog brains or fish eyeballs in a culture where those are considered a delicacy by the natives: What is the smallest possible quantity I can consume without being rude, how can I minimize the contact between my sensory organs and this nominally edible substance, and how do I camouflage the gag reflex I know is lurking? All of us know perfectly well that if dog brains are a delicacy in someone else's culture, they can't possibly be poisonous, and we will not die from eating them. At the same time, it's a struggle to construe the taste as delicious or the texture as within the normal range for something to put in our habit-bound mouths.

But it *isn't* dog brains or fish eyeballs, friends have said to me in wonderment. It's just *chicken* ... Chicken is what you fix when you want something everyone will eat. In many cases, it's an accommodation to widely shared and understood health concerns. A conversation very much on point from the situation comedy *Friends*:

Rachel's Dad: Why don't I order chicken Kiev for all of us?

Phoebe: Uh, I'm a vegetarian.

Dad: But it's *chicken!*

Phoebe: Well, I don't eat that either.

Dad (exasperated): I'll *never* understand you lesbians!

Part of the issue, clearly, is that many of the tricky conversations happen during public occasions. I know people who, when invited to a gathering where food is a primary dimension of the event (and some time count up the ones you go to where it *isn't*— I bet you don't run out of fingers), find some matter-of-fact way to tell the host or hostess that they are vegetarian, or they keep kosher, or they can't have any salt. Even after I got to a point of claiming vegetarian as an identity I was entitled to, I had trouble saying that in response to an invitation.

I know there are many people—and I consider them the healthy ones, not me—who assume their dietary needs or preferences will not be a problem. They are able to share relevant information with someone who, having invited them to take part in a social occasion, can be assumed to like them well enough to want to accommodate their legitimate needs. Somehow, I don't think many of them were raised in the South. Here are conversations I have had around this issue:

At my parents' house, during a family reunion:

Aunt: Aren't you having some of this ham I baked? It's REAL good.

Me. No, thanks, I'm fine.

Aunt. You're just having *potato* salad?

Me. I'm going back for some green stuff in awhile.

Aunt (with a longish look) You're not having any brisket, either?

Me. I don't eat meat.

Aunt. You're saying this to a *rancher*? You want to put us out of *business*?

Well, she was a bookkeeper at a ranch, and I haven't yet heard of ranching being in a financial crisis because of exploding rates of vegetarianism. But the affronted tone was real: Vegetarians are an offense and a threat to ranchers, the farmer and the cowboy can't really be friends, and more is on the line than what I'm eating today.

At a party:

Hostess: Here, give this one to Jairo. This one's yours (hands me a plate served with beef lasagna, chicken breast, salad, and a roll).

Me. I'll just have salad, thanks.

Hostess (a stare): You're on a DIET?

Me. No, I'm vegetarian.

Hostess: Is that how you're trying to lose weight? YOU don't need to ...

Me. I'm not trying to lose weight.

Hostess: But this is just a *little* bit. (4.0) Okay. (3.5) Here, hold this, I'll go get another plate from the kitchen.

Me. I'll go ...

Hostess. No, no, it's fine, I can get it quicker than I can tell you where to look.

A part of this conversation I objected to was the idea that I wasn't eating meat because I was on a DIET. Besides the fact that it wasn't true, the odd connection of avoiding meat to dieting leads a surprising number of people to try to talk me out of that crazy idea. I wonder resentfully, why is food a subject for social influence at *all*? Why would someone try to talk me out of being vegetarian any more than they would try to talk me out of being Orthodox Jewish or allergic to peanuts or struggling with life-threatening high cholesterol?

At a sit-down dinner:

Host: Here, Kristine, I made THIS one for YOU, because I know you're ...

Me. Oh, thank you, how very considerate of you, you shouldn't have gone to so much trouble.

Host looks at me expectantly as I lift a forkful.

Me. Does this, um, have chicken in it?

Host (beaming): Yes it does! I made it special for you.

Me. But I'm *vegetarian.*

Jairo. Well, *sort* of vegetarian—

How can the person I share my life with feel free to claim I'm only *sort of* what I say I am?

Clearly, eating and food are more than just physical processes needed to sustain life. Because eating often happens in groups, eating what the group does makes you a member of it, and refusing to leaves you outside of it: We eat black-eyed peas on New Year's Day in the South, for good luck, and if you turn down the black-eyed peas you aren't one of us. Oh yes, we cook them with ham or bacon—that's not a problem, is it?

When vegetarianism doesn't make sense to those around you, it threatens the interpersonal ties people make in that most primal of ways, offering food. If you try to give reasons—political, environmental, or health related—you risk sounding like you're accusing others of being ignorant or wrong in their own choices, no matter how carefully you try to explain your own as personal ones.

If you can't eat peanuts or drink milk because you have a life-threatening allergy, no one tries to coax you into it. If you keep kosher because you're Orthodox Jewish, I don't think anyone tries to convince you that hot dogs are OK because it's the Fourth of July and we're all Americans. Those are things you can say just once and count on the subject being dropped. Outside of those legitimate frameworks for resistance, though, it gets so much more difficult to explain your food habits. Vegetarianism seems to be perceived more often as an individual preference, another version of being a

Picky Eater, because it's something you choose to do rather than something your religion or your physical condition demands of you. When I have said to people that my motivation was really personal taste rather than political conviction or health concerns (at the risk of TMI, after 15 years as a vegetarian my cholesterol is nonetheless so high I have to take medication for it), I got some hard stares. If it's a preference, you can damn well set it aside and eat what the rest of us are eating. The fact is, after all this time without meat or chicken, it does make me physically ill. Chicken-stock soup is a nightmare, even if all the chicken is taken out of it.

I'm glad I'm not a politician: During presidential campaigns I read about the tradition of political candidates eating alongside the voters while on the campaign trail, and the complexities that can bring for people with dietary convictions (which sounds like something that could bring jail time): In 2004, Joe Lieberman, Orthodox Jewish, had a hell of a time finding something kosher to eat at the Iowa State Fair. Pass up the corn dogs, nix the pork on a stick, what's left? A deep-fried Twinkie (which the "solemn and amused" candidate pronounced "indescribable"). Dennis Kucinich, a vegan, organized an animal-products-free dinner in downtown Des Moines, a place where rib-eyes and pork chops are institutional rituals. The bravery of these acts, in a game where the stakes amount to professional life and death and success rides on persuading voters that you're similar to them, is hard for me to imagine. It makes my own moments of discomfort seem like minor inconveniences, but also makes me wonder: Why is food so symbolically important? It's clear enough that food is *physically* important, but why do reputations and relationships and cultures and love itself become what's riding on choices between one kind of food and another?

After a decade of this veggie life, it feels like as much a part of me as my failing eyesight or my lack of political activism. I have to work through how, and even whether, to say something to people that, I know from experience, won't necessarily make sense to them. I have to decide which will be more painful: saying ahead of time that I'm vegetarian and trying to calm the near-panic that sometimes ensues, or saying nothing and hoping I can manage the situation in the moment without too much awkwardness. There is power in being able to say out loud, this is who I am, take me or leave me; and a powerlessness and violence in having to stay silent. For that power to extend into what we eat—something both central and, somehow, often treated as mundane—the symbolic web must be dense and complicated indeed.

Reflections and extensions

1. I thought about titling this narrative "The silent vegetarian" when I realized I had reached a different point in the process of becoming one: I now tell everyone who invites me to dinner that I am vegetarian. I point out (gently, I hope) when there are no vegetarian options among the catered buffets offered at departmental events. I've learned to ask in restaurants for things that are not on the menu (and avoid restaurants that are non-veggie-friendly). Either the world is changing, or I have. Can you think of a way to tell which has changed?
2. Being a smoker is now a much more significant bodily choice than being a vegetarian. Do you frown at or scold smokers you know? Are there times when you see smoking bans violated but stay silent because of the social awkwardness of complaining? If you are a smoker, do you ever feel you have to hide that fact from people you know? How and when do you do so?
3. Although I experienced stigma attached to being a vegetarian in the early years I was one, it was nothing like the social pressure still faced by LGBTQ people to hide who they are. What other imposed silences (whether self-imposed or socially demanded) do you know of that do violence to people's identities? How many "closets" are there for people to stay in or out of in your speech community? What are the relational and cultural stakes involved in coming out of those closets?

Part II

Fictional narratives

Andiamo

¿Quieres que conservemos una dulce
memoria de este amor?
Pues amémonos hoy mucho, y mañana
¡digámonos adios!
(Do you want us to keep a sweet
Memory of this love?
Well let's love much today, and tomorrow
Let's say goodbye!)

Gustavo Adolfo Becquer, 1868

Winds on Chesapeake Bay were coming from the northwest, stiff bursts through the warm October air, but the weekday had largely emptied it of sails and wakes. Five nautical miles from Annapolis, a 36-foot sloop skimmed and heeled, its dual triangles white and almost alone against countless shifting hues of the water.

"Come left just a little."

"You mean come to *port.*" Griffin smiled, lean in a red windbreaker. His profile stayed pressed to the binoculars.

"Can you see that house over there on the island, in there among the trees? That's the one I was telling you about." Elizabeth squinted to where he was pointing across the water. Behind a rocky beach sculpted out of a grove of poplars was a masterpiece, all glass and

---

Transcribing Silence: Culture, Relationships, and Communication
by Kristine L. Muñoz, 165–180.

soaring archways and a roof that seemed to be suspended in midair above the house.

"I have to concentrate here, skipper."

"It's *captain* to you." He turned to look at her, still smiling. "You're doing great; I'm going to let out the sail a little. We're getting good wind behind us."

"I should stay on north?" She peered at the compass in front of the wheel, bracing her feet on the deck as the boat heeled to the right. "I hate having to do this with the compass, I don't get to see anything."

"So let me take it for a minute, you look at this house and tell me how they made that roof work."

They changed places, murmuring *mmmm* as they squeezed past each other behind the wheel, and Elizabeth peered through the binoculars.

"All I know is it's called a cantilevered ceiling, or roof. I can't really tell you how it works, but it's something complicated and invisible that holds up a part of the house from the inside to give it that look, like it's suspended in mid-air." Her husband would know, but Otto was at home in Houston, at this very moment teaching Principles of Design to sophomores at Rice. Even those sophomores might know, actually.

"How come you can't see *any* of it from outside?" Griffin asked. "Not a column, not a wall, not a post ..."

"That's the point, if you could see how it was held up there wouldn't be any trick to it."

"OK. Take the wheel; I need to do something about this sail that's catching on the runner."

They changed places again, and she watched him climb halfway onto the cabin. He tugged at ropes, untied them from cleats, retied them, jiggled something loose off the sail, all in movements that caressed, smoothed, stroked. Elizabeth thought, *I bet I've heard more about this boat over the years than I have about his little boys.* She smiled at his concentration, the way his blue jeaned behind wriggled with effort, and the miracle of seeing this boat at last on such an impossibly beautiful day. Then the sail eased to the left and the glare of sunshine off the water made her turn her eyes down toward the island, toward the house with the impossible roof.

Andiamo—Elizabeth loved the name, "Let's go" in Italian. Her friend Sofia told her *andiamo* could also be directed at someone, meaning "You, get moving." The boat settled back closer to the water, the side rails easing away from the waves, and Elizabeth sat back onto the seat. The jib went from taut to flapping wildly. "DAMN," Griffin said, "too much of a good thing." He pulled harder on a rope. "Those gusts are really coming out of nowhere."

"Why is that front sail going crazy all of a sudden?"

"The mainsail's out so far it's blocking all the wind from it. I don't want to pull this in too far ..." his voice got lost in the wind. The flapping from the jib got noisier, and the boat seemed to shudder. "*Ooops.*" He put a sneakered foot onto the seat to climb further out on the cockpit.

"Anything I should do?" The water raced past them, greenish brown, choppy.

"Got a line hung on the cleat, I can't get the jib in. I'm hoping I can reach it from here." At six feet four, there are few things he can't reach on this boat. He brushed wisps of blond hair back from his forehead, peered forward. "No, I need to go up there." He slid back down to stand in the cockpit.

"Put on a life jacket," she urged.

"Oh, I'm not *going* anywhere," but he looked past her at the waves. The wind wedged a scream into the clanking of the jib. "Maybe I'll use the safety harness. Come right a little, slow us down some." He ducked below into the cabin while Elizabeth took deep breaths and tried to focus somewhere other than on the uncontrolled front sail, the mainsail popping up and down, the jerking of the wheel under her hands, how hard it was to stay pointed more or less at the island. This boat wasn't like the little sailboats she'd been on as a child. Those boats had one sail, that you had to watch carefully when you came about so it didn't smack you in the face, but they were on inland lakes where the wind only came from one direction at a time. More often there was too little of it to get up any speed, and a sail often turned into a swim. At worst you heeled over too far and capsized, and there was a well-understood way to get the boat back upright. Here on the Chesapeake there was more water, more wind, more sound, and it took her breath away. And if this thing capsized ... She has watched Griffin's ease and tried to relax into it, but it was really only at anchor in the evening that her heart didn't pound.

He came back up, buckling a webbed harness around his waist, and untied one end of a rope on the cabin top. "Should I take this nice hat off?" he grinned at her as he clipped the rope onto the harness. She had bought the hat for him during their weekend in San Francisco, two years ago. "Or just watch it fly off into ..."

It happened in an instant that—because all of her life was divided into before and after that one—lasted forever. Struggling with the wheel, Elizabeth felt the boat surge too far to the right, her face whipped with a gust of wind at the same time it hurled the mainsail across the deck. Maybe Griffin heard it, maybe he felt the boat lurch, maybe his sailing experience led to instinct; he threw an arm high and ducked. His arm took much of the impact of the sail, but six feet plus do not curl quickly into a ball. The boom clanked against his head. He was off balance from ducking, the boat lunged onto its rails again, and the force of the boom took him over the side into the heaving, surging water.

Elizabeth wrenched the wheel hard to the left, then squirmed out from behind it. The horror of what she saw, blood and waves and a crumpled man attached to the boat by the thinnest of ropes, drove her voice down into her chest. Her mouth moved, but no sound came out, like every nightmare she'd ever had, only this one had cold shrieking wind tearing through it. The boat heaved again, and the boom swung back the other way; she fell backwards against the opposite side of the cockpit. Her legs felt useless and rubbery as she struggled to get up and move to the high side of the boat, further from the raging hungry water. She held on to Griffin with her eyes, hearing a wordless pleading chorus in her head rise above the flapping and clanking of the sails. The webbed vest was pulled up under his armpits, but his head and shoulders were dragging through the water. His head was a bloody mess, his arms were hanging limp, his face was a shade of gray she'd never seen. A wave washed briefly over him, slapping him against the side of the boat.

"My God," she heard herself say. "My God, my God. What do I do? Griffin—" The certainty that he could not respond sucked all the air out of her chest again. The sail flung itself back and forth across the cockpit; she had to duck to avoid it.

Elizabeth stared at the floor of the Coast Guard boat, a wooden rack over fiberglass, all of it spotless. She pulled the blanket, soft and blue and smelling of fabric softener, as tightly around her as it would go, though it was warm inside the cockpit, out of the wind. The boat raced noisily across the water, bouncing over the waves. A man in a surgical mask and gloves held a flashlight to Griffin's eyes, put a bag over his mouth with a bulb attached, murmured things she could only halfway hear: "pupils responding to light, symmetrical dilation. Respiration labored. Pulse at 100."

"What happened, ma'am." The calm voice was asking, again, and Elizabeth had to respond. Boom came over. Hit his arm, then his head. Knocked him overboard. In the water about 30 minutes. Don't know if he stopped breathing at any point. Seemed to be unconscious the whole time.

"Does your husband have any drug allergies, ma'am?" he asked from behind the mask.

"Codeine and penicillin," she answered without thinking. Something flashed in her head—a lightning bolt, an icy current down through her— "This isn't my husband. My *husband* is allergic to codeine and penicillin." Both pairs of eyes were briefly on her. "This is ..." She stopped. *This is a man who is supposed to be in New*

York working on a class action suit, instead of on a boat with someone else's wife.

"What's his name, ma'am." The voice was careful.

"Griffin Connally." She spelled it automatically, like Griffin always did.

"Does *he* have any drug allergies."

"I don't know." Her face sank toward the spotless wooden floor, and she put her hands up to stop its path. The boat's motor sounded louder than before, the thump-thump as they sped over the waves pounded harder. *I don't know his allergies, I don't know about his insurance coverage, I don't know why he got involved with me. I know he loves that boat like I love my daughter, like I love ...* She stared at her hands, white against the brown flooring. *Like I love Otto.*

The men went back to their jobs, one of them writing things on his clipboard, the other leaning over a sodden, still Griffin.

They were loading him into the ambulance on shore when the next icy bolt hit her: Aside from her purse, that it occurred to her to grab only because it was hanging on a peg near the cockpit, everything she'd brought with her on this trip was still on the boat in the middle of the Chesapeake. Laptop computer. Sweatshirt with *Rice University* on the front. Pajamas in the forward berth, maybe stuffed under a pillow, maybe lying on top of rumpled sheets. Shoulder bag with her plane ticket back to Houston for tomorrow morning. She felt another wave crash over and inside her, threatening to drown her.

"What will they do with the boat?" she asked the Coast Guard uniform beside her.

"That's kind of up to you, ma'am," he said. "We can call a tow company to bring it in, we can take you back out there—" his voice faded on the second option; he was the one who'd taken the sails down when they got there and dropped the anchor, the part she should have remembered how to do but couldn't. "You're better off getting it towed in here to the marina; that'll be expensive, but it's better than leaving it out there." His vowels were pure East Coast, his r's disappearing —*bettah, out theah—*

"That's fine." Expensive? Could she give them her credit card? *Annapolis Marina North* on the credit card bill, when she told Otto she was going to a conference in Amherst this week? What was expensive? $500? $5,000?

A voice behind her broke through the questions jangling in her ears. "Ma'am, if you're coming with us to the hospital, we need you to get in now." She stared at him, a muscular young man about Maren's age, head shaved on the sides with a bushy stripe of black hair running from forehead to crown, a silver ring glinting in one ear. Any other time she would have wondered how he could be an ambulance technician, and would have said so. Now she needed him—or someone, anyone—to stop asking questions and tell her what to do. The Coast Guard man beside her coughed, shuffled his feet.

"Go on with them in the ambulance, we'll take care of the boat." Had he read her confusion? She let the earringed man help her in beside the stretcher, keeping her eyes on Griffin's arm, trussed now in a large splint across his stomach. A white neck brace started at his collarbone and hid his face.

The ambulance ride was as bumpy as the Coast Guard boat had been, and sudden swerving around corners and near-stops made Elizabeth hang on to the edges of the seat with both hands. For the first time since the sail had whipped across the deck, her mind started to clear. The EMT's were talking in low voices, to each other and into a radio, and she understood enough to know Griffin was not yet stable. Compound fracture of his arm, shoulder dislocated, head injury the biggest worry ... This was not something he would be treated for and released; he was in serious trouble, and she was going to have to figure out what to do. The hospital would contact his wife, who would ... The screen in her head went blank again. Griffin's wife would be surprised indeed to find out he was on *Andiamo* instead of in New York. Elizabeth could somehow be on her plane tomorrow morning, letting Griffin figure out how to explain why he was on the boat instead of in a law office. Maybe Pam would never know he wasn't on it alone? just a boating accident, lamentable but not the end of the world? Maybe she'd just be glad he was alive and not press for the details? What about the pajamas and laptop on the boat? What would she say to Otto about not getting home with her prized laptop?

The quiet urgency in the Coast Guard men and the ambulance people told her that Griffin could be in the hospital for a long time, could even ... she slapped the thought away. How would she find out if he died? Would he speak to her again if she left him? Would she be doing him a favor to leave before Pam got there, or abandoning him at his worst moment? She made herself look up toward his head. Surely he would glance down at her and grin, the way he looked over his shoulder at her just before it happened. He would tell her what to do, whether to stay or go. She couldn't see his face at all now, only the neck brace. Seeing him turned from a strong, laughing man into a wet, still thing, Elizabeth wanted to weep.

"Ma'am, we need you to stay here." Her eyes on the gurney rolling away from her down the hall, Elizabeth stopped but didn't turn around. "We need to get some information from you."

"But I ..."

"The doctor will come tell you as soon as he knows something." A woman in a maroon smock stood behind a high desk marked RECEPTION. She had short dark hair, wire-rimmed glasses, the tone of someone in charge. Her nametag said *Bonita Blasson*. "They're doing everything they can for him, ma'am; the best thing you can do is stay out of their way. Why don't you come sit down over here, and we'll take care of this paperwork." Elizabeth moved toward the chair at the side of the tall desk, and a different woman in the same color smock sat down across from her.

"His full name, last name first?"

"Connally. Griffin. William."

"Home address?"

"I..." A pause. "... don't know." She swallowed. "He lives in Laurel."

"Maryland?"

"Yes."

"Home phone?" That, she knew. "Your name?"

"Elizabeth Rattrey."

"Your relationship to Mr. Connally?" A phone rang. "Bonnie, can you ... Excuse me, please. I'll be right back."

Your relationship to Mr. Connally ... The question hung in the air. *What do you THINK? We are adulterers and liars who have deceived the people we're married to, and even though we love those people deeply we have loved each other, too.*

The woman returned.

"Relationship?"

"Friend."

"We'll need to notify a next of kin." The eyes, behind wire-rimmed glasses, stayed fixed on the computer screen.

"Try the home phone number." A sweep of panic made Elizabeth's voice curt.

"And who should I ask for."

"His wife. Pam."

"Can you tell me what happened?"

Elizabeth repeated the details of the accident, squeezing her hands together. Twisting them, hard, seemed to help; she could breathe almost all the way down. She wondered whether any of her agony and confusion was even registering with this person in the maroon smock. The woman knew it was a boating accident, but for all she knew they'd been on that boat for two hours, not four days. Get a grip, she thought, just tell the story.

Elizabeth had tried twice to write her involvement with Griffin into her stories. Once, both of them were minor characters in her novel, their relationship something the lead character envied in the life of her sister. Another time they were the focus of a short story, but halfway through she realized there was no story there, just a long musing about relationships that the social world didn't understand and thus judged harshly. She put aside the short story, then deleted it from her hard drive and backups in a fit of anxiety that it would be found. Probably just before one of her long trips, envisioning as always the plane crash that would leave a bereaved Otto—or worse, Maren—sorting through her life and finding a nasty postmortem surprise. She worked it out of the novel, too, partly for the same reason and partly because Joyce from her writing group pointed out that it didn't develop the central characters. The desire to tell the story has not left her, but it is not the question she was just asked.

"Can you tell me anything about Mr. Connally's insurance coverage?" The voice was neutral, and the woman looked up as she asked. Elizabeth focused on her name tag: Cynthia Ringer.

"No, I can't. Sorry." Her mind floated—*I can tell you how much he loves a French chardonnay to toast the sunset. I can tell you what he looks like with his baseball glove on trying to catch a fly ball at a Red Sox game. I can tell you the songs he plays on his guitar and how sweet his voice sounds from the deck of this boat that was his dream and now has gotten him and me into this mess. I can't tell you his home address because I've never been anywhere near it, never been to Laurel, Maryland, in fact, but I can tell you how he sounds when talks to his wild little boys—and how he grins when he calls them that—on the phone.*

"Would you like a glass of water or something?" Cynthia Ringer's face was pink with concern. Elizabeth felt nauseated and tired.

"Can you find out something about Griffin for me?" she asked, gripping the edge of the desk. "Can I see him?"

The concern faded back to firmness. "No, we have to wait until they have him stabilized. We're about done here, so if you want to go on into the waiting room, you might be more comfortable there."

When are you calling his wife, and what will you tell her, thought Elizabeth, but her mouth didn't move. She picked up her purse and followed the signs into the waiting room. A black woman sat on a sofa, staring at a soap opera on TV. Her graying hair was tidy; a toddler sat in front of a box of toys on the floor. The woman glanced up at Elizabeth as she came in, maybe taking in the damp jeans and ratty Red Sox sweatshirt, then looked back at the TV. Elizabeth sat down in an armchair and looked up at it as well: pretty people moved around, talking, making faces, moving their bodies quickly, sounding intense and alarmed. One of the women onscreen started to cry, tears flowing down perfect cheeks but magically leaving her makeup undisturbed. *Why are you watching these make-believe people with their make-believe problems?* she thought about asking the woman on the sofa. *Don't you have someone in there with a REAL problem?*

Her gaze had drifted to the other woman, who was looking back at her through narrowed eyes. There was no way not to speak.

"What are you here for?" Elizabeth asked.

A long pause; she wondered about emergency room etiquette. Maybe you weren't supposed to ask.

"My other grandbaby got into some fingernail polish remover. My daughter's in there with him."

The black woman looked back at the TV. A longer silence hung over them as Elizabeth wished she hadn't said anything.

The nametag with *Bonnie Blasson* came to the doorway. "Ma'am? We can't reach anyone at Mr. Connally's house. Do you know where his wife works?"

"At a library." Her voice caught in some weeds, she had to repeat it. "I don't know which one. In Laurel."

"Public library?"

"I don't ... One of the college libraries."

"They'll find her." She was gone.

The black woman was looking at her.

"Boating accident," Elizabeth said. "A friend." The neatly coiffed gray head moved slowly. *A friend* hung in the air. The toddler ran a plastic truck across the floor, making growling noises.

"I've never been in an emergency room before." Elizabeth was so unprepared for this to come from her mouth, it might have been the TV. The gray-haired woman studied the child in front of her as she spoke.

"Never had any children?"

"Yes, a—my daughter's grown now. She was born at home."

"Well how about that." The toddler banged the truck on the floor. "Trey, watch out with that, baby, you'll break it." A commercial came on, louder, and Elizabeth winced. "I can turn this down," the woman offered. "I'm not really watching it."

"Thanks." Without the sound filling the room, conversation was inevitable.

"What happened?" the woman asked.

Elizabeth marched through the tale in a few sentences. "He's always so careful, I couldn't believe it. At least he put the harness on first, or who knows what could have happened."

"Will he be OK?"

"They're still trying to stabilize him. I haven't heard anyone say for sure that he will be, but ... God, he looked awful." She was having trouble breathing. "I don't know what to do, whether to wait here with him or go—I'm supposed to fly home tomorrow."

"Where's home?"

"Houston. My husband teaches at Rice; he's an architect."

"They'll find the wife; she'll get here."

"Yeah." Elizabeth's chin sank onto her fists, and she rocked forward and back. "She didn't know he was on the boat, she thought he was working on a class action suit—he's a lawyer—someone will have to explain to her—" the words trickled to a stop.

The woman looked thoughtful. "My name's Elsie," she said.

"Elizabeth."

"How long have you known him?"

What the heck, she thought. *If I were boring her she wouldn't keep asking questions.*

"Five years or so ... I was at a writer's conference in Boston and he was there with someone from his law firm. We got to talking at a cocktail party, and then this big group went out to dinner, and then we stayed in touch after the conference" *and my mother died about then and Otto couldn't deal with me because his mother left them when he was little and mothers are something he just can't handle, and I knew that about him and we've had a remarkably successful marriage despite that, but Maren was in high school dyeing her hair purple and coming home at 3 a.m. smelling like pot smoke and yelling every time she opened her mouth, and I couldn't figure out how to BE a mother when mine was suddenly gone, and Griffin was willing to answer eight e-mails a day and talk on the phone whenever I was having one of those earth-pulled-out-from-under-me-moments, and then I had another conference in Tucson, and he made some excuse to be there, and I really never imagined we would keep finding ways to see each other, but then we did. I have never stopped loving Otto, if anything I have appreciated him more because he understands other parts of me that Griffin gets impatient with and because if Otto were here right now he would know exactly what I should do. As far as I know Griffin loves Pam just as deeply, and there has never been any idea that either of us would leave our family.*

The silence started to seem lengthy. "And we've been friends ever since."

"But you haven't met his wife."

"Not *that* kind of friends." For once, Elizabeth felt a giggle starting, and was relieved to see Elsie's mouth curve upward. "The kind of friends that, if I'm here when she gets here, she says 'Who the hell are you and what was Griffin doing on his boat on a weekday and what's going on here?' just like the soaps." She nodded up at the silent television.

"What are you going to do?" Was it an offer of advice?

"I'm open to suggestion."

"I think you need to get out of here before the wife comes."

"How will I know what happens to him? How will he explain what happened?"

"Let him worry about that."

"But he isn't even stable yet, they don't know ..."

"Let's just see what they don't know." Elsie stood up, her chin at an angle that Elizabeth envied. "Trey, you stay here a minute baby, Grammaw's coming right back." Elizabeth and Trey looked at each other. Would she really just go, leave Griffin on his own? The question was the same as an hour ago: Would her staying make a bad situation worse?

Elsie reappeared with a tall, hospital-garbed woman with somber brown eyes. "This is Elizabeth," she said in a firm voice, and the tall woman reached out to shake her hand.

"I'm Dr. Rovens," she said. "You're a friend of Griffin Connally, is that right? You were there when the accident happened?"

"Yes, that's right."

"I think we can let you in for a few minutes, he's conscious." Elizabeth felt tears finally start, but could not have put a name to the emotions. She glanced over at Elsie, who nodded. Dr. Rovens turned to walk back down the hallway. "He inhaled a lot of water and has a bad break in his arm, but the head injury isn't as bad as it might have been. A concussion, but no signs of any internal bleeding or damage. He's responding pretty well, under the circumstances."

"He'll be alright?" Elizabeth was short of breath again.

"We still have to see about swelling that could get worse in the next few hours, but he's not in any immediate danger."

Thank God, thought Elizabeth. *Thank you, thank you God.* She steeled herself to what he might look like; she could never watch hospital dramas on TV. The sterility of the room, the white sheets, white bandages, white everywhere, were somehow comforting after the blood and brown waves of the bay. His face was pale, but no longer gray; his eyes were half-open. A tube down his throat kept him from speaking.

"They're towing the boat in," Elizabeth heard a strange voice that had to be her own. "It's OK." Griffin's eyes opened wider and his unbandaged arm waved a little in her direction. "I'm OK, too. I'm trying to figure out ..." She couldn't ask him to decide for her whether to stay or go. "They're looking for Pam," she started again. He nodded and blinked. "They found her?" Another nod. "She's on her way?" Another. *So they told you all this, but not me ... a "friend" in the waiting room doesn't get the updates ...*

In the end, all they have together is a shameful secret, with nothing noble or unique, really, holding it up. Not enough strength to stay and try to explain this to Pam, just enough loyalty to go back to the boat and collect her clothes and laptop. Their having loved each other was an illusion they cherished for awhile, but you don't leave someone you love in a hospital bed with a concussion. Hundreds of miles from where Griffin was supposed to be, his side of the affair will be exposed. Hers may or may not be, but all Elizabeth wants for now is to be on her sofa in Houston, with Otto next to her grading papers. She squeezes Griffin's hand, wanting to hang on a little longer. No, his look says. *Andiamo.*

Reflections and expansions

1. There are various kinds of love that "dare not speak (their) names," one of them being romantic relationships that fall outside of cultural expectations for monogamy. Who do you think knows about Elizabeth and Griffin's relationship, and why (or why not, and how) would anyone else know? Is there something about being in love that makes it hard to stay completely silent about it?
2. Given that both Elizabeth and Griffin still love their spouses deeply, do you believe they actually loved each other? Why or why not?
3. What kinds of lies had to be told for this ill-fated boat trip to take place? Which of them would have had to be spoken aloud, and which of them simply details left unsaid?
4. Elizabeth's conversation with Elsie follows a well-known pattern of strangers having conversations when they are thrown together in a public place that the people involved have not had, and perhaps never would have, with friends and family. Because the usual explanation for these conversations is the freedom of knowing you'll never see this stranger again, observation of such conversations is a revealing look into what must be unsaid for personal relationships to continue. Still, there is much that Elizabeth thinks but does not tell the sympathetic stranger. Why doesn't she?

5. One way for Griffin and his wife Pam to keep their marriage together is to focus entirely on his recovery from the accident, leaving unasked all the questions Elizabeth was mulling in the emergency room. How likely do you think that is to happen? Assuming these events really do put a complete end to contact between Elizabeth and Griffin, would it be better for them to follow that route—don't ask, don't tell—or to hash it all out completely?

6. A classic study by Katriel and Philipsen (1981) describes *real communication* as a culturally situated symbolic action with strong evaluative consequences. In that world, silence about relational issues, such as those faced by Griffin and Pam, and probably Elizabeth and Otto, is neither morally justifiable nor sensible in any way. To say that expectations to talk things through are culturally situated insists that they are not universal, that there are in fact other ways to manage such problems—like silence. What does your culture expect of people in these situations?

Crush

The four interns were anxious when they finally found Building R-486. On the mezzanine above the atrium they edged inside the door marked *Engineering* and stared across a forest of cubicles. To the left was a kitchen area with round tables and square chairs; directly across were offices with frosted glass fronts. "I think that may be a conference room," Matt ventured, craning his neck; but there was no clear route between the cubicles to the opposite side.

"Do we just go around," Will asked behind him, "or ..." A frosted door opened and a man with dark-rimmed glasses leaned out, frowning at them.

"Are you the interns?" he accused. The four nodded like naughty children. "Well get in here! We're all waiting on you!" Matt heard Rob breathing heavily behind him. They all glanced at each other and squinted around the room. The rows of cubicles seemed truly solid. "Over there!" the man snapped, pointing to his left.

He stood aside and glared as they passed him into an airy conference room with floor to ceiling windows. Outside, manicured lawns

Transcribing Silence: Culture, Relationships, and Communication
by Kristine L. Muñoz, 181–195.

of Midwestern Manufacturing lined the spaces between industrial buildings. Russell Porter was easy to spot as the boss, even before he spoke: medium build, reddish brown hair, a casual glance that directed them to empty spaces around the table without a word or a gesture. He leaned his head toward a woman on his right, talking softly to him, as they settled into chairs.

"The *late* interns," said the man with the glasses.

"Sorry, we ..." started Will.

"No problem." Russell Porter looked back at the woman while she finished, and turned his head to the side to say something they couldn't hear. "We're just now ready for you. Let's introduce ourselves—tell them what we do so it's obvious who they come to for help."

"Don't *ever* come to me for help," the man with glasses growled, and people chuckled.

As the names and introductions flowed past him, Matt's eyes drifted toward the woman next to Porter. He didn't hear her name; did she say it? She was petite, with black close-cropped hair and dark eyes. Her shirt had accents of a shade of blue that glowed against her skin. When Rob was the first intern to speak, she smiled at him, and Matt had to catch his breath.

"Um, Rob Gordon, uh, I'm an intern this summer," he gasped.

"Where do you study, and what's your area?" she asked. Her voice was low and musical. Matt had to put his eyes somewhere other than on Rob's sweating face, and gazed at the laptop in front of the black-haired woman so it wouldn't seem like he was staring at her. A stack of folders was on her other side, edges squared and tidy. In front of her was a yellow legal tablet, and her slender hand moved a silver-barreled pen across the lines. She nodded as Rob talked, wrote on the page when he paused. Matt found himself wanting mightily to be the silver-barreled pen.

Simone's voice slid into the pause, her words flowing smoothly after Rob's uneasy sputter. Purdue—previous internship experience involved ... Chicago last summer ... Matt tried to imagine the dark woman's name. Sofia? Maybe from Greece? Whitewashed buildings against a sapphire ocean sparkling between deep green mountains flooded his brain. He imagined her in a swaying summer dress, light and transparent, instead of the pale blue sweater draped over her shoulders. An outdoor cafe with glasses of wine on weathered wooden tables, a plate of olives and cheese, took shape before him. He heard her laughter, felt a breeze off the water, saw a sailboat surging through the waves, smelled bougainvillea draped on the walls behind them.

Then her brown eyes were looking at him across the table, and he groped for words. Matt Cortina. Grew up in Montana, finishing—uh, just finished—his third year at Montana State. First time in the Midwest. Focused on circuit board assembly in commercial aircraft.

"Have you had Jay Chandra in class yet?" she asked. "I think he's still teaching."

"I did have that pleasure," Matt noted her white, straight teeth. "And I'm alive to tell the tale." There was a chuckle around the table, and Simone examined her scarlet fingernails.

Next, Will pulled out a ten-minute string of details as though finding them at random in a paper bag: He decided to go to college in California, even though he grew up in Texas and really missed being able to step out his back door in the morning and shoot a rabbit for breakfast ... he paused and grinned around the table, waiting for a laugh, but all eyes were on hands, the ceiling, computer screens ... not much aerospace in Texas any more, after Obama shredded the space program, but we do have a lot of military bases ...

"What are you hoping to learn in this internship?" the black-haired woman broke in.

"Oh, how to get my butt in the chair on time in the morning and not leave before the whistle blows." Will grinned again, and Matt studied the grain of the table. He felt Simone sigh next to him.

"Well, I'm Priya Patel," the dark-haired woman said, and Matt felt the Grecian coast and white-washed buildings fade away. The Taj Mahal slid into its place, Priya Patel in front of it in a flowing garment of peacock colors, brilliant green and stunning yellow and subtle touches of purple and scarlet. Pri-ya, the sound a bird might make on the first warm day of spring. Her voice was surprisingly low, and she had just enough accent to evoke the exotic. "I'll be your primary point of contact this summer, though Russ will join us as he's able. We'll plug you into some of our ongoing projects and also make sure you have some time for your own projects in your specialization. Julie will get you set up with cubicles"—a round-faced blonde woman grinned, and Will waved at her—"computer accounts, show you how the microwave works in the break area—"

"I *know* how a microwave works," Simone muttered, and Matt realized he was the only one who could hear her. She smiled, glancing his way.

"—and we're glad to have you with us; we hope to make this a valuable learning experience for you."

"Just stay out of the way!" growled the man with glasses, who had given his name as Doug. He had a pointed nose in a thin face, and a gut big enough to bulge against the table. Julie tittered and several of the others smiled as though this were actual humor, and now Matt sighed.

After that first day of following Julie around, choosing passwords and finding bathrooms and reading plant safety guidelines online, the interns became more independent of each other. They sat in project group meetings in the frosted-glass conference room, peered at machines grinding or clanking or whirring on the manufacturing floors in other buildings, shouted questions to the operators. In their cubicles they searched the web for details to turn into reports, made and answered phone calls, wrote countless e-mails, struggled to learn acronyms. At lunch time, they each edged close to groups that formed in the break area around TV dinners and sandwiches, and when that failed sat together or went back to their cubicles to eat. Every Friday morning the interns met in the conference room with Priya, and sometimes Russell, to talk about their projects.

That time became the center of Matt's existence. He noticed that Priya filled up his attention, both during the meetings and at odd times in between, though he wasn't quite sure why. Simone was lithe, elegant, and smart as hell; over lunch, she laughed at his jokes and touched his forearm with her fingertips. She always seemed to find what he needed on the web before he could really describe what he was looking for. When they both stood up, seeing her eyes almost directly level with his unsettled him. Priya stopped by his desk sometimes to ask questions, give directions, correct this or that detail. Then she disappeared, leaving the lightest scent of sandalwood behind her. His eyes followed her, and he had no control over them. He searched for her in conference rooms, scanned the doors and cubicle walls several times an hour to see when she might appear. Simone was usually a few feet away, ready to look up, talk, and laugh. It made no sense to him.

On Fridays, Will invited the other interns to his apartment to drink Bud Light with his three Texas roommates and play volleyball in the expansive swimming pool. Rob splashed loudly and swore when the ball went into the net. Simone went once, coming late and staying only long enough to do three swan dives off the board, orange bikini flashing around her lightly tanned limbs. Matt went twice, until he knew enough guys in his own building to play soccer in the park across the street. He texted his roommate Kenneth, working construction in Bozeman, a few times a day:

> Tall chick wearing a white suit. I want to get her dirty.
>
> 8 a.m. sucks no matter what your doing that day.
>
> Laundry last night, no lunch today :-{
>
> Do these khakis make my dick look big?
>
> Hot boss asked me to come to her office after lunch. Whaaaa ...?
>
> Hot boss wants me to run adhesive test on circuit boards. CALL ME!
>
> Hot boss smells good when she walks by. Hard not to follow her around.

Kenneth texted back:

> STAY AWAY FROM HOT BOSS.

Matt chuckled in his cubicle, then slid his phone back into his pocket when Rob peered over the divider. Later he responded:

> Will you care if I never come back to Bozeman?

Kenneth:

> GO MARINERS! SHOW THOSE FUCKING PADRES!

Matt:

> Padres die 7 p.m. MST.

Two days later:

> Will HySol E-90FL hold to 2000 PSI on substrate metal? Why am I asking somebody holding a fluorescent sign that says SLOW on it?

Later that afternoon:

> Tall chick says HySol wont work. Dont know whether to believe a female.

Building R-486 got colder inside as summer got hotter, and sprinklers watered the emerald lawns for hours every day. Matt learned about circuit boards, chips, and adhesives. His ears burned when Priya stopped by his cubicle, his concentration crumbling as he peered over the top of his cubicle to see where she was. He pursued details of resistance to vibration, temperature and air pressure with intensity that confounded him. Was he really this interested in adhesives and circuit boards, or was it the thought of telling Priya he'd found out something new that drove him? He started to text Kenneth—"Hot boss making me crazy"—but then deleted it unsent. He found himself thinking adhesives/circuit boards/Priya's smell/

Priya's small, finely drawn ass, as he played soccer or rode to work with Will. Simone continued to seek him out at lunch time, and he only half-listened to her. "DUDE what is WRONG with you?" he imagined Kenneth saying. "Simone is *hot*!" Matt knew that she was, and that Doug seemed to have a joke to tell her or advice to give on her project every time he walked past her cubicle. Will always drifted over when Doug was there, laughing at the jokes and asking questions that kept conversations going a long time.

Matt's ability to tune them out improved as the summer baked and frosted them. He could feel when Priya was in her office, whether her door was open or closed. He packed his lunches most days, thinking someday she would come to the break area with her own, sit next to him, offer him a cracker or maybe a sip of her iced tea, and he would look her in the eyes over the top of the glass ... When she did show up, she had a cup of yogurt and an apple in her hand, and sat a few tables away, smiling and chatting with anyone sitting nearby. *She's dying to turn around and look at me*, he imagined. Or: *I could just get up, walk over there, pull out a chair and sit down, ask her something about where she's from and how long she's been at Midwestern*. But he never did.

Near the end of July, Priya showed him how to schedule a lab test of the adhesive he had researched. He watched the assembler, a lean man in blue jeans near his dad's age, pull out a tray and ease the cover off. "Last one we have of these," the man said with a certain reverence, holding up a chip the size of a matchbook. "They cost eight grand apiece." He looked at Matt. "You making that much this summer?"

"Uh, almost," Matt muttered. Okay, about half that.

"You better hope this works." Not sure what to say, Matt just nodded and watched as the older man bent his head over the circuit board.

A few days later, the engineering interns followed Priya to the lab, two buildings further up the street. The company was sponsoring a trip to a minor league baseball game in the next town that evening, and Will and Rob chattered about everyone from the office that was going. "You're coming, aren't you Matt?" Will asked, and Rob glanced over at Simone.

"Sure, of course," Matt said. "We're down to one more week, need to get out and see something around here."

"You're coming, too, right, Simone?"

"Well, if we're ALL going—" She may or may not have brushed her arm against Matt's as they went through the door at the same time.

"Priya, you need to come with us," Will said. "We're *all* going and we need our supervisor to—you know—SUPervise us."

"It's *team*-building," Rob chimed in.

"We'll see," she said, and pointed at a bin of safety goggles near the door. Matt looked intently at the goggles, fireworks in his chest, a vision of sitting next to Priya for *nine innings* springing into his head. He would be so relaxed with this adhesive test out of the way. Minor league baseball would mean beer flowing freely. Next week he would be on a plane back to Bozeman. He would ask for just one individual meeting, say he wanted to talk to her about classes to take. She would suggest they stay in touch. The thought of not seeing her every day made him feel a little sick, and what if she didn't go tonight? The rumor was that Midwestern only made one job offer to an intern in each area, and they all assumed that Simone would be this year's. That one meeting might be his only chance—to what? Tell her he couldn't stop thinking about her? Tell her she smelled like a forest after rain and he would never forget that smell, ever? That she made his life complete and he couldn't go on without her?

Priya said hello to the operator, called him Greg. "So let's see how this adhesive works," she said, putting on her safety goggles and smiling at Matt. He felt all the air leave his lungs and tried to smile back, but only got halfway. The interns crowded into the bay, close to Greg, and Matt smelled a forest after rain. "Watch these gauges," Greg told them, and explained the measurements each of them showed: pressure, heat, vibration. A loud hum started, and Matt watched the needles moving around their circles, slowly, then more quickly.

Then the one in the middle did something odd: It reversed and went back to zero. "What the *hell,*" Greg muttered, and threw some switches. "This should never ..." Matt felt Simone glance over at him, and focused more intently on the control panel. All of the needles slid back to their starting points. "Stay here," Greg snapped, and put on heavy leather gloves and a mask with a smoked-glass visor. Matt tried to ignore the feeling of the floor collapsing underneath him, his stomach caving in on itself, the hot steamy air of the lab turning somehow to ice, the murmurs of Will and Rob behind him. Something brushed his shoulder—Priya's slender fingers, giving the slightest squeeze and a look that was concerned, but calm. A dream, but he barely felt it.

Greg came back into the bay, pushing the mask up and holding out the circuit board. There was a charred, ragged area in the middle. "Chip came loose," he said. "Adhesive didn't hold. Short circuit, burned the whole thing out." He looked at Matt with a mixture of pity, contempt, and something close to rage. "That was the last one of these chips we had—takes 10, maybe 12 weeks to get a new one." Matt stared at the ruined circuit board and worked at keeping his knees steady, hearing Priya murmur her thanks to Greg and usher them out of the bay, toward the door of the lab. Will, Rob and Simone lagged behind; Matt didn't blame them.

He knew by the way everyone looked up when they came into the office that they had heard about the circuit board. No one said a word, not "Hi" or "How did it go?" nor even an irritated grunt from Doug. Priya tilted her head for him to follow her into her office. He dimly registered her closing the door behind him, motioning for him to sit in the chair at the table. She sat on the same side of the desk where he was.

"What do you think happened, Matt?" she asked.

"I have no idea." He stared at the floor, then the table, then tried to get his eyes all the way up to hers—didn't quite make it. "The adhesive was E-90FL, it really should have held at that vibration and temperature. I read the documentation over and *over,* I ..."

"When you ordered it, did you input the information into the ERP system yourself, or did one of the buyers enter it?"

He glanced up. "I really don't remember. I was talking to the buyers about so many things, this was weeks ago ..."

"Then that's where you start looking. Go through your e-mails and see if you have one that says you entered it or they did."

"Actually, I'm pretty sure I didn't, because it was taking me awhile to catch on to the ERP system." He stopped short of saying, *I was wandering lost as a troll in the woods.*

"OK, you want to be completely sure that the adhesive we used for the test is the one you researched, because it should have worked. Start with e-mail. If you don't have one that says who did what, you need to go all the way back through the ERP and find out who placed the purchase order, who received the product, who did the receiving inspection, and where along the line something went wrong."

He spoke past the iron in his chest. "I might have just gotten it wrong about the adhesive."

"Yes, that could be, but let's rule out some other possibilities first." He felt her gaze, and looked up. "I have confidence in you, Matt. I think this may not have been you." She gave him a little smile. "You didn't want to go to that baseball game anyway."

He found he could grin back, weakly. "No, of course not." *And beer,* he thought mournfully. *And a soft summer evening with endless possibility, and who needs ten more minutes with these dark eyes, those fingers on my thigh instead of my shoulder*—and then the misery, part humiliation and part terror, flooded back.

Nine hours later, Matt's eyes had been on the computer screen for so long the lines were blurring. He sighed and leaned back, rubbing his forehead with his hand. He'd been all the way through his saved e-mails, having to look up names of people he'd written to but didn't remember who they were or how his path had crossed theirs. He had wandered the impossible maze of the ERP—enterprise resource planning system—for so long nothing was making any sense. Endless acronyms, so many steps in every order for every project he was involved with all summer, different levels of approval at every step. His stomach rumbled, and he remembered the last time he ate anything was a microwaved hot dog and a can of Coke at noon, which felt like a past life now. He groaned and stood up to walk over to the kitchen area; maybe some leftovers in the refrigerator from the potluck?

As he stood in the glow of the open refrigerator door, he heard a key turning in the lock to the outer door. What the fuck, he thought, it's after midnight ... He imagined a security guard telling him he had to leave the building, his shame and failure unchanged by the tortured hours in front of the screen. The refrigerator held a half-eaten tuna sandwich zipped into a plastic bag, a carton of skim milk, and two dried-out lemons.

"Matt?" He reared back and pushed the door shut, embarrassed that he'd been reaching for the sandwich. Simone stood behind him, blond hair pulled into a ponytail and a leather bag over her shoulder. Pink sneakers glowed on her feet, and her white shorts were startling, in the half-light, against her tanned legs. His hunger roared, and she looked delicious. She smiled at him, slowly, knowing.

" ... fun at the game?" his voice was a croak; he had to force himself to speak loudly enough to be heard.

"It was OK." She shrugged and slid her hips onto the table behind her, sliding the bag off beside her in one smooth motion. "You're still working?" He nodded, noticing her eyes were holding his, and that he was wide awake now. "I've noticed that about you all summer," she said. "You work really hard."

Well, yeah, he thought, at a loss. What do I say to that? Does that mean: All that hard work and you STILL fucked up? He realized she wasn't waiting for him to respond; her purring voice went on, paused, went on. Something I've wanted to tell you ... never seemed to be quite the moment ... we're never alone in this office ... I find you very attractive, ever since that first day when we all ... Her eyes were molten, pouring through his weary brain, only now he didn't feel tired at all.

They both heard the sound of a key in the outer door again. Matt imagined the security guard coming in and seeing the two of them, Simone's leg now bent up under her chin, one foot on the table, Matt almost touching her knee—would the guard leer knowingly and leave, or yell at them? His shoulders tensed.

Priya came through the door, and Simone's knee un-bent, her leg sliding back off the table next to the other one.

"Well, hello," Priya said, and Matt couldn't tell if there was surprise in her voice or not. "Matt, how are you getting on?" Her slightly rolled r's were his favorite sound, familiar now after a summer caressing them in his mind. Her t's, a little sharper than American ones, just enough to be exotic.

"Haven't found anything," he managed to say, easing further away from Simone. "Nothing really clear in e-mails, the ERP is—well, kind of confusing ..." Did something brush his thigh? He looked down at Simone, whose eyes were still on him, and she may have licked her upper lip very slightly—it was hard to tell in the dim light, with the refrigerator door closed.

"It's a mess, isn't it?" Priya shook her head, smiling.

"I can help you look, Matt," Simone's purr straightened its back a little, but not completely. He sucked his breath in. It wasn't bad enough he blew up an $8,000 chip, Priya will think she walked in on a late-night slap n' tickle *in the office*? But how can he say he doesn't need help when he's just admitted he's got nothing, he's confused, and it's past midnight?

Priya cleared her throat. "Matt, what do you think? Are you close?"

She was looking at him, her gaze direct, and Simone's eyes had never moved from his face. *What I want is for* you *to stay here and help me*, he wanted to say to Priya. Hell, why not say that, when it's true? When she's his supervisor? Who—hang on—just showed up here at midnight?

But what does her question mean—"are you close?" Is he supposed to say *yeah, I'll figure it out*, or *actually, I could use some help*—but then Simone will hear that as an invitation to stay. If she stays, will she help him out of the jam he's in, or start something physical, which he should want much more than another hour or two wrestling with a computer program that reveals his stupidity?

Then he smelled something very faint. Not Priya's forest-after-rain, woody delicious smell, but Bud Light. He glanced at Simone, whose eyes seemed a tiny bit unfocused until she snapped her attention back to him. Of course—she's toasted. She came over here from the baseball game, and helping him with the ERP system is the last thing on her mind.

Still ...

"Yeah, I think I'm getting close," he said. "Thanks, Simone, but you must be beat." Her eyes opened wider in surprise, and she opened her mouth to say something. OH those perfectly shaped lips, and where they could be ten minutes from now—

Priya's lips smiled very slightly. "We'll leave you to it, then," she said smoothly. "Simone, I'll walk out with you." With a brief stare at Matt, Simone slung her bag over her shoulder and slid off the table. Priya's smile stayed put while Simone stalked past her, then she looked back at Matt. *Thank you,* he mouthed. *You're welcome,* she mouthed back. It was intimacy, as sure and satisfying as though they had kissed.

He walked back to his cubicle, the light from his computer screen and the desk lamp blending smoothly with the light from the hallway when the two women went out the door.

A week later, a humid August afternoon. The parking lot was a blast furnace as the interns gathered outside for a shuttle bus to the auditorium where they'd met at the beginning of the summer. One more official event: filling out forms, turning in ID badges and keys, before they scattered. Will was joking and high-fiving with friends from other buildings, Rob talking earnestly with a woman assigned to escort them. Simone was poring over her phone, texting and scrolling without a glance to anyone else. Matt texted with Kenneth:

Home this weekend dude. Frisbee Saturday or Sunday?

Sunday 3 p.m. prepare to die.

Newbies any good?

One a speed demon, another very hot.

Matt grinned, and wiped sweat off his forehead. The shuttle bus heaved into view at the end of the street, and relief sighed through the group.

A beep from his phone.

Don't get lost OK Matt?

It was Simone. He kept his eyes on the screen.

Of course not—hey congrats on the job offer.

Thanks. Wish we had spent more time together this summer.

Yeah, well, he thought, but didn't touch the keypad.

Another beep: Kenneth.

Anything happen with Tall Chick?

Nope.

Hot boss?

Matt looked at the two words for a long time, and felt himself smiling. Then he slid the phone into his back pocket, picked up his backpack, and joined the line to embrace the icy welcome of the shuttle bus.

Reflections and expansions

1. Once you act on a crush, it isn't a crush any more. It's a romance, an affair, a hookup—but not a crush. What do crushes provide that those other relational types prevent? What are the decision rules, spoken and unspoken, for balancing the risks and benefits of acting on a crush? In what cultural understandings and expectations about relationships are those decision rules grounded?

2. An often repeated maxim of creative writing is to *show, don't tell,* although most experienced writers know the reality of good writing is more nuanced: There has to be some telling as well as some showing, in order to move the action along and not confuse the reader. This narrative, like some others in this volume, intentionally ended on an ambiguous note: The reader doesn't know what Matt's response was to Kenneth, or even whether he solved the problem of the adhesive failure. The benefit of that ambiguity is that the reader can imagine his or her own, preferred ending. The risk is that the reader will be confused and frustrated that the writer left him or her to his or her own devices. Should unstated conclusions be encouraged, or made illegal?

3. In ethnography, there are two parallels to this dilemma. One, mentioned in the preface to this book, is whether to make theory points explicit in the text, rather than letting readers draw their own conclusions from narratives alone. The other is how to pull together details from different sources of information—an interview, a research finding from another study, a newspaper article describing a broader pattern of an event the ethnographer has witnessed or heard about—into a persuasive case. What happens to your understanding of ethnography if you read a case study in this way: as a balance between describing, interpreting, and situating findings within a broader conversation, versus relying on description (showing, not telling) and letting the reader, as the end user, be the one who interprets and applies the findings?

Along a winding road

"What a fan*tas*tic …" Penny stopped just inside the door and gaped at the high ceiling draped with white crepe paper and pink balloons.

"*Yeah,*" Marcus agreed, taking her elbow. "Let's get out of the way." They moved to the side, near the guest book, and let the current of wedding guests flow past them. A five-piece folksy band was playing at the far end of the room; white linened tables filled the rest of the space except for a small dance floor in front of the band. The building was a round wooden creation of a master carpenter, called a barn (perhaps for want of a better term) but meant for human revelry rather than animal shelter. The cement floor was polished and immaculate, the walls clean pine, and for this celebration of late-life love it had been made into a billowy tent, everything pink and cream and white.

"We have to stand near the fan," Penny told him over her shoulder, and moved further along the wall.

"Hot flashes?"

"Aren't you hot? Isn't it hot in here?" She tugged at his shirt collar, a crisp yellow button-down he'd worn to the office.

Transcribing Silence: Culture, Relationships, and Communication
by Kristine L. Muñoz, 196–204.

"I'm okay." He grinned at her, enjoying a hint of gleam on her forehead, making her hair curl. "You look great." Was this green blouse new? He wasn't sure, but it set off her gray eyes.

"So do you." He was always a tidy dresser, even on a warm summer Saturday; she smiled back, running her finger inside his collar as though neatening his hair, an excuse to touch him.

"SO. The wedding." She'd started the story on the way in from the parking lot, their two cars head to head on the grass, before the loveliness of the inside of the barn interrupted her.

"It was really sweet ..."

"Let's get punch." His arm around her waist, he steered her toward another side table with a silver fountain with pink foamy liquid streaming down its sides.

"God, yes, good *eye*. So it was very sweet, Jean came in with one of Malcolm's daughters—the first husband, he had daughters from his first marriage before her—he had two but I heard one of them wanted no part of this." Marcus laughed at the face Penny made—her storytelling always a full-body experience. "The groom, I think his name is Barry? He came in with his grown son and daughter, that guy over there is his son, the one with the ponytail." She directed his gaze with a nod. "And the priest said something nice about how each of them had already shown they were good at marriage, they loved a spouse till death them did part ..."

"The guy's a widower, too?"

"Apparently, oh YES, let me tell you, I was on my way out" she paused for a long gulp of punch. "This is solid sugar, but oh well. Cold and wet."

"Champagne in it?"

Penny tasted it again. "I don't think so—Sprite. Maybe Mountain Dew." They giggled, their heads together.

The band was too loud for the enclosed space; she put the fingers of her free hand through his belt loop and tugged him closer. "You were on your way out ..." he cued her.

"Yeah, the line was really long and moving slowly because they just lined up right outside the door of the church to shake everybody's hands and hug and stuff, and it was taking forever so I went around the side to get out, and the receptionist from my doctor's office was there! Charlotte is her name, but of course I couldn't think of it, she's one of two that work there and they look enough alike that I can't tell them apart." She was wearing the earrings he gave her for their 20th wedding anniversary; he watched the emerald studs bob while she talked. "It turns out Charlotte is related to Barry; she told me what the connection was but I don't remember, something like her husband's sister is married to Barry's brother. She told me—well, she didn't say his family is *upset* about this but she kept saying, we all just *hope* it's for the best." Penny grinned wickedly, delighted. "Never once said how they felt about Jean, the bride, well she *is* kind of an acquired taste; said Barry's first wife just died, like, two years ago"

"How long ago did Jean's husband die? What was his name?"

"Malcolm. I think it was three—maybe four years ago. Well two YEARS ago didn't sound like exactly yesterday to me, but Charlotte went on and on about how it's been real hard for the daughter, Barry's daughter, and how they were real close to Barry and his wife, they lived with them when they first got married, Charlotte took care of her when she was sick—she died of lung cancer, don't you know, and Jean's husband died of emphysema."

Marcus shuddered. "Guess they had a lot to talk about."

"If they talked about it at all. And then Charlotte says, they're remodeling the house Barry and his wife lived in, it's been in the family for like a hundred years out on this farm, and they're putting in a new *kitchen,* new *appliances,*" Penny's eyes widened, replaying a horrified reaction.

"Sounds awful."

"Yeah, I wonder how much of this Jean is aware of. It was funny to get this side of it from Charlotte, who I barely know—and the way she kept saying 'We all just *hope* it's for the best' started to sound kind of eerie. Like what they really hope is that Barry will come to his senses before they tear out those historic old appliances." Their heads bent together again as they laughed. "She said she would *never* ... well, that who knows what she would do if, God forbid, something happened to her husband, but she couldn't imagine going through the trouble of breaking in a new one. Jesus it's hot. Do you have a handkerchief?"

"Do *I* have a *handkerchief*?" Marcus snorted and pulled a neatly folded square from his pocket. "Where do we look for food? I'm hungry."

"I think it's in the other building next door. You didn't take anything to work with you?"

"Didn't think I was staying so long; I meant to have something on the way here, but then I was running late." They started back toward the door.

"Listen, if anything happens to me I want you to not listen to anybody, get remarried if you want to and let the new missus remodel the damned kitchen any way she wants. Tell yourself I would want you to be happy, because I would, and the kids would, too." She dabbed at the back of her neck with his handkerchief. "I hope you don't have to nurse me through some horrible illness along the way."

"Yes, *dear*. You keep that handkerchief if you want." She stuck her tongue out at him and rolled her eyes, and he squeezed her to him as they moved together through the crowd.

Between the heat, the loud band, the big crowd, and the lawn waiting at home that Marcus kept saying he needed to mow, they didn't stay long at the reception. Penny drove out ahead of him, more sure of the way back to the highway along gravel country roads that all looked the same. He called her on her cell phone as they turned onto paved road, saying her car was more gray now than red, from the road dust. She laughed and then the signal cut out because they were so far out in the country, and that was the last thing she ever heard him say.

Never even saw the fucker, is what got him. The road was so curvy and the trees were so close, they should have trimmed them back farther, you couldn't see anything until it was on top of you. Plus the other guy was speeding, and the reason he was over on Marcus's side of the road was he had to cut the corner closer to make the curve, and he must not have seen Marcus either because it was a head-on crash. Dead on impact, the drunk in the '89 GTO and the husband and father in the '97 Chevy van. There was no time for their lives to flash before their eyes, like people say it does when you die. All Marcus had time to think was, *Thank God he didn't hit Penny.*

The maniac driver missed Penny by inches, because she swerved and he swerved and there was just enough of a straight stretch in the road that both managed to react. She swore at him and looked in the rear-view mirror, saw the black car yank away from the next curve, the one she had just come around, and went back to the juicy story Charlotte had shared about the bride and groom, laughing a little. How Jean remarried was one big mystery, after everything that first sick husband had put her through, and now she had a whole *family* to win over ...

It wasn't quite an explosion she heard, more of a dull thump, or a boom. She didn't immediately think much about it and kept on driving, loving how the trees bent so gracefully over the road, how green and tall the corn was in the fields on the other side of them. Then something about how the black car had barely missed her when it sped past crossed with the image of Marcus in the van in her rear-view mirror seconds earlier. She looked up in the mirror and slowed down, waiting for him to drive up behind her. The car went slower and slower, and that 100-degree Iowa day turned icy cold.

"How could I have *said* that, the part about if I die would you please remarry?"

"Penny, your saying that did not cause the accident."

"I know that. Of course it didn't."

The rain was driving against the kitchen window.

"I know it didn't."

Jessie is a nurse on a pediatric ward where children come, horribly mangled or diseased, sometimes to die. She can be trusted to hear all that cannot be said to the children, Penny's colleagues, her family, Marcus's. She also does not ooze into psycho-babble: *Your head knows you didn't cause this but your heart still thinks you did and that's why you're in such Godawful pain and you just have to be there for yourself.*

"Is it ridiculous to wish we hadn't been so happy? Because I know people who are so miserable together that if one of them died, it would be a relief to the other. They'd say all the right things about missing them and what a tragedy but on the inside they would be really pleased."

"We all know people like that, yes."

"Susan and Doug across the street. Have you ever been around them at a soccer game? They scream at each other worse than they scream at the kids on the field, and that's bad enough."

"More tea?"

"Isn't it martini time yet?"

"It's 3:30."

"I could have a martini if I wanted one."

"Want a martini?"

"I want to be 18 again when alcohol solved all my problems. Martinis just give me a headache."

Penny put her head on her arms, smelling Pine-Sol on Jessie's table top. "Always so clean," she murmured into the scent, and felt a flash of hatred for Jessie's clean house and her healthy, very much alive husband.

"I'm not cut out for this widow business," she said, loudly enough to be heard.

Jessie agreed. "Coretta Scott King probably thought that, too."

"Why did I *say* that," Penny moaned, rolling her face to the side so the tears flowed into the sleeve of her sweater instead of making water spots on the damned clean table. "If I had just not *said* that about remarrying—I meant it, though, I did. I did want him to be happy if I died." Her body shook, as it had been doing on and off for a month, since she saw through the cornfields on Old Dodge Road how little was left of the van after the black car blasted into it at, the police report estimated, somewhere close to 70 miles per hour. "I didn't know ..."

"Of course you didn't know this was going to happen." Jessie knows not to touch her, too.

"I didn't know that *life goes on* could sound so horrible. People really do mean well when they say that. There's no way they could know how cruel it feels to hear it—*my* life, the one I really liked, doesn't go on; it can't. The life I liked had Marcus in the middle of it and whatever is going to go on now won't, so how can you call that life? How can you say it's going on?" She was yelling again, and the sobs were uncontrollable.

Jessie looked at her, tears in her own eyes.

Jean didn't hear about Marcus being killed on her wedding day until she was back from her honeymoon. Penny didn't hear from her for a year, partly because she didn't know her that well and presumably because Jean didn't know what to say. Finally Jean sent a thank-you for the wedding present, apologizing for how late it was.

> *Barry and I love the figurine—did you know I collect Lladro, or was it a lucky guess? Sorry this has taken so long, we have been remodeling for what seems like years and everything has been a mess.*
>
> *Widowhood isn't an experience I would wish on anybody, and I'm so sorry you joined me in it. The world ends and there's nothing to say that changes that for a very long time. Then, someday, words come along. I don't know what those will be for you—"life goes on" is the label we give but what's underneath, whatever comes along that makes that true, has to be different for everybody. I hope the silence is not too unbearable for now, and I'm always happy to sit quietly if company would help.*

Penny read this over several times, seeing again that nobody, including those who have suffered, knew what to say when the unthinkable happened. It would be so easy—too easy—if saying nothing at all were an option; but people are just too tied to words for silence like that. If the crash on Old Dodge Road hadn't happened to Marcus, if it hadn't happened to Penny, she would have been at exactly the same loss for what to say to the person it did happen to. Something about that thought—*I wouldn't know what to say any more than you do*—was reassuring. Something about knowing silence was harder to do than finding the right words made all the wrong ones (*If I die would you please remarry/your saying that did not cause the accident/Marcus would want you to be happy*) stop tumbling around inside her for a minute, and an instant of stillness came along. Silence and quiet, she decided, are different. With enough silence, someday she will be blessed by quiet.

Reflections and expansions

1. As mentioned in the Introduction, anthropologist Keith Basso studied silence among US Western Apache tribes. He concluded that members of that culture often dealt with awkward situations—first dates, being around someone who is drunk and angry, being with someone who is sad—with silence rather than talk. What would it take for members of the culture Penny and Marcus inhabit to acquire that habit from a different speech community? What would a first date be like if the expectation was that neither party said a word to the other, but learned about each other by listening and watching how they interacted with other people?
2. What does it mean for partners in a romantic relationship to compliment one another on their looks, since some of the usual expectations for ritual compliments when people are dressed up for a special occasion are presumably relaxed? What would it mean for romantic partners to say nothing verbally about the other's physical appearance, regardless of whether the occasion is a wedding reception or the end of a long day working in the yard?
3. Advice columnists frequently give suggestions about what to say, and what not to say, when someone has suffered a loss: "I'm so

sorry" and leave it at that is one of the most frequent. Yet people who suffer unthinkable tragedies still frequently hear well-meaning people say something unintentionally hurtful: "Bet you wish you had stayed longer at that reception, huh?" "At least you had a wonderful 15 years together." "God only gives us the burdens we are able to bear." Religious references are particularly delicate in the US if you don't know for certain whether the hearers are believers, but they are also quite commonly offered in condolence: "You and your family are in our prayers." "Marcus is in heaven now, watching over you and the children." What would silence mean in response to each of these kindly-intended utterances of solace to the bereaved?

Draft.doc

Jeremy Blake stared at his computer screen, sweating despite the soft breath of summer coming through the open window next to him. The groggy just-woke-up feeling that had led his hand toward the coffee mug on the desk ran out of him like a tide, and the mug stayed untouched. The birds racketed in the trees outside and Bobo sniffed around the bushes at the back of the yard, marking them at random on his first patrol of the day. A fresh smell of dew on grass he'd mowed late yesterday afternoon tickled through the screen, mixing with the sharper smell of coffee and the scent of the breadmaker, set last night to have a loaf of honey whole wheat warm and ready by the time the family woke up.

None of this registered with Jeremy as the words on the screen burned his eyes.

> Dear Peter,
>
> I can't go on like this. God knows we've had bad fights before, but yesterday's battle left me feeling

Transcribing Silence: Culture, Relationships, and Communication
by Kristine L. Muñoz, 205–217.

> just too wounded—beyond repair this time. It's not enough that I'm meeting you in the Poconos, with the usual lies and risks that involves; I have to be there Friday instead of Saturday or none of it counts. I think we're at the end of the line—I'm sorry. I have to take care of my family and myself, and there isn't, I fear, any more room left for you.

He knows Peter. Or thinks he knows who this is. A coworker at Jacqueline's bank for a few years; he moved to Boston for another job awhile ago. When he worked in town, Jacqueline went between being grateful for Peter's support, reporting the occasional lunch or beer after work, and groaning over him being pushy, controlling, demanding. She hadn't said anything about contact with him after he left the bank, but this tells a different story. She is due to leave for a conference one week from today—Saturday—in Pennsylvania.

"Daddy?" Jeremy started. "Why are you up so early?"

"Hey there, pumpkin." He searched for the button to minimize the screen, but it was tiny, his eyes weren't focusing—he turned and held his arms out to her instead. "It's not so early, it's nearly eight o'clock. I got up to get some work done before you needed me."

Tracie wandered across the study, her pink nightgown brushing the floor, and snuggled onto his lap. He turned the chair so both of their backs were to the screen. "But I allllways need you," she yawned. "What's for breakfast?"

"There's fresh bread ready, smell it?"

"mmmmm"

"And we have some of that apple butter Chuck made to go on it."

"I don't like Chuck's apple butter." Jeremy was losing track of the conversation, his mind on the message on the screen behind him.

"How about you find some cartoons to watch for awhile and then I'll—we'll figure something out for breakfast."

She smiled. "I can go keep Mommy company." As quickly as the thought came to her, she slid off his lap and trotted out toward the stairs. "MOMmmmmy, time for cartoooooooons!"

Yeah, go keep her company, he thought. If she's alone up there. His mind was racing, tumbling over itself, a sharp pain starting below his ribs. What was this message doing here, in HIS directory where HE would be sure to find it—she must want him to know. What a foul, sneaky way to tell him—how long had this been going on? Peter moved on, when was it, three years ago? four? so *all this time* she's been— His eyes roamed the walls of the study, looking anywhere but back at the treacherous screen. He heard his breath raspy in the quiet, heard the faint music of the TV turn on upstairs. Jacks, Jacks, he wanted to moan out loud. How could you *do* this, what do we tell our *daughter*. His eyes were starting to bother him.

"Do I smell Jeremy's Famous Wheat Bread?" His wife's voice came from the stairs. He froze—this wasn't the moment to unravel their marriage. Forcing himself to look back at the screen, he searched for the button to close the file. There was a beep, a message on the screen:

> do you want to save changes to c:/jac/work/draft.doc ? Yes No

Hastily punching NO, he stared at the string of letters on the screen. This wasn't in his directory, it was in hers. In her work subdirectory, where he would never have reason to go; where in fact, because she works for a bank and this is a small town, decency and confidentiality would make it an invasion for him to go. How did I get there? he wondered, confusion taking over, fog seeping back into his brain. Was I that sleepy, that I thought I was in my own directory, opening ... what *did* I think I was opening?

Jacqueline's voice had faded; she was turned around at the bottom of the stairs, talking to Tracie. Jeremy's heart hammered in his chest, but numbness was settling into him. He had to think this through before he said anything to her. He wasn't going to sniff around for more information, geez, how humiliating. He would just ask her, Jacks, what is this I found ... Jeremy how did you FIND this, what were you doing in my work directory?

He shook his head. For now, on with Saturday morning, act like nothing's wrong, like he doesn't know anything. His world had just come completely undone, and he hadn't had a single drop of coffee yet.

That weekend lasted a year. Saturday, Jeremy went through the motions, washing the car, taking Tracie to her dance lesson, stopping by a bookstore to pick up a new history of the Civil War they special ordered for him. He felt a terrified need to watch himself, not to let on what he knew, to hide everything going on inside him. He watched Jacqueline closely, when she didn't seem likely to notice, and headlines flashed in his mind: The Adulteress Fixes Lunch. The Woman Who Lies to Her Husband Says She's Going for a Run, *but where is she really headed?* He turned his eyes away any time hers swung close, so she couldn't see the burning inside. Exhausted before dark, he slept fitfully that night, scooting out from under Jacks's arm to the far edge of the bed.

Sunday, he found himself close to tears in church, lacerated by the fragile, ironic images: The perfect family together in a pew, Tracie in purple capri pants and a pink top, coloring and whispering to him through the service—he didn't hear a word—so innocent and happy, so sure of her world. He felt like they were posing for a painting, more a cartoon now: The intact married couple sharing a hymnal. The six-year-old hugging her parents together.

For those two days he rocked between disbelief and a raw mixture of grief and rage. Weekends had always been such happy times, easy hours of looking around for things that needed doing and feeling relaxed about whether they got done, warm treacly delighted moments of watching Tracie ride her bike or sweeping Jacqueline into his arms and upstairs to the bedroom. Ordinarily, that happened at least once on a weekend, and he wondered if she noticed by Sunday night that it hadn't. He thought about gamely giving it a shot, pretending, having sex somehow so she wouldn't catch on; but couldn't imagine doing it. In the angry moments he thought of violence: he would hit her, he would shoot her, he would pick up a kitchen knife with her back to him, he would hunt down Peter and ... but the images failed him as quickly as trying to imagine having sex with her. In the bleak times he saw a graveyard that was his life from now on. Life without Jacks waking up next to him, trying to explain to Tracie why Mommy and Daddy didn't live together any more, life without Jacks's seared salmon steaks— He shook himself like Bobo after a swim, trying not to make a list of everything that would be gone from his life if Jacqueline weren't there.

Monday morning was a relief it had never been before. Jeremy woke up before the alarm rang and gathered together his gym bag in the faint light coming through the curtains, drawn against the early summer dawn: shaving gear, towel, golf shirt and khakis on a hanger. He dressed silently in shorts and Tshirt, tied his sneakers, and left without kissing Jacqueline goodbye.

Chuck was already there, of course, brown thighs pounding on the treadmill. Muscular, a full head of curly brown hair, $200 running shoes. Jeremy has admitted to Jacqueline how deeply his envy of this friend runs; that fact seemed to figure in to how much paler, thinner, more inconsequential than usual he felt as he returned Chuck's wave. He climbed on the exercise bike, across the room, instead of onto the next treadmill over, wanting freedom from the obligation of small talk.

That lasted only a few minutes, just long enough for the anger to make him jumpy and the sadness to make him hopeless. As they mixed together into profound confusion, Chuck left the treadmill and came over to the elliptical, close enough to the bike for the kind of shouted conversation Jeremy hated.

"Have you met with the Dixons yet?" Chuck barked. "I have this girl looking for a condo, new in town, she might be interested in having a look at theirs."

Jeremy shook his head silently.

"You know of any other ones, mid 70s, maybe 80, she could take a look at?"

"Like how big?" That was it: ask a question, seem interested, Chuck would be off and talking and not require anything other than the occasional nod. He'd end up saying, Let's have lunch, and then they'd go through it all again, so it wasn't like he was missing anything. Jeremy wandered off into his head again. So many questions pounding around in there, one every fourth revolution on the bike. Was it really Peter Barrows from the bank, all those years ago, or was there another Peter—another peter, he thought grimly—he'd never heard of? When did it start? How did it start? WHY did it start, why did she do this, was it him, was it her, was it them ... the questions pounded on an endless loop. Who, when, why; when, why, who; why, why, why?

"Do you know why the Dixons are splitting up?" he asked Chuck, surprised to hear the words burst out of him.

After a look of mild reproach—the question made it clear he hadn't been listening—Chuck answered. "I think there was some tomcattin' involved, and Sally got tired of it and showed him the door." *How do you know this,* Jeremy thought fiercely. *Is* my *wife's affair all over town, too?*

"Hard to blame her for that," he said. Chuck glanced at him, moving in silence for awhile.

"Maybe not," he said. "But that's a pretty big meal ticket she's giving up. She might not like being a social worker so much if she starts having to live like one." He laughed, enjoying his own wit. "Listen, you free for lunch?"

"Sure." Jeremy's response was automatic, then he nearly groaned. What he really wanted was some time alone, not another hour listening to Chuck entertain himself. On the other hand, maybe Chuck could help him figure out what he should do about Jacqueline. He's a close friend, and they often chew over work dilemmas. Chuck complains about his wife often enough. That thought plunged him further into gloom, in two directions: One, his best friend, the one person in the world he can talk to about anything, is also the problem he needs to work out. He isn't looking to complain, gripe, or whine; he needs to figure out what to do. Two, he cannot imagine any conversation in which he would tell Chuck Simmons that his wife was having an affair.

The timer on the exercise bike sounded, and Jeremy slowed his pedaling to cool down. At least this half hour, usually the longest of the day, had gone by quickly.

"See ya at lunch." Chuck got off the elliptical. Jeremy was grateful to see him head back toward the stairmaster, rather than coming in with him to the locker room. Something reared wildly inside him, though, that he had to ask.

"How did you know this about the Dixons?" He hated the prim, correct sound of his voice; he wanted to sound casually curious, not pained and tense. Chuck didn't seem to notice.

"Maybe running into Bill Dixon at all hours in restaurants and bars," he said, "with at least two or three different sets of cheekbones over the years. Sally is a ..." He paused, searching for words. "She has some sharp edges to her, being political and all, and the company I saw Bill keeping seemed to be, if nothing else, easier to just hang out with." He wiped his face with a towel hanging on the stairmaster and eased himself onto the pedals. "I mean, obviously I don't know for sure, it's just a hunch I have. But this is a pretty small town to let people see you out and about with a string of different girls."

Jeremy went through the routine of showering, shaving, getting dressed, every step automatic, done exactly the same way in the same order probably hundreds of times, with Chuck's voice replaying itself. Small town. Just a hunch. Sally was ... had some sharp edges to her ... two or three sets of cheekbones ... she got tired of it, showed him the door. Sally showed him the door. Can't much blame her, can you?

What, exactly, was he going to do? Show Jacqueline the door? Bill and Sally Dixon didn't have children. They lived in a condo with a property owner's association that did all the yardwork and told you what color you could paint your front door, not in a 1920s farmhouse they had replaced nearly all the plumbing in, added a bathroom and a sunroom to, planted roses around. Bill Dixon was an engineer in

Naperville, 20 miles away. They lived here to be close to Sally's job and had only been here about 10 years, and as soon as they separated he moved to an apartment in Naperville. Marcus has loved Jacks for 15 years, since sophomore English class when she turned around and asked him if she could borrow his notes on Beowulf. She is as much a part of him as his arm, his eyes, his lungs.

Well, he wasn't going to do *nothing,* either. He would find a moment when he could discuss things calmly with her, he would say, look, tell me what's going on, I need to know ... What does he need to know? Whether the note he read was accurate, that this—whatever it was—was really over with this guy? Does he need to know for sure that it's the Peter he thinks it is? Does he need to know if Chuck's been seeing *her* around town with different sets of cheekbones? He does need to know why she did it, that he absolutely needs to know. Is it something he's not doing, something she's not getting in their marriage? When did this business with Peter, whoever he was, get started? Is she really ending it with him?

He wandered through paperwork at his desk much of the morning, and left a message on Chuck's cell phone that lunch wouldn't work out. He needed to be somewhere else, doing something else, anything but here pretending everything was fine. He went home, fixed himself a sandwich, turned on NPR. The voices were resonant and professional; the stories of faraway people with troubles of their own, most of them of the life and death variety, drew him out of the quicksand of his own thoughts. He caught himself staring at the computer, which he'd avoided like roadkill ever since Saturday morning. He could go back into Jacks's directory, could look for other letters, other evidence. Travel itineraries. Hotel stuff.

He shuddered, disgusted with the idea of snooping this way, and went out into the yard. Standing there in his office clothes, the sleepy summer afternoon folding itself around him, he saw what to do. He put on cutoffs and a Tshirt and attacked a ring of day lilies that had gotten weedy and overgrown around the oak tree. When the earth proved too hard for a shovel to make headway, he grabbed an axe from the shed. He chopped at the musky, tangled growth, yanking the lilies out in handfuls, enjoying the sweat pouring off him and the taut feel of muscles across his shoulders. Once the lilies were out, scattered across the lawn, gashes in the dirt where they had been rooted, he leaned on the axe and looked at the tree. Could he chop that down, too, or maybe start on the planks of the deck they'd put in five years ago and just finished paying for?

"Jeremy? Are you making a mess over there?" Janelle McCreedy called across the hedge. "Isn't it too hot out here to be working so hard?" She shaded her eyes with one hand, a bony figure in seersucker shorts and a crisp white blouse.

"It's GREAT," he boomed, hoping she wouldn't want to chat.

Fat chance. "Where's Tracie these days, off at camp?"

"No, she's at the summer program at the rec center." He moved into the shade closer to the hedge, so he wouldn't have to yell.

"Is she enjoying that?" Janelle keeps encyclopedic tabs on every child, adult, and pet in the neighborhood. She would file away his being home in the middle of a workday, infrequent but not unheard of, noting his yardwork with far more approval than if he had pulled out a hammock under the tree. It dawned on him that Janelle might know more about some areas of Jacks's life than he did. He chatted with her, wondering what she knew, how he could find out, whether he wanted to know.

"I had *such* a nice time last week when Jacqueline took me out to lunch," Janelle was saying, and Jeremy's attention came back to her.

"She did?"

"Oh, yes, didn't she tell you? We went over to that new restaurant in Benton, the Thai place. I didn't think I would like Thai food but your wife said, now come on, give it a try, so I did, and you know *what,* it was delicious."

"She's adventurous like that," he muttered.

"And while we were out she took me to run some errands, wasn't that nice of her? I could have gone myself, of course, but it's so much more relaxing when someone else is driving."

He nodded, his mind starting to wander again.

"And that lemonade stand she got the neighborhood kids organized to do!" Janelle swiped at an invisible bug. "I heard they made 50 dollars!" Her laugh was loud, unrestrained. "I told her, a few more weekends like that and every kid in this neighborhood could have a college fund going!"

"She's probably drumming up business for the bank," he offered. "Get them all started thinking about investments early." He smiled as Janelle laughed again.

"That's a good banker you have there!"

"Yep." Good banker, good mother, good neighbor. Even a good wife, in so many ways. Did being unfaithful cancel all that out?

The heat and bugs got to Janelle after awhile, and she went inside, leaving Jeremy to separate the mess of stalks and bulbous roots from the loose dirt and cart the plant matter back to the fence. It was slow and backbreaking, far less satisfying than chopping away at the ground had been, and the wild buzzing thoughts seemed to give way to a tired calm. He no longer remembered the note he'd found on the computer very clearly, so two things about it were stuck sideways. Why was it labeled "Draft," as though there were a final version still ahead? And what was this about going to the Poconos? Jacks traveled on business, but usually within the state. She went to visit family and friends sometimes, but they were all on the West Coast. He didn't know quite where the Poconos were but it was somewhere out east, Pennsylvania, New York, something like that. That much, he would ask her about.

"Do I remember you telling me about some trip coming up?" he asked that night, as he reached for another helping of green beans. Tracie was playing a complicated game on the computer upstairs, finished with dinner in lightning speed as usual. He hoped he sounded casual, vaguely absent-minded.

"Investment convention in October, then Christmas at Mom's. One of them?" Jaqueline pushed her hair back from her face as she looked up from her plate at him. God, she had gorgeous eyes, gray and blue, an ocean with a rainstorm coming. Those eyes had kept words from coming out of his mouth in answer to her request for Beowulf notes 15 years ago, and nearly stopped him this time, too.

"Where's the convention? I was thinking there was something out east."

"Minneapolis." Something rushed wildly through him—relief of some kind. She wasn't really going to the Poconos, there was some other explanation for that note he'd found, this was all a mistake.

But her eyes went down to her plate, and her hair fell forward again, hiding them. "I had thought about a mini-conference in Pennsylvania that sounded, maybe, better than the usual stuff at the convention, but I decided against that." She took the skin off the last of her salmon, doing it delicately with her knife and fork instead of just peeling it away with her fingers. There was something an inch too careful about this, and his insides sank back onto tense, angry spikes.

"What *kind* of mini-conference." The spikes were in his voice now; he couldn't help it. He felt cold and hot at the same time, furious and terrified.

"Umm." She still didn't look at him, didn't say, just a conference, and what's with this tone of voice? She pushed the pieces of salmon around her plate slowly, as though the task required deepest concentration. "It was organized by this Boston group and has to do with software innovation and how you can develop, or tailor, or something, software packages that are particularly suited to your clients." A long pause, the only sound her fork scraping the plate very softly. "When I first heard about it I thought, well, I might get more out of that than the usual big regional convention that I always go to, where there are so many people to see and talk to and it's really hectic. I thought something smaller, quiet, where the focus is on individuals, on particular kinds of clients and what they need ..." She blinked several times, still looking at the plate. "I wanted to listen to what clients need. I thought maybe I wasn't hearing them, just trying to get through the day quickly and efficiently, get 'em in get 'em out, not slowing down and listening to them."

"That sounds pretty important." Jeremy was shocked to hear how encouraging he sounded. As though he understood this.

"Well, maybe it is." She looked up, brushed her hair back again, one quick motion. "But then maybe it's too much trouble, maybe Pennsylvania's too damned far away for three days, maybe their software innovations are not that great. Maybe the way I'm doing things is fine, and I ought to do *that* the best I can and not be taking chances, adding something else on to everything I already know and do." She looked up, her eyes wide open. She looked so strong and certain. "I love you, Jeremy," she said. Not as an afterthought, not as a routine, unthinking duty, but as a conclusion she had reached after deep and lengthy study of the salmon on her plate. He felt some of the spines melt away. Not all of them, of course; so many had grown since Saturday morning when he had stumbled on the note that would both end her affair and ignite his knowledge of it. But some. Enough to think that there would be evenings side by side on the sofa watching TV and afternoons spreading mulch and Sundays close together in the pew at church, that those would happen again because some questions got left unasked and some deceptions got forgiven, and because every day, no matter how shocking and horrible it was, eventually gave way to another one. Maybe there was something to be said for not saying what you knew or asking questions about what you didn't know.

He put his fingertips lightly to her cheekbone. She looked at him, those ocean-storm eyes steady now, and they finished dinner in the most companionable of silences.

Reflections and expansions

1. "I love you" is one of those utterances for which the expectation of reciprocation is, in US American culture at least, the strongest. What does it mean when Jeremy does not respond "I love you, too?" What goes unsaid in that moment?
2. Chuck and Jeremy are close friends in this story, and they communicate about Jeremy's worries in ways stereotypically associated with men: indirectly, or not at all. If this had happened in the opposite direction and Jacqueline was the one convinced her spouse was having an affair, do you think she would have talked it through with someone?
3. What impact would it have on a child to find out one parent was having an affair, and to know that the other parent does not know? Children have notorious difficulty leaving matters unsaid, and must be socialized to know both when they are required to be silent and when they must keep information secret. How do they learn to leave unsaid what is unsayable in their culture?

Another word for nothing

It began that year that autumn lasted forever, hanging over the Midwest like it couldn't bear to leave. Connie went back to teaching while Belinda stayed with an Indonesian babysitter in family housing. Every day at noon she locked her office behind her and shuffled through the leaves along the creek, around the intramural fields, and through the maze of apartment buildings, spicy smells swirling around her. Sitting on a neatly covered mattress on the floor of a back bedroom, she nursed Belinda while her mind wandered through meetings, classes, the students left standing at her door when she made her escape. Belinda looked up at her sometimes, more interested in eye contact than sucking, and Connie tried to be aware and attentive, a Good Mother. Her attention always wandered after a few minutes, back to the student who kept interrupting her lectures or questions to ask Russell when he got home, the bank balance, the grocery list, should she vacuum today and mop tomorrow or could she manage both before "Parenthood" came on? Belinda's green eyes watched her face as Connie frowned

---

Transcribing Silence: Culture, Relationships, and Communication
by Kristine L. Muñoz, 218–248.

and smiled and made mental notes and tried not to hurry the baby along. Sometimes she closed her eyes and felt the holy intense pleasure of the sucking, heard the thirsty gulps, smelled the warm baby smells of Belinda's soft blond hair and the inside of her own clothing, lightly scented with milk. At night Russell smoothed the interrupted sleep by bringing Belinda into their bed for Connie to nurse her. The drowsy cuddles of the three of them were the deepest satisfaction Connie could remember, moments when they all had everything they needed from each other.

In October they drove down to see Russell's mother in Kansas. Wilma made lemonade, and they sat out on the veranda, still needing shade in the middle of the day. Belinda sat on a big blanket surrounded by Tupperware and other toys, and Connie was freed from conversation with her mother-in-law by way of a green-eyed ash blond miracle. Wilma didn't want to hold the baby much, preferring to watch her. What talk there was touched on other things, mostly the repairs she needed Russell to do after he finished the one he was working on. Her eyes sat hungrily on her only grandchild's head, the soft body inside terrycloth, the white legs curling and uncurling beneath her or waving in the air. The baby bestowed placid two-toothed smiles lavishly on her audience and burbled her benediction on their harmony. Connie watched Russell being a son all day, listening to his mother's stories over dinner, fixing her venetian blinds, combing through her bank statement to see whether they really were cheating her every month as she suspected. When he climbed into the oak sleigh bed that night, Connie reached for him with hands, feet, thighs, reclaiming him into their warm-breath space, Belinda in a crib in his mother's room to give them the hope of a quiet night. They made love, and his energetic attention to her body made her feel cherished, nourished. For a moment she was not a mother, not a dairy, not an intruder on his mother's life, but a loved one, THE loved one, the one who excited a dark-haired fine-muscled man and made him groan with delight. They both slept heavily, resting together in the hollows of each other's bodies.

They left early Sunday afternoon so Belinda would fall asleep in the car. She woke up before they were halfway home, first fretting softly then tuning up rapidly to a full scream. "Whatsamatter, sugar, what's the problem, need a fresh diaper?" Connie reached back to check and Belinda grabbed at her arm, wanting to be held. "No, you're not wet and you don't stink."

"Hey, hey, hey," Russell boomed. "Come on now, we got hours to go."

"Need a blankie; are you cold? You can't be hungry." Her shrieks took on a piercing tone, and Connie covered her ears. "BeLINDa take it EASY. Should we pull over and take her for a walk around?" Russell nodded, turning on the blinker. The baby pulled at her ear, her face reddening from the screaming. "Oh shit, bet that's an earache."

It was. Connie walked her around a rest area, remembering her mother blowing cigarette smoke into her ear when she had earaches as a little girl. Who knew why that seemed to work; the best Connie could do was hold her hand cupped over Belinda's ear, blowing gently into her hand, willing her breath to be warm and healing. Russell called the doctor's service from his cell phone.

"They said take her to an emergency room," he said, snapping the phone shut. "I told them about her waking up suddenly like that and pulling her ear, and they think that's bound to be ears, so ..."

"Couldn't they just call in a prescription?" Connie's voice was short. "Given that they agree with us that it's an ear infection, that she's had one before, that ..."

"I'm telling you what they told me," Russell said. "Can you drive, and I'll see if I can figure out from the map where the closest hospital is?"

They waited nearly three hours in the Minnville Community Hospital emergency room, waiting for a football player to have a broken ankle set and an elderly man to have his chest pains monitored. A farmer came in with his hand wrapped in a dishtowel, reddened with blood, muttering something about a tractor, as Belinda went between dozing on Connie's chest and screaming with pain, her back arching. Russell stretched out on a sofa in the waiting room and was asleep almost immediately. Connie stared at him, her arms aching from holding the baby upright. Couldn't he tell how uncomfortable this position was? How could he possibly sleep through his daughter's moans? Wouldn't you think he'd offer to give her a break?

Finally, they were ushered behind a curtain; the doctor looked in her ears as Belinda tried to wriggle away from him and confirmed what they already knew. Some antibiotics and a painkiller later, Connie drove them home, Russell asleep in the back with his head slumped on Belinda's car seat. She glared into the rearview mirror at him and tried to focus on her lecture for tomorrow. It was nearly 2 a.m. when she sank into bed, every muscle aching with fatigue, her eyes burning, and she pulled as far away from Russell as she could manage. Because he went on to bed while she nursed Belinda, he didn't seem to notice she didn't kiss him goodnight.

Between the huff and the weariness, neither of them set the alarm, and Belinda slept past dawn for the first time in her life. When Connie rolled over and the clock read 8:30, she concluded with sleepy gratitude that it must be Saturday. A line from her lecture scheduled to begin 45 minutes later filtered through her mind—"It's really a myth that Eskimos have 200 words for snow; the fact is they have exactly four words for snow." Something flashed in her brain, red alert, she snapped upright in bed.

"RUSSELL GodDAMN it it's 8:30!" He grunted and rolled over, his feet hitting the floor with a slap.

"What happened to the alarm?"

"Didn't go off how the HELL do I know." She grabbed at jeans and a sweater from her closet; Belinda tuned up from the next room. Russell stumbled toward the bathroom. The scream sounded just like last night, now that the painkiller had worn off the ear infection was clearly still in full bloom. "Could you PICK UP your DAUGHter please." Connie's teeth gritted together so tightly the sounds barely emerged. She pulled the sweater over her head and reached for the hairbrush on the dresser, too quickly; her fingers hit the edge straight on. "OWW, damn, damn, damn"

"Are you OK?" Russell came into the room, Belinda redfaced and wailing in his arms. "Here's mommy, baby girl." Belinda stretched her arms piteously toward her mother, who was writhing around her bruised fingertips. "Um, hon, not to be critical but take a look at the front of that sweater ..."

"GEEZ baby drool on EVERYTHING what would I give for ... Okay sweetie, okay, I'll hold you, just hang on would you please? Just let me ..."

"I can take her to Ratna's," Russell offered, jiggling Belinda on his stomach and making faces, trying to distract her. "Maybe some Tylenol will help this?"

"Yeah, and some more pink stuff." Connie struggled into a different sweater and looked at the clock again, and moaned. "I can't feed her or I'll be late, but if I don't I'll be a mess by ten o'clock."

"Here, sit down with her, and I'll get your stuff together." Connie sank onto the rumpled bed and reached for the baby, her mind racing. Belinda's sobs dissolved into hiccupy slurping, one hand clutching her sore ear, diamondlike tears between her dark lashes.

"Okay, socks." Russell sat down in front of her, rubbed Connie's foot briefly between warm hands, and pulled her socks on. She looked down at him and giggled. "Shoes."

"Not those, the brown ones!"

"Whoops, of course, the brown ones. How could I possibly forget. Now, you taking your lunch?"

"No, there's no bread."

"Leftover lasagna?"

"Okay, that'd be great, shovel some into a dish, and an orange, and one of those little candy bars."

"Got it."

She made it to her lecture with 3.2 minutes to spare, and it went surprisingly smoothly. Back in her office, the message light on her phone was on. Don't let that be Ratna, she breathed, please, please, don't let that be Belinda screaming—

You have two new messages, the tinny voice informed her. Please, please—

The first was a deep voice she had to struggle to identify. "Hi, Connie, Ben Stevens. I wondered if you and I ought to talk soon." Ben Stevens, Ben ... Oh. New Guy. Blondish hair, mustache, biker boots. Sort of a swagger, but apparently bright. Joined the department last year while she was first absorbed in her pregnancy, then on maternity leave. Grad students say his name a lot and either sound very earnest, if they are male, or arch their eyebrows if they are female. His voice rumbled on, and she drew impatient circles in the air with her hand, hurry up, hurry up. "So if you want to let me know a time that's good for you, I'm in the office all day today and then tomorrow ..." Mental note to call him or find him; click to the second message. "Herro Connie dis Ratna. I sorry but Berinda keep cry, keep cry ..." Indeed, the too-familiar wails rang in the background as the recording played on. Connie sighed and slumped forward, laying her forehead on her desk.

"Um—hchkHUM." A deep voice cleared its throat behind her. Connie snapped her head up and slammed the phone down.

"BEN, hi, I was just going to return your call." He had a large file folder in his hand and looked uncertain.

"Well here's the stuff I was talking about, for the review, I thought I'd just leave it with you ..."

"Right. Review." Her mind whirled, Ratna's voice, Belinda's screams, a blond mustache moving in front of her. *You are no matinee idol in my book,* she thought; *what's the fuss about*? "What review."

"Curriculum. You and I are supposed to review the basic critical thinking course and come up with a revision that would allow it to be more widely shared among the faculty." He did have a nice voice.

"Oh yeahhhhh" She smiled; he grinned back. "Now it's coming back to me. We should meet. When's good for you."

"Now would work for me, we could just look through this stuff from previous years and maybe come up with an outline or something. It's in order by semester, pretty straightforward." He shifted his weight off the doorframe; she ran a hand through her hair.

"Now. Uhm." Wasn't there a reason now wouldn't work? "Sure, have a chair."

"This is a *really* nice chair." He settled into the green brocade easy chair across from her, his compact frame fitting easily between the arms.

"Thanks. A present from a former student."

"An appreciative one, apparently."

"As they all should be."

"Of course, of course, if only they would see that." His hair shone in the sunlight coming through the window, and his white denim shirt was spotless. Only the mother of a baby could admire someone for their clean clothes, she thought.

He had careful notes about the course, complaints and comments gathered from faculty and former students, outlines of similar courses from other universities. Connie listened to him talk, and relaxed. Here was someone who needed nothing from her, who was even prepared to make her life easier. Gratitude swelled in her for the peace of the moment, and spread itself thickly on his glinting hair and impeccable white shirt.

"Ben, that's terrific," she said when he paused. "I'm not sure what you need me for on this." He laughed, looking up through fine eyelashes over, she noticed, quite fine green eyes.

"I do need some sense of how much of this I'm suggesting has been tried before, what I'm lacking here is the history of the course beyond, before its current form."

"Oh, well that I guess I know." She reached for the page he offered her, and the phone rang. DAMN. She winced. That would be Ratna again, knowing full well she was out of class nearly an hour ago. What if she let it ring? Her mind raced, tantalized. Lots of people did, if they had someone in their office. It feels like ignoring the cries of a drowning person to her, and she knows her child is screaming for her mother ... On the other hand, for ten more minutes she can scream at Ratna. Connie smiled brilliantly. "Explain to me again this part about ..."

She didn't even call when she left, just put a note on her door cancelling her office hours, and drove instead of walked over to family housing. Suddenly worried that something might have gone terribly wrong, she breathed soft prayers: "God, let her be OK. I'm sorry it took so long, please let her be OK, please let it be just the earache ..."

Ratna was a little wild-eyed when she answered the door. "You take long time, baby cryyyyy, cry cry." Belinda snurled into Connie's arms, her sobs turning to hiccups.

"Did you give her more Tylenol?" Connie's hips swung automatically into the baby-sway that had become second nature as she hugged Belinda's sweaty body close to her. "You're OK, sweetie, it's OK, take it easy, deeeeeeeeeep breaths, lovey, it's OK."

The baby calmed as she nursed; her face cooled, and she slumped into a deep sleep. Connie leaned back on the bed with her as she dialed Russell's number.

"Russ, she's been crying all morning and her fever's still way up there. Maybe she needs to be at home in her own crib or something." A ceiling fan twirled slowly; Connie felt herself melt into the mattress. She heard Ratna cooing to her own four-year-old as she fried something wonderful in the kitchen. *Oh please feed me too,* she thought. *Just let me lie here and have a nap and then bring me a bowl of something gingery—*

"Maybe so. Want me to come and get you?"

"No, I drove over. I wondered if I took her on home, could you be there by three or so and I could make the faculty meeting."

A long silence. "Connie, I was an hour-and-a-half late this morning."

A longer one. "I understand that. We're discussing junior faculty reviews today."

"Which requires your presence?"

Connie chewed her lip, picturing Mike Drew looking around the table at the meeting, saying, "Who are we missing?" The ceiling fan didn't move the air around quite fast enough; the smell of curry and onions was starting to be overpowering.

"If you can't do it, Russ, you can't. I'm just telling you what I'm up against."

He sighed. "Will 3:30 help at all? I guess I can bring this report home."

"It definitely will; that way I'll be there for the second half anyway."

"You got it. Drive careful; kiss the girlie girl for me."

"Yep."

Home in her baby powdered crib, Belinda slept another soft hour. Connie sat in the rocker, patting her back while she read the files of the junior faculty. All the windows were open in the house, unbelievable in late October, and her gaze wandered out to the front yard where the trees were just starting to turn to fire. Belinda's room was the color of butter, and the light spread through the air, still more summer than fall. Finally she dozed, the contents of the file plashing onto the floor between her feet.

"Oooo-oooo-oooo," an odd bird sound worked through her half-asleep mind. "Oooo-eee-ahhhh-oooo." Connie frowned, trying to think what sort of bird cooed like that—Pigeons? maybe doves. What would doves be doing in Central Illinois? A rattle of the crib brought her the rest of the way back to consciousness, and she slowly opened her eyes. Belinda was standing, holding the bars of the crib and grinning widely. "Ooooohh-ah-ooo-ooo-ahh."

"Oh yeah?" Connie smiled back at her. "Is that what you think?" Belinda bounced and her rubber-ball knees gave way. She sat back onto the mattress and looked so surprised that Connie laughed out loud. "Silly round feet!" She swung her up and out. "They don't hold up very well, do they?"

"Anybody hooooooooooooooome?" Russell called from the front door.

"Daddy!" Connie said, squeezing Belinda tight. "Daddy home! Daddy, whatcha doin' home so quick? Just when we're in a good mood and ready to play, Daddy shows up for the good part, huh?"

He always looked handsome and businesslike in his tie, though Connie rarely saw him this way. He brushed Belinda's cheek with his chin, the stubble making her giggle, and gave Connie a long kiss. "How's my little sickie kid?"

"Not sick anymore, Daddy, miracle of antibiotics once again."

"You takin' off?"

"I have time for some lunch, I haven't eaten. Have you?"

"Not really, an orange and a piece of cake this morning."

"Hold the kid, and I'll heat the lasagna." She held onto him as she passed the baby to him, enjoying the laundered smell of his shirt. "Family hug."

"Family hug." They swayed together until Belinda grunted, hot and crowded between them.

It was clear in the meeting that Davis and Rheingold were on track for tenure; Ben Stevens was still anyone's guess. His work on Derrida was original and would be important, if he got it out the door on time. Apparently there had been several rejections, though at least they were at the Right Journals. Connie heard herself volunteer to read his work, despite a general distaste for anything Derridean. Later, as she read it, she had to admit he made the argument more interesting than most people did; maybe that's why it was rejected so often. Or was it that when she heard it all in his Ben Stevens's voice, even Derrida was beautiful?

She was ready to stop nursing before the leaves were completely off the trees, but hated the thought of giving up the midday walks. They were a lovely break in the day, and Belinda was often at her best—not sleepy like in the morning, nor late-afternoon fretful. In the end, it was a three-day conference in Chicago that made the break for them. By the time she got back her breasts were hard with drying-up milk. Belinda had bottles at bedtime and seemed not to notice.

Connie and Ben had lunch early in November, sitting outside a bar called Malone's that served sandwiches. She gave him suggestions about reworking his papers to make the News more prominent, and he took notes while she watched the sun glint off his pen, the corner of his sunglasses, his blondish hair. As they parted company on the street corner, thinking of wanting some exercise and trying not to be intimidating, she suggested they play raquetball at the community center. He seemed pleased, a little surprised, and agreed. When they played, her serve plainly surprised him more; it was a close game. In the shower, Connie ran her hands across her stomach, leaning her head back into the hot spray and replaying the game. The delight of having her body back, light and quick again, after so many months of nursing bras that were always wet, made her shiver. She left the water running while she rummaged through her bag to find the aromatherapy soap Denise gave her on her birthday.

The soap's strong scent washed thinner in the shower, surrounding her delicately. She rubbed it over her breasts, her belly—the stretch marks were fading a little, there were muscles there somewhere. She got tired too early today, or she'd have had Ben on the ropes. She ran him around pretty good anyway. She smiled again at the thought of him, sweating as he dashed to cover the corners.

"We have *got* to do this again," he'd said as they walked off the court. "That sneaky backhand..." That smile ...

She shook herself. Time to get out of here. Belinda would be fretting and Russell wondering what was taking so long. Stepping out of the shower with her towel, she checked the clock—only 4:30. She could still soak in the hot tub a few minutes and be home a little after 5:00. Although, if she left now she could be early and have dinner well underway by the time they got there. Connie swayed from one foot to the other, chewing her lip. Her gym bag was open, her bathing suit was inside, she could smell the hot cedar of the jacuzzi just beyond the frosted glass door to the right.

What the hell, she'd make omelettes. She hurried into her bathing suit, stashed her bag under a bench, and skittered into the jacuzzi enclosure. Doing anything unplanned felt deliciously wicked, and she hung her towel on the bar beside the tub almost furtively. But, ah, the bubbles called out to her tired muscles, the steam lifting away all thoughts of babies, husbands, papers to grade. She sank in up to her shoulders, eased down till her earlobes were just above the water and the bubbles were a mad roar. She closed her eyes and moaned, vaguely aware of another figure in the mist; but the ecstasy was beyond decorum.

"HckHHMMmm." A familiar throat clearing. "Someone will hear and call the cops."

She kept her eyes closed, embarrassed. "I should have known that would be you."

"I pick my times, don't I?" Behind her eyelids, Connie envisioned shoulders, chest, mustache. Would he be scrawny, hairless, pale, an academic's body? Would he be flabby, paunchy, freckled? Was he eyeing her breasts and thinking, So THAT'S what childbirth does to a woman's body ... The clouds of steam, the unexpectedness, made it all seem unreal. She squared her shoulder blade around a jet, the heavenly pounding making her moan aloud again.

"Forgive me, I don't get out much."

"You're among friends." She heard a smile in his voice.

"Friends." She didn't quite snort. "Now there's a concept. I have at least as much time in my life for friends as I do for jacuzzis."

"I'll bet." Something sympathetic in his voice made her open her eyes at last. Ben's head leaned against the edge of the tub and he looked as relaxed as if he were taking a nap in a hammock. She drank that in; when was the last time she was that deliciously tranquil?

"I think I read somewhere that that's typical," Connie said. "Women have fewer chances at friendship after they get married; men have more. And kids, of course, change everything." Damn, she was whining. She searched for a lighter note.

"There's something about age that makes it harder, too." His voice purled through the steam; he laced his hands behind his head and stared up at the ceiling. He had finely muscled arms; Connie stretched her calves, pushing against the opposite side of the tub, careful not to brush against his legs. "Moving around a lot, you run out of energy to connect to new people everywhere you go. You figure you'll hang on to friendships you had in the last place, but then realize everybody that's important to you is in another time zone."

"It's also complicated when most of the people you meet are ones you work with," she agreed. The heat was starting to make her lightheaded.

He nodded, laughed a little. "Tell me about it. Grad students always so ready to go for a beer, then you're on the committee that decides whether they pass their exams or fail. You figure they know that, of course, but do they *know* that? Do they think you'll stand up for them if their work's no good?"

She studied him, his eyes on the ceiling.

"Do you ... " she wasn't sure how to put this, "share your life with anyone?"

The green eyes swung down, met hers briefly, swung past to the window behind her head. "Not anymore."

"Ah." Now she vaguely remembered a woman at a party once, when he first arrived. "That must be ..." its own set of difficulties, she meant to say. "Delightful," is what came out of her mouth. She winced broadly as he laughed out loud. "No, no no, I don't mean that at all, forgive me, it's the hot tub, I don't even think that."

"No, obviously it never crossed your mind." They moved on to talk about grad students and colleagues. Connie lingered in the warm easiness as long as she dared, pushing away thoughts of a screaming Belinda, a scowling, puzzled Russell, omelettes slapped onto plates with a slice of bread. Speeding home through the autumn twilight, she smiled at the glow inside her—it was a long time since that honeyed heat had been just *there*, under her ribs.

She noticed the silence before she came through the door. No screams, or even coos, from Belinda. No "hellllOOOOOOO!" from Russell before the door squeaked shut. She shivered a little in the quiet, hung her coat on the hook in the hallway. "Hello?" she asked softly.

"We're in here." A voice just as soft; a spoon banged once in the kitchen. Connie strode through the hallway, eager for something to bring back the chaos she'd anticipated on the way home. Even for scowls—she didn't care about scowls.

"Hi, gang." Belinda looked up from her high chair, red cheeks and mouth wreathed in creamed peas. Russell's back was to the door, his broad shoulders a U-curve, his head almost on the tray of the high chair, one hand cradling an empty highball glass. He didn't turn around; Connie kissed the back of his neck. "You're here early." She mugged at Belinda, hoping for a laugh; she got a solemn look instead.

"Since three, in fact."

"Three?" Connie searched her mind for a forgotten promise, a reason he might be home at that hour. Nothing. Silence. Finally: "How come?"

"I was laid off today."

"You..." she sank into a chair next to the table, "what?" Something dropped several stories from the bubble of sweet warm mood she'd had between her ribs to below her knees. She stared at the floor, then at his pale yellow shirt, the brown forearm, fine black hairs, resting on his knee. The highball glass in his hand.

"I no longer work for Peterson Architecture."

"For how long?" He turned to look at her, and she saw it was a stupid question.

"Forever, presumably."

"But if business picks up ...?"

"I believe that if business were going to pick up, it would have done so by now. Generally, they wait as long as they can before laying people off." He stood slowly and reached across the counter for the scotch. "Can I pour you some solace?"

Her head whirled. She hates scotch, he knows this, but maybe she should have one to keep him company. What did a Loyal Wife do in the face of such catastrophic news? What should she say, she who made her living with the written and spoken word? She was startled to realize she wanted to ask Russell himself.

It was an endless, largely silent evening. After Belinda had been bathed and coaxed into pajamas, Connie wondered whether to take her into the living room to play or keep her out of Russell's sight. Finally, she asked him.

"Do you want to be alone, or would company be better?"

"I don't care." The shrug was worse than a snarl. He stared at the TV, fingering his glass instead of the remote. Neither of them had eaten; neither seemed to notice. Connie tried not to eye the level of the scotch, now sitting in front of him on the coffee table. She took Belinda into her bedroom and held her on her lap in the rocking chair, hugging her hard, wishing she hadn't stopped nursing.

"What do we do, little girl? what are we gonna do?" Belinda just stared at her, green eyes round in her pale face, while Connie looked wildly around the room. Once—so recently—a haven of golden sunlight and autumn smells, of baby coos and powdery whiffs; all she could see here, now, was a mortgage. For the second time that day, she groaned out loud.

Aside from paleness around his eyes, Russell showed no signs of a hangover the next morning. Before Connie and Belinda left the house he had begun what became a pattern for the next several weeks: calling people he knew from other firms, at companies he had worked for recently, at the national office of his professional association. All architects, it seemed, had experience with being laid off; they were used to calls looking for leads on jobs. He went to the unemployment office, standing in line for an hour each week to pick up a check that was just under half of his regular salary. By the time she came home, whether that was three o'clock or five, he was ready for company and often, a scotch. The bottle he'd finished that first night was one they bought for a party the first year they were married. It had been in the cupboard under the sink, then, for five years. That one was replaced with a new one the next day, which was then replaced every week or so with another one.

Connie admired how calm and diligent he was with his phone calls, his rounds to the various offices involved in collecting unemployment. They celebrated the interviews he went to, three within the first few weeks; then said nothing to one another when there were no calls with offers. Belinda, who had been sleeping through the night almost always, went back to fretfulness between 2:00 and 4:00 every morning. Russell slept more soundly than before the scotch, and Connie hated to disturb him, telling herself she needed to learn to doze off more quickly holding Belinda in the rocking chair. The glorious lingering fall turned to a wet, snowy winter, but they turned the thermostat down to save money on heating bills.

Sometimes, when Connie dragged herself through the freezing dark towards her unreasonably whining child, she felt a dangerous rage invade her. "Rotten kid," she muttered, "horrible, rotten, feral child." She had a trick for those moments, one she'd used when Belinda was a newborn and Connie was home with her during the day. She imagined a closed circuit TV camera in the corner of the room that switched on whenever she came in. Watching her from the other end was an entire committee of Children's Protection Agents, clipboards in hand. She imagined Belinda's pajamas wired with tiny sensors that transmitted information to the committee on whether she was being handled gently or whether the fury was coming through her hands. She pictured smiles of approval on the faces of all the committee members as she softly changed a diaper, cooed delicately at her ungrateful screaming baby, and rocked her to calm, then sleep.

The university was a haven she escaped to in the morning, dragged home from slowly in the afternoons, and thought about—absently, guiltily—on the weekends. It was warm there, the coffee pot was always full, and people needed her for things she could give them. Ben was there, with news of an acceptance to a journal of one of the essays she'd helped him with. They played raquetball or had lunch nearly every week, talking about anything except babies or jobs or marriages. There were pub runs on Fridays, sometimes with other faculty, more often with grad students. She sat next to him, when a grad student didn't get there first, and wished she could touch him. He never touched her, whether he wanted to or not being unclear. Connie had time for one beer, two if she got Russell to pick up Belinda, before the weekend dragged her back into The Mess. She suggested once that they get a babysitter on a Friday, Russell could join the group at the bar for awhile, and then they'd go out to dinner, maybe a movie. He wrinkled his brows and said, "Sounds like a lot of money to hang out with people I don't particularly enjoy." Presumably he meant her colleagues, not Connie herself. At the last Friday gathering of the semester, the students were loud and joyous to be free of exams, excited about holiday ski trips or weeks of sleeping late. Ben kissed her on the cheek as she left, squeezed her hand and said, "Stay warm; see you in January." She smiled wanly at him, then cried all the way home in the car.

Calling that month of Sundays a holiday seemed the most bitter irony of their lives. Russell got a call from a contact in an architecture firm in Peoria, an hour away by car, that the company was going to announce plans for expansion just after the first of the year; his resume was at the top of the pile in the personnel office. Confident his luck was changing and that his enforced time off from work was about to come to an end, Russell turned to fixing things. He banged and clattered and bought wood and nails and a new handsaw, while Connie tried to write an invited chapter for a book about feminist literary theory, shivering in the chilly house and working harder each week not to stare at the price tags on the tools and materials and bottles he brought home. Belinda caught a bad cold and was miserably teething, so they spent New Year's Eve at home by themselves. Russell walked her around the living room, singing along with Buddy Holly songs on the stereo, swinging her up toward the ceiling then down low near his knees, to distract her. Connie dozed on the sofa, smiling faintly at them both, and wondered where Ben was, how he was spending New Year's.

Russell hadn't heard from the firm in Peoria by the time the semester started late in January. Worried about money and thinking that having something useful to do with his days (house repairs having petered out gradually as the days wore on), Connie suggested in her most I'm-open-to-discussion voice that Maybe Belinda Could Go to Ratna's Just a Few Days a Week, and Stay Home the Other Days. Russell stared at her, chewing his baked potato—thoughtfully, it seemed, until she saw the muscles in his jaw tense like electricity had jolted through them.

"I will NOT be a NANNY!" he shouted, and picked up the butter dish in front of him. Connie watched in shock as he hurled it against the wall opposite his chair, the butter sliding down across the pansies on the wallpaper they'd put up together the week they moved into this house. Belinda stared at him and started to scream. He gave the baby a look as unknown to Connie as his having thrown something in anger, stood up hard enough to knock his chair over, and walked out the front door into the freezing darkness. She heard him gunning the car to startled life as she pried Belinda out of her high chair and swayed with her, jiggling up and down. "Breathe deep, sweetheart, both of us, breathe deep. Just breathe. He didn't mean it. Daddy didn't mean to scare you, it'll be OK. He'll be OK."

By the time he came silently home, after midnight, they were both asleep in the big double bed where Connie had so often, countless nights, felt his arms around her like a safety net, warm, soft breathing on her neck, sweet gentleness all around her. She felt him pull the baby softly away from her, heard him soothe her back to sleep in her crib, and was wide awake by the time he came back to their room. He left his clothes in the hamper and slid in naked behind her. His hands—the ones that had picked up a butter dish and smashed it against her posied wallpaper—were clumsy, uncertain. She could smell cigarette smoke and beer, bar smells. Eyes open, staring at the heavy curtains in front of the double paned glass, she never moved. After awhile, he sighed deeply and rolled over. Things can't get any worse than this, she thought almost hopefully, feeling alone in the dark. Every couple has hard times, things they work through. You stick together through those and come out stronger on the other side. This can't go on forever.

February passed, quiet and polite. Cautioned, perhaps, by his explosion, Russell drank less. There was a halfhearted, futile undertone to his job seeking—he had checked the possibilities in the area several times by now. He made up for it by pouring his energy into Belinda, picking her up early from the babysitter's, being sweet and patient with her early evening tantrums, even getting up to rock her to sleep most nights when she woke up. If things were a little cold and distant between him and Connie, surely that was mostly her coming home in such a bad mood so often. It was the time of year she always felt most hopelessly drowned in work: graduate admissions, a search committee to hire another faculty member, longer lines of students. She alternated staying up past midnight on the computer with falling asleep over dinner, and always seemed to be struggling to pay attention when Russell talked to her. Spring Break, she promised silently, I will make it up to both of them. I'll have most of this behind me and we'll take Belinda to the babysitter and I will just be home and focus entirely on him. Unless he has found a job by then. Surely, he will be working by then.

Early in March, a wildly improbable warm snap hit the Midwest. Human forms emerged from the cocoons of winter, and the air seemed soft and sweet as a daydream. Anything seemed possible, healing and connecting and new leaves turned over. Russell went to an interview, so gorgeous in his suit, a pale pink shirt in honor of springtime, a perfect blue tie with tiny maroon arrowheads on it; Connie couldn't imagine he wouldn't get an offer. Ben asked her to guest lecture in his graduate class the Wednesday evening before Spring Break, three days from a glorious week of rest. "We sometimes quit early," he said, his eyes perhaps lingering an instant—it was hard for her to tell. She took her chugging heartbeat as a hint and wound up her lecture by 8:00, then watched the clock as discussion went on in fits and starts. She'd told Russell she would be home by 10:00, so if they were out by 9:00 there would be time, wouldn't there, for a quick beer at Malone's. If it were not mentioned to grad students maybe none of them would come along, none of them would know Ben and Connie were going there alone. At 8:47 Ben laid his hands softly on the table, smiled at her, and said, "Thanks for coming, Connie." It was too lovely to be true.

Thirty, maybe 45 minutes later, the bar dark and throbbing with body heat, loud music. Two empty beer bottles in front of them, a full one in each of their hands. "Going to conferences can be dangerous don't you think?" Ben's finger traced a line across the knuckles of her right hand, he looked her in the eye, then his finger was between the first two of hers, the second two ...

The music stopped suddenly and a hole yawned into the sound. Through giggles and protests from the crowd came a voice on a microphone they'd never heard used here: "Connie Mason, emergency phone call. Connie. Mason." Ben's eyes widened, his shoulders hunched into a question mark. She felt something plummet from her chest into her feet; who knows she's here, and how? She pushed her chair back and squeezed through people who swayed and stared and repeated her name as she passed. The music started up again, to cheers, as she reached the bar. The dreadlocked man behind the beer taps handed her a cordless phone. "Jefferson Hospital," he mouthed, though she heard nothing over the beat. The phone felt like a grenade.

"Hello? Yes, this is Connie Mason. Wait, I can't hear a thing, hang on ... OK, this is better, try again? Yes. She what?" Connie slumped against the wall in the musty corridor leading to the bathrooms. "How ..." She pressed her hand to her head, her voice gone. "My husband." Another struggle to breathe. "I'll be right there." Slapping the phone shut, she looked up at a dusty yellow light bulb hanging from the ceiling, no shade, just a bulb. Ugliest thing she'd ever seen. Engraved on her mind forever.

The bartender had his back to her so she just set the phone on the bar and shoved through the crowd toward the door. They all seemed tall and unmoveable, trees packed too closely in a forest, dense underbrush— Now something pulled at her arm, a vine. She tried to wrestle away, seeing clearly only the block between her and the car.

"CONnie, your coat, your purse." It was Ben, trying to hand them to her. "What's wrong?" She just stared at him, grabbed her coat and purse out of his hands, turned to go. "Connie, what happened?"

"Jefferson Hospital," she gasped, and then fled.

It was like trying to run in concrete. The sidewalk was a living enemy between her and her ash-blond baby. Her breath was ragged smoke in the cold darkness; one foot slid treacherously away, and she landed hard, on her hip. People around her murmured concern, tried to help her up, she shook them off. Feeling nothing in her hip except a slight awareness of damp, she walked more slowly to the car, digging in her coat pockets for her keys. Naturally they fell to the ground; she cursed loudly as she reached down for them, pain suddenly registering in her hip. Finally, she was next to the door, her hands numb, her body shaking with the cold. She forced herself to breathe deeply as she struggled to find the lock; surely an hour had passed since she hung up the phone; they would be wondering what was keeping her.

"Please start," she whispered to the car, her coat next to her on the seat as she shivered uncontrollably. It roared into life. Careful, she thought, something finally registering from her fall on the sidewalk. Careful, an accident will take much longer ...

She drove cautiously to the hospital, the defroster roaring, her eyes so wide open they hurt. Belinda. Fall. Head injuries. Quite serious. The voice through the phone chased wildly through her head. Get here fast.

The light in the emergency room hurt her eyes. The person at the desk seemed to know, before she said her name, who she was. The One They Found at a Bar.

"Your husband's over there, in the waiting room," she said. Connie turned and saw him, slumped in the now-familiar posture, his shoulders a drooped curve. A memory flashed, him asleep on the sofa while they waited for Belinda's ear infection to be diagnosed, a lifetime ago. She sleepwalked over to him, all the hurried urgency drained away, replaced with not wanting the next hour of her life ever to happen, not ever. *Stop right here and let me get off,* she thought.

Her hand lightly on his shoulder made him jump. He stood up and engulfed her in the embrace of someone drowning. His hair, always perfectly in place, was disheveled; the too-familiar smell of scotch wafted down from him. He held her, his shoulders shaking with sobs. She stroked his back— "It's OK, it's OK, tell me what's wrong." For an instant she forgot Belinda was the reason they were here; she could think only of calming him, holding him, reassuring him. Everything's OK, honey, take a deep breath.

"Belinda." He gulped, held her more tightly, buried his face in her hair. "She was crying, she wanted you to put her to bed, I tried, and she wouldn't lie down, couldn't go to sleep." More gulps, a marathon runner going uphill. "I put her in the laundry basket, you know, the way we did when she was tiny, and put it on the dryer, thinking that would calm her down." The sobs started again, noisier now. "She tried to stand up—she—it fell off—she hit her head on the drain pipe ..."

Connie stroked his back still, mechanically now. Deep clammy cold was seeping through her. "Is she—will she be alright?" The carpet was grimy in the far corner of the room, had maybe never been cleaned. She felt Russell nod against her head.

"They think so. Oh, God, Connie, I feel so terrible, I should have realized ..."

"It's OK, sweetie, it's not your fault, I'm sure ..." A tiny voice whispered in her head, how could you not realize that standing up would be the first thing she would try; she's used to the bars in her crib ...

"Mr. Mason?" The voice behind them was icicle hard. Connie kept her arms tightly around her husband as they both turned to look at whoever this was, probably trying to blame him, thinking WHO would put a baby on a dryer, not knowing how many times that had lulled her to sleep. Fool doctors, thought they know everything—

They gawked, clinging to each other. Beside them stood a police officer, a wall of black, a shiny badge, a name plate just above Connie's eye level. For an instant it didn't compute—why was a doctor dressed in a police uniform? Then another confusion—what was a police officer doing in a hospital?

"Mr. Mason, I need you to come with me." Connie tightened her grip on Russell's waist, feeling something drain away from him.

"Ms. Mason, you come with me, please." A gentler voice, a woman, on the other side. Connie looked at her—a doctor dressed as a doctor.

"But what—why—" Russell was holding her so tightly to him. "Our baby— " He whirled to face the doctor. "How's Belinda, did she ..."

"Let's talk over here, Mr. Mason." The police officer's name badge said *Josephs*.

"But my daughter—"

"Dr. Myrins will fill you in on your daughter after we talk."

Connie's head swam. *You can't take him away from me,* she thought; *where is my daughter? Just bring her out here and we'll go home, the three of us. We don't want you, we don't need you. Just let us go home.*

"This way, Ms. Mason." The doctor's voice was low, coaxing; her hand was on Connie's arm.

"Not without my husband," Connie snapped, yanking her arm away.

"I'm afraid the police need to talk to him first, Ms. Mason. Come on, let me catch you up with Belinda's—" The sentence ended abruptly.

"Can I see her?" Finally, an image of Belinda, alone and afraid, calling for her, came through the fog. Russell dropped his arms to his sides, squeezing her hand. Connie watched him walk away, taller than the officer, maybe older, too. How could this be?

Dr. Myrins was talking, and Connie hadn't heard a word. "I'm sorry? I want to see Belinda."

"Let's sit down over here first, Connie." *Why do you know my name,* Connie thought bleakly. *I don't know yours. I don't want to know yours. I want my husband, who is very sad and scared, and I want my baby, who's hurt her head.* She let herself be led to an office off the hallway, behind the nurse's station.

"Russell says Belinda will be OK," she said abruptly, standing in the doorway. Dr. Myrins turned to look at her.

"I'm afraid that's not the case," she said. "Belinda came in with very serious head injuries, and I'm very sorry to tell you that she didn't make it."

"She didn't make what?" Connie heard how stupidly this came out, but could only stare at the doctor's black hair.

"She's dead, Connie." The room whirled around her and there was a fog, suddenly.

"She can't be."

"Please sit down, here. Let me get you a glass of water."

"She cannot be ..." the word stopped behind her teeth. "I have to see her."

"You can see her." The doctor was just a voice now; Connie couldn't make out eyes or hair or teeth any more, for the fog. "I want you to be aware, first ..."

"I need to tell Russell," Connie blurted. "We need to go in together. I can't go by myself."

The doctor's eyes came into focus, looking grave. "There's something else you need to know." Equal parts gentle and firm. How do you manage that tone, thought Connie crazily. "Your daughter shows signs of having been shaken to death."

There was a tiny speck of something in one corner of the woman's eye, as though she hadn't washed her face. Connie felt frozen, nauseated. She stared past the doctor at the desk behind her, littered with papers, an empty coffee cup, a framed picture of a man with a beard.

"That's impossible, Russell put her on the dryer to help her calm down; see, we did that all the *time* when she was a baby ... he *told* me, she was fussy, he put her in the laundry basket and she tried to stand up, she fell off and hit her head. That's what happened." She felt a surge of relief, because this was a story that made sense, and nothing the doctor had said made any sense. "She wasn't ... he didn't

... She hit her head when she tried to stand up and fell off the dryer." Stupid, stupid doctors. Idiots. Poor Russell feeling so badly already, and they would have the nerve to suggest to him ... she had to get to him, to keep that policeman from upsetting him.

"Her injuries aren't consistent with that story, Connie." The voice rang hollow in her ears. "She had intercranial bleeding; there are bruises on her upper arms ..."

"But that *could* happen," Connie broke in, "that could happen when he was picking her up, I know he must have ..."

"Connie, listen to me." The doctor's mouth moved slowly. "Your daughter is dead. Her injuries are not those that happen when a child has a fall. I'm sure this is difficult to take in, but you have to believe me. Your baby was shaken violently enough to cause severe bleeding, which killed her. Your husband ..." her voice trailed away. "He will be taken to the police station with the officer you met to answer some questions."

"When will he be able to see Belinda—when can I talk to him?" Her mind was whirling again, faster than before. Nothing was making sense, none of this could possibly be happening to her. This was a bad joke, a dream, a hallucination. Another wave of nausea hit her. If she had gone home straight from the class instead of stopping off for a drink (how did they find her at Malone's?)—if she'd told Russell about the hidden camera from Children's Protective Services—wait, is that what makes them think he shook her? Did they see him do it on camera, do they have a video? Wait, there wasn't really a camera—or was there? She shook her head slowly. She was losing track of what was real and what wasn't.

The officer appeared, breaking the long silence. "I've read him his rights, but I told him he could see the baby before we go." He leaned down and looked Connie in the eye, close enough for her to smell his aftershave. "It is not in your best interest, or his, for you to ask him at this point what happened."

"Do you want to go in together?" the doctor asked. "You may want to wait until he leaves, Connie."

She turned her head slowly toward the doctor. Her whole body was a block of ice. Faces, words, physical sensations seemed to be sliding by just out of her reach. Out of the blankness she heard a wooden voice say, "No, I'll go in with Russell."

She tried to look up at him as they were led down the hallway, but could only take his hand. He squeezed hers; she could feel him shaking. They both hesitated at the doorway, putting off the moment. When finally he stepped inside, pulling her with him, she couldn't look at Belinda's face either. One small, baby-pearly white foot was sticking out from under the sheet, and Connie focused on that. With her free hand she stroked the toes, the sole, waiting for peals of laughter to come forth from the tiny form so motionless next to her. She couldn't look, she couldn't hug Russell, she could barely move. She couldn't understand any of this, because none of it could possibly be happening.

Crazy as it was, the thought was a life jacket. None of this is happening, she whispered to herself. Things like this don't happen to people like us. Russell is A Good Father and I am A Good Mother and we are A Happy Couple Who Love Each Other and these things don't happen to People Like Us. She could feel Russell shaking with silent sobs next to her, but couldn't lift her arms to put them around him. This police station business was just ludicrous, he would be home in an hour with apologies from them for the terrible misunderstanding. Their child was dead, that much was sinking in, but they would deal with this together, they would reach down into the powerful love that weighed so much more than anything life could throw at them, and they would survive it together. For this moment, though, she couldn't get her arms to move.

Finally, he squeezed her hand, hard, and turned to leave the room. She stood there confused—do I go with him, or do I stay here with my daughter? She almost asked the doctor. In that moment of hesitation, Russell walked off down the hallway. She watched his broad shoulders get further away from her down the sterile corridor, hearing her body scream NO!— but the only sound was a sharp little moan—"Mmmf"—like she'd stubbed her toe.

"Is there anyone you can call?" The doctor's voice was gentle again. The fog in her mind cleared slightly. Of course, of course. Call someone, someone who will help her figure out what she's supposed to do, because she never prepared herself for a moment like this. A question on the exam that she hadn't studied for. Someone has answers to this. Ben. She will call Ben. She felt giddy. Of course. Ben will figure this out for her.

She knew his number, but had to try three times to dial it right. She was flushed now, sweating, dreading the need to call him at eleven o'clock on a week night and say please come to the hospital and do something about my life, but he would understand. He would respond calmly, reassure her, be here so fast, "It's OK, you're among friends..."

The phone rang loudly in Ben's darkened apartment. "Who the hell ...?" He raised his head.

"Pretty late to be getting phone calls," Rita laughed. "Your fans don't know when to leave you alone."

He smiled down at her, red hair spread over the pillow, and stroked her cheek with his finger.

"Maybe a follow up question from class tonight," she purred into his ear.

"Too bad, I'm involved in a tutorial session." He heard the answering machine pick up and strained a little to hear.

Connie hung up without leaving a message. Ben ran his hand down Rita's thigh and lost himself in her delights.

A week later, the night pressed against the windows, damp and full of sound. Malone's was crowded and Ben's mood leaked through his fingertips, tapping on the tabletop without stopping. Connie saw the effort it was for him to focus on her, how hard he searched for questions to keep her talking. When she fell silent, his eyes drifted up toward the TV hung in the corner, some playoff game explaining the crowd, the noise, the tense energy. She shrank deeper into her coat.

"Sounds like you're handling this well, all things considered," he said. There was a sheen to his words, a degree too enthusiastic.

All things considered.

His fingers drummed, his watch glinted on his wrist. She felt a wisp, a tug—what a battle it was once not to stroke the fine hair on his forearm, just above his wrist.

Once.

She didn't realize she'd said it aloud.

"Beg your pardon?"

"Huh?"

"Once what?"

She smiled weakly, glassy eyed, letting him take that as confusion.

"You said 'once.'"

"Wonder what I meant to say."

"Once upon a time?" The grin hurt a little, she could tell.

"Once I get over this?"

Pause.

"Is that a song title?" the words fell together in haste.

"Not that *I've* heard."

"Guess that's not what I meant."

"What DID you mean?"

"Did I mean anything?" She sounded lost. "Did I really just say 'once' and stop?"

"You did indeed." His mouth twisted a little. This was all too odd to pretend it wasn't.

He picked up his beer and took a lavish swallow, his lips all the way around the opening in a way she hated. She stared at her own, untouched green bottle, her eyes fleeing from the sight of his too-widely-opened lips. The lamp over the table threw a circle of light through the bottle, turned it green and spilled it over the oak table top.

The silence had become a question. Finally, she looked over at him.

"It's over, Ben."

"What's over." A short laugh, barked. "What IT is it that's over."

"Us. You and me."

"We're over?" His playfulness was unconvincing. "WE are OVER?" He rolled the bottle around in his hand, and she looked away. "How can WE be over?"

"What 'we' am I talking about, you mean?" She nodded. "A reasonable question that I will not try to answer." Her eyes roamed, caught on silky blond hair several tables away, and her breath snagged in her chest. Belinda's soft white skin beneath hair just that blond pressed against Connie's cheek for a second, a flash, a brutal taunt. *My baby's dead.*

Ben saw she had flown elsewhere. "Connie, maybe this isn't a good time in your life to be cutting yourself loose from people."

"You mean beyond those already lost to me." Her voice was calm.

"Well, this is a terrible time for you; I'm sure everything seems ..." his voice trailed away. "I mean I can't imagine what this must be like, I want of course to be there for you."

She stared at him. 'I want of course to be there for you,' she nearly mimicked him.

"Ben, you heard me."

He nodded.

"See you, then." She stood up and looked at him once more. "I'm sorry."

He nodded, eyes fixed on the table top, tracing lines of graffiti layered into the wood over decades of students' talk, flirting, arguing, studying, dreaming. "Randy Michaels loves me" was carved in tiny, flowing script.

She threaded her way out of the bar, standing silently and staring at people in her way instead of asking them to move. She felt fragile: if someone touched her, or she brushed against someone, she would shatter into hard, sharp pieces. The night air was cool, fresh, still slippery with the rain. *I don't have to go home,* she thought, then said it under her breath. I don't have to be home at any particular time. Her mouth curled into a grimace. *You see my baby is dead, my husband is in jail, and I have just found out that your friends can't always be there for you when you need them, if in fact they were friends in the first place. I am free to do whatever I want.* She shuffled down the street, legs aching, seeing only her feet moving along the wet sidewalk. People steered around the slight figure, muttering softly to herself. I am completely alone, she mouthed.

Is she the one from the paper?

SHHHHHHHHHHHH!

A Janis Joplin song came into her mind, one she had hummed, sung aloud with the radio so long ago. *"Freedom's just another word for nothing left to lose ..."* She gasped, held her sides, air wasn't getting into her lungs. The car was still a block away. Her knees crumpled beneath her and she huddled on the damp leaves, clutching them with numb fingers, wanting to feel the cold, the slipperiness, to feel anything at all except the oceans crashing inside her. Freedom. *My baby's dead.* Nothing left to lose. *My husband's in jail.* Nothing left to lose. *Freedom.* If she made a sound, if she started to cry, she would never stop. She would wail and shriek and thrash until they took her away to a cell. Cell. Hell. *This* is hell, and she will be here forever. She rocked back and forth, silent, while a chill March moon shivered around her.

Reflections and extensions

1. As mentioned earlier, being able and willing to "talk things through" is commonly understood to be crucial for a healthy relationship in some cultures, including the US middle class. When, and how, did that ability slip away from Russell and Connie? What had to be left unsaid at the various moments in the sequence of events that led to the baby's death: when Russell first lost his job, when he started drinking more, when he bought expensive home repair equipment, when Connie had an enjoyable conversation in a Jacuzzi with a younger colleague?
2. Connie will have to explain to people that she had a daughter who died as an infant. What stories are available to her? What do you think she will begin to leave

unsaid about how the baby died, and when and to whom will she eventually speak the truth?

3. Why does "freedom" become part of Connie's numbed thought processes at the end of the story? What has she not said to herself or perhaps to Russell that makes the idea of freedom both relevant and utterly painful at this moment?

Conclusion

Breaking the silence

Learning and teaching ethnographic writing

We are all apprentices in a craft
where no one ever becomes a master.

Ernest Hemingway.

If *Hemingway*—Papa, Ernest—said that, what can the rest of us hope for? And he was, after all, a creative writer (largely fiction, but some literary nonfiction like *Death in the Afternoon,* which was the first Hemingway work I read). Surely, learning to write scientifically is different than learning to write creatively.

Taking 20 years (and counting!) to write this book has shown me that teaching ethnographers to write is complicated by the varied identities, forms, and audiences of ethnographic writing. Ethnographies are meant to represent human lifeworlds in ways that are systematic, and at the same time evoke richly textured worlds inevitably immersed in contradictory detail. Unlike its cousins, such as literary journalism and memoir, ethnography is part of social science. Social scientific writing aims to be clear, objective, and original, and requires diligent practice and good models to learn from.

Transcribing Silence: Culture, Relationships, and Communication
by Kristine L. Muñoz, 249–276.

Creative writing needs to be evocative and original, and also requires diligent practice and good models to learn from. Ethnography needs to be both clear and evocative, as well as original. Models may be useful to some extent, but ethnographic practice centers on unique case studies (as does creative work) positioned within broader scholarly conversations (like social science). Questions about what ethnographers need to learn about writing, and whether writing can be taught, are (in some communities at least) left unasked. A few years ago I thought about organizing an ethnographic writing conference/retreat. When I ran the idea past some ethnographers I admire, the response was puzzled, unenthusiastic, even a little embarrassed for me having raised the question. What would you talk about? Writing? What kind of writing? What would you *do,* sit around and write?

That community is only one of many where ethnographers are taught, employed, and (endlessly, like all academics) evaluated. There is another community, both broad and deep, where teaching, discussing, and working at writing itself are at the heart of ethnographic practice. Instead of silence, there is constant deliberation, even argument. There is instruction, practice, and considerable talk of writing strategies and processes. The conceptual center of this conversation has been sustained consideration of how an ethnographer's own perspectives, experiences, and emotions should be represented in, and thus made part of, the ethnographic record. Since at least the mid 1980s, ethnographers in several fields—notably sociology,[1] anthropology,[2] and in my field of communication studies[3]—have examined these issues through conversations about narratives and writing.

Once I noticed how vigorously talk about writing was silenced in my social scientific neighborhood, when it was clearly the daily bread of others, I became fascinated by that silence, as I was by others (the secrets, the taboos, the taken-for-granteds) described in this book. I thus conclude with some observations and suggestions about teaching and learning ethnographic writing. Although my own engagement with the issues centers around this particular scientific/

creative divide, I hope to offer some guidance for others whose lives have reading and writing at the center.

Naturally, I start with a narrative. As I describe the process through which I learned, unlearned, and relearned to write, I focus on times of silence, when something about writing itself seemed unsayable—at least in the neighborhood where I lived. Then I try to put into words (always a risky move) some advice based on what I've learned.

The narrative: A confession

I learned early, as did Louisa May Alcott, that narratives were a great way to get grownups' attention. A family story repeated too often for my taste involves a tall tale I related at age five, insisting it was true. My mother said that the story was so convincing they almost believed me. "We kind of worried whether you knew what was real and what wasn't," she said. Once I could read, there was nothing better in life than getting lost in a book. Once I could write, I could get lost in worlds *I made up myself.* My parents genially supported all this, thinking it was harmless as long as it didn't go on for too long. There was a creative writing unit in freshman high school English, and for those three weeks I felt like I was suddenly able to breathe underwater: There were hours of magic in every day, both writing in class and being completely absorbed in the homework. As a typical adolescent, there was no way I would say out loud that I was delighted by something school-related. When the three weeks ended, school was back to being mostly hell. A few years later I took journalism and wrote for the school newspaper. That beat algebra and chemistry, and came close to Spanish class for making me feel competent, but it wasn't *magic.*

My sophomore year at the University of Texas at Austin I signed up for a creative writing class, thinking this was too good to be true: I could get grades, and credit, for what I loved most to do? Alas, it was indeed too good to be true. The first day, the professor assigned us a brief writing exercise that we turned in at the end of the hour.

The second day, he read one aloud, which happened to be mine, stopping every few lines to point out how incorrect it was in terms of the exercise. Even though he didn't read my name and did point out a few things I had done well, just not in line with the exercise, I have never been in such public pain. I left the room in tears and dropped the class, knowing this meant that creative writing was now a part of my childhood best forgotten.[4] Again, I told no one; clearly that meant not only was I no good at writing, I couldn't take the heat of honest criticism.

After a study abroad year in Spain and writing a paper for independent study credit led me to graduate school, the task before me was to learn to read and write Science. I understood the task, as most graduate students do: to learn to Sound Smart. Originality was important, but only counted if it fit into a conversation that was already going on. One showed knowledge of conversations in the field through citations of other work, and showed original thought by way of arguments constructed in particular ways. I had no complaints about the arrangement, never connecting the creative writing I wasn't doing to the regulated forms of social science writing I was doing. Besides, qualitative ethnographic writing was less strictly regulated than experiments and surveys.

Once I had finished my dissertation, produced some social science publications, and was starting to think I might have the hang of it, I went back to reading for pleasure for the first time since graduate school (when "reading for pleasure" was an oxymoron). I found the same joyful abandon in reading fiction that I had as a child, and now I had children to read to as well. I didn't have a lot of leisure time, but I knew just what to do with it.

Getting lost in fiction again slowly led me to start writing fiction again, with a difference: Now, instead of being a way to entertain and amuse grownups, it was a furtive act that I was embarrassed to admit I spent time on. A friend of mine, also an academic, says she had an easier time coming out as a lesbian than she did as an equestrian. For both of us, the most important parts of our lives as children were things we thought we had to give up in order to join the serious world of adulthood. Were we silenced by real judgments about what was appropriate for a college professor to do with her time? Or did we silence ourselves with our own perceptions and fears? Is there any way we could have told the difference between the inner and the outer pressures?

Adding to this was the contradiction of academia's difference from other professions. Work time is flexible, and you have control over your schedule that others envy, but the work *never* ends. For many of us, it never stays behind in the office. There is always a deadline looming, or already past, and everyone else seems to be producing more than you are. As Terry Caesar pointed out in an essay about bosses in academe,[5] success means internalizing a system of rewards and punishments that no human being could possibly command: "The gun to our head IS our head." For years, I allowed myself to write fiction only during non-business hours, early in the morning before the children were awake or on Saturdays. Sundays I needed to *work,* and whatever this hobby was, it wasn't work. I was embarrassed to admit, even to Jairo, that I was writing, um, fiction, because that was something *real writers,* not somebody like me, wrote.

In 1994 I wrote a narrative about the murder of one of Jairo's relatives in Colombia (an earlier version of *A death foretold,* in this volume) in order to take part in a National Communication Association preconference that Dwight Conquergood was involved in. It became a narrative of my first immersion in Colombian culture and the interpersonal dynamics of becoming part of an extended family. Conquergood, with characteristic generosity, read it and encouraged me to pursue it. It had not occurred to me that this piece, with its raw emotion and honesty, would ever be published, or even read, beyond the people taking part in the preconference. I was finishing my first book then, a social science argument that Colombian culture was organized around interpersonal connections as the fundamental basis for human identity. I went through the essay a few more times, this time focusing on making it a *narrative*—with developed characters, dialogue, and descriptions of the physical context—and clarifying some connections to the claims I'd made in the rest of the book about Colombians' patterns of communication and relationships. I added it to the social science book as an epilogue. To my surprise, no one along the road to publication told me to take it out.

When the book came out, people commented specifically on the epilogue as the part that had most impact on them. I realized two things. One, I was now well and truly out of the closet: I was a writer of narratives, in addition to social science. Two, there are arguments better made in 20 pages of narrative than in 200 pages of social science.

By that time we lived in Iowa City, a mecca for creative writing for more than 50 years. Although the Writer's Workshop is an elite crowd, there are weekend and week-long writing workshops in the summer that are moderately priced and take all comers. They cover every genre and topic, and many of the teachers are Workshop alums. People come from all over the United States, and beyond, to take part in them. Those workshops are structured to be far gentler, more life-affirming experiences than the famous one. I took one shortly after I got tenure, and then others, and my narrative writing habit started edging its way into daylight hours. My favorite teacher, Marilyn Abildskov, later worked with me as an editor, and I began to quote her as often as I do Robert Hopper.

That's when I "discovered" (in the same sense that Columbus "discovered" the New World) the vast genre of literary nonfiction, particularly essays.[6] Ethnography and fiction came ever closer together as I gradually relaxed my self-imposed rules about writing narratives during work hours and allowed myself to write both fiction and nonfiction. I still believed I would never try to publish the narratives. They were the writing that made my life complete, and I needed only to rejoice in the increasing freedom to focus my attention on that luxury. I particularly resisted the idea that I was "working at" narrative writing. If that was work and social science writing was work, what was I doing for pleasure?

I did start to send electronic copies of my narratives to close friends, ones who would insist they loved them (no more sophomore creative writing teachers for me!). One of those friends owned a small publishing business in Spain, and he asked me whether I had enough stories to fill a book. They would publish it to expand their line into English, and pay me in copies. If it sold well enough in Madrid to cover a foreign transaction fee for a money transfer, they would pay me 40 percent of the total (it never happened). That edged closer to public exposure, but still felt safe. I would give copies to friends, and besides them, who in the United States would ever read this book?

All this time I was working with graduate students and finding that writing was the focus for most of their (considerable) stress. They worried about speaking up often and wisely enough in their graduate classes, but usually just their first year. Anxiety over writing started smaller and built to a climax as the dissertation came closer. Some said they wished they could include what they thought and felt, and how they experienced the phenomena they were studying, in their writing. Social science (or high-theory humanism) was a straitjacket they wanted to fit into, while chafing against the silences required to do so: Personal experiences, even those relevant to the subject, were off limits (although in recent years, some Iowa grad students have done autoethnographic writing and performances in the public venue of department colloquium). Any emotional reaction they had to the research process, the subjects, or their data had to be hidden to avoid the ultimate damnation of "bias." I sympathized, told them my own struggles, and urged them to read ethnographies that pushed traditional social science boundaries without giving up on it altogether. We read autoethnography in methods seminars, and the students grew restless: Why were they not "allowed" to take narrative approaches to their subjects? Why did their own lives and perspectives have to remain unsaid when they explored the topics closest and most important to them? Why weren't there classes offered on *writing*?[7]

I asked them whose permission they needed to write freely and joyfully about matters they were passionate about, because they certainly could count on mine. Even as I said that, I remembered the shame and terror I felt in that creative writing class, how hard it was to admit I was writing narratives alongside social science, and how perilous it felt to claim that each was part of the other. There were more outlets than ever before to present and publish narratives as scholarly contributions: the Ethnography Division in the national professional organization (NCA); interdisciplinary journals, such as *Qualitative Inquiry* and *Journal of Contemporary Ethnography*, that actively celebrate such work; commercial and scholarly presses (Left Coast, Stanford University Press) with series devoted to it. My resolve to consider narratives a "hobby" rather than work, and not to try to publish them, was now a self-imposed silence. By keeping my creative work separate from my scholarship, I was in fact part of the oppressive separation the students felt so strangled by.

The Obermann Center at the University of Iowa then made one of the greatest contributions to my intellectual life so far. An interdisciplinary discussion group called Intergenre Explorations formed in 2011, and I got to know colleagues from several departments who were each working on projects that departed from the conventional forms of their disciplines. A theater scholar, always a historian among performers and directors, wrote and delivered a performance about her personal history with horses. A visual artist engaged in environmental activism and created a documentary film about it. A literary historian and theorist wrote a book about writer's block that dealt extensively with the emotional impact of pressures to publish, and co-organized a conference on the material conditions of knowledge production, asking the radical question: Does it really have to be this painful? Compared to these projects, my attempt to do communication theory through fiction and nonfiction narratives seemed tame. In this group we read work that none of us would have otherwise encountered. We performed, screened, read, and discussed each other's work. We talked a great deal about the risks and insecurities involved in crossing genre lines.

For me, the insecurities were all about writing. Could I really write *fiction* and send it into the world for people to read? Did I dare to claim that narratives about my own experiences as a department chair, a vegetarian, an intercultural marriage partner, were ethnographic? The members of the Intergenre group showed me that the outcomes of their risk-taking were priceless, and encouraged me to see my own as, if nothing else, worth a try. Something that came up often, in various forms, in the discussions of that group is that we all gave each other *permission* to step outside the boundaries of our familiar territory.[8] It was not lost on me that graduate students had been asking ME for exactly that same permission when they encountered auto-ethnography. It may be that "DO it!"—*it* being take chances with the work you have invested your heart, soul, and far too much identity into—is something that really has to be said out loud. And not just once—over and over again.

I close, then, on some things I learned about writing. I offer these suggestions as a way of saying, to social scientists who are tempted to come out of the closet in some creative direction or another: DO IT!

Re-learning to write ethnography

Craft

Craft is one of the words used often and knowingly by people in the Iowa Writer's Workshop. It is always a noun, never a verb, which confused me. Finally, I asked my teacher Marilyn what this large, stretchy category of an absolutely essential part of Real Writing was. "Everything that happens after a first draft, I guess," she shrugged. I have since found that an enlightening description: Craft includes cutting excess words (both Howard Becker and Stephen King claim this to be the primary goal of second and subsequent drafts); rearranging pieces to make more sense; honing word choices so you can use fewer of them, with more impact; poring over transitions until they make your argument, the narrative arc, or both, more compelling. Editors help with this process, but the better you get at sensing problem areas—wordiness, vagueness, a sagging plot, a vanishing argument—and being able to address them on your own, the sharper your writing skills. Besides, you don't always have a patient editor to do the close reading needed to polish a first draft into a better one.

Another common way in which ethnographic writers often need to hone their craft requires skills associated with creative nonfiction:[9] building complex characters, balancing showing with telling (or scene with story), describing places and action in ways that are vivid and compelling for the reader. "At that point, though, aren't you *making stuff up*?" fretted a history colleague (a historian! Who knew they were such rock-ribbed empiricists?). Creative work is not science, and vice versa, although the lines between the two, especially in ethnography, are drawn in rushing water. There are many ways to approach the issue of what the differences and similarities are. My take is that good writers, both scientific and creative, care about their audiences. There should be trust and agreement between a writer and an audience: The audience has to know what they're getting, in terms of Truth and Accuracy.[10] Writers must know what their audiences need to be enlightened about or convinced of, and they must work to provide it. Writers also need to feed themselves, both physically and spiritually. I will return to questions of feeding oneself, and audiences, shortly.

In the meantime, however, in ethnography, good social science and creative craft are not mutually exclusive. The research and writing skills required to produce empirical ethnographies are quite consistent with those required to produce fiction: The details of sailboats and boating accidents that went into *Andiamo,* the signs of a shaken-baby death in *Another word for nothing,* and the engineering world and interns' places in it in *Crush* all came through observation and asking questions very close to the ethnographic practices I use. Kirin Narayan takes up this idea to follow her passion for Anton Chekhov into ethnography.[11] She proposes that, although best known for his fiction, Chekhov built his stories from careful observation of the world around him. Both Chekhov and his characters show ethnographic prowess for capturing the subtle detail that reveals social structure and symbolic systems of meaning. The power of these descriptions and interpretations makes them timeless: In describing the particulars of a communal life, Chekhov and his work illuminate the human condition. Narayan uses excerpts from Chekhov and others as the basis for practical advice for writing, shifting and adapting to genre conventions while always keeping an eye on the analytic possibilities of narrative.

Another point about craft: The fact that it rhymes with "draft" should be considered no coincidence. Multiple written drafts are not delays in submission, publication, or delivery, nor (if done correctly) are they repetition. One of my first published articles went through 19 drafts before I quit counting in despair. These being the early years of my first faculty position, I suffered mightily: I did not (I thought) have the time for 19 drafts! I had to get this essay published and move on to something else! Looking back, it seems to me those multiple drafts were the concrete, almost physical, level of learning to write a particular kind of argument. Twyla Tharp talks about muscle memory as it relates to artists:[12] With many hours, days, even years of practice, artists absorb the skills they value on an unconscious level. She talks about artists, from dancers to novelists, who learned from the greats they admired by copying them. Raymond Chandler, for example, wrote extended imitations of the style of Hemingway, his favorite author. Proust spent 12 years translating and annotating his favorite author, art historian John Ruskin. My version of this is that I no longer simply highlight passages when I read. With almost everything I read, fiction and scholarship and everything in between, I have active conversations. I still highlight, and now I put lots of sticky flags on pages. I write questions and comments in margins of books I own, and keep long notes in different programs that work on different devices (Endnote or Refworks for computers, Notability—which lets you audio record into a file attached to a .pdf that you write in—on i-things). Apart from vague ideas that this will make for more efficient searching of things I've read before, active engagement in noticing and saving well-crafted prose builds writing muscle. It is part of the experience that makes writing flow more smoothly now than it used to. When I carve out time for writing days, I plan for half or more of the time I spend "writing" to be primarily reading.

I am also less inclined nowadays to declare reading to be work or pleasure, rather than simply something that catches my interest. Being further along in my career and my children being grown obviously gives me more freedom and flexibility. I have never met any avid reader, however, nor any professional who makes their living with words who had all the time they wanted to read and/or write. I do propose that wandering and exploring beyond the boundaries of the deadlines in front of me has improved my writing, because the excitement it gives me to read in completely engaged ways feeds my energy to write. Maintaining that energy, I propose, is as crucial to learning to write as any attention to craft, genre, or conversation in the field. Figuring out how to keep going, year after year, draft after draft, requires sustained attention all its own.

Perseverance

Multiple written drafts, forays into new intellectual/creative territory, and determination to continue in the face of rejection all create a demand for support, from both inside and outside, to stick with writing long enough to learn the craft. I have three thoughts about that: steady habits, rewards versus fear, and balancing writing that pays the bills with writing that feeds the soul.

Connecticut has long had a state nickname as "The Land of Steady Habits." This seemed hilarious to me when I heard it in history class, but it is an idea that I find central to ethnographic writing. It's also a thought echoed in almost every writing book I've ever read: Make writing such a firmly entrenched habit that (a) you do a great deal of it, (b) you are not intimidated by a blank screen or page, and (c) you do not wait for the ever-elusive Muse to strike, because she is far too fickle to count on when you want to make a living at something that requires writing.

There are many systems for doing this, and the one I've found most productive is described by Julia Cameron as morning pages.[13] Her perspective is one that combines spirituality and creativity, and encourages readers to see everything they habitually do as creative. You can take that or leave it—I found it a nice perspective on teaching—but the morning pages idea is simply to write three pages of longhand first thing in the morning. Write whatever is on your mind, even "I have nothing to say today and I'm tired of doing this" over and over until you fill the three pages. On writing days, my mind is often on something I'm writing: I stopped at a transition because I didn't know what should come next. I still need to read some things before I can move to the next point. I want to look again at some data besides the examples I have already put into the text as illustrations and see if the argument is still headed in the right direction. I can start morning pages with the equivalent of small talk—here's what happened yesterday; here's what I need to remember to do today—and then move to beginning the writing task. I find that takes some of the pressure off to get just the right words into just the right place; pressure that, in my experience, is neither productive nor pleasant. Because I've done morning pages at least six days a week for roughly 15 years, sitting in front of a screen with a keyboard is not in itself an intimidating place to be, any more than getting into a car or standing in line to get on a bus: It's just the way the day starts.

I was too attached to word processing technology to ever do morning pages in longhand, and the three-page rule is flexible if I'm pressed for time. If the writing task for the day seems really difficult, I write *anything but that* in morning pages. With Cameron's system as with any other,[14] you have to find a rhythm, a style, a medium, that works for you. I find morning pages both relax me, because they are such a familiar routine, and keep some kind of muscle well-toned. When my fingers touch a keyboard, most of the time they pause only briefly before they start moving. They know what to do, the kind of muscle memory Twyla Tharp described.

Every habitual writer seems to have a process that he or she holds onto, sometimes with the seriousness and energy reserved for spiritual practices. That might be times of day that work best, modes of production they hold sacred (pens? pencils? specific kinds of paper? laptop? desktop? electronic modes for first drafts, printed hard copy for revisions, or vice versa?). One of my favorite conversations to have with graduate students when we talk about writing, then, is "How do you write?" The value of going around the table hearing different responses, all of them delivered in the same firm tone of conviction ("It has to be GREEN pens on a YELLOW legal pad"), is that everyone finds out that other people have magical beliefs about writing just like they do. For scholars to believe magic is required, writing must be *hard*. If other people need magic like I do—if we all constantly have to work at writing, instead of it being a gift that some people have and others do not—it must be hard for them as well as me.

Many people have found writing groups or partners to be important allies in persistence. If you have a standing check-in with a person or a group that you have agreed to be accountable to for progressing on your writing projects, you have something beyond your *own unsteady willpower*[15] to fall back on when the inevitable barriers to progress appear. Many others have written about how to organize and sustain writing groups, among them psychologist Paul Silvia.[16] Along with setting a writing schedule and sticking to it, he recommends four guidelines for academic writing groups:

1. Set concrete goals for group members and monitor them as a group.
2. Focus on writing goals, not goals from other areas of academic life.
3. Use rewards (social outings, coffee) and punishments (interventions) to keep group members accountable.
4. Have separate groups for graduate students and faculty.[17]

I am told that the separation principle (4) also holds for undergraduate institutions that encourage close working relationships between faculty and students.

In any writing group, the critical dimensions are a sincere commitment to focused attention on writing, a willingness to be accountable to one another, and trust in the collaborative energy of the enterprise. One particularly inspiring group of women I know started such a group while they were graduate students at Iowa. Ten years later, they each have finished dissertations, articles, and books. They saw each other through graduation, then tenure, marriage, and parenthood, and they still gather once a year for a week-long writing retreat. Did these steady habits require money and time, as well as energy? Yes. Was the first requirement staunch commitment, and has it paid off for them professionally as well as personally? Yes, and yes. I have found accountability easier to sustain with one person at a time, so I write with partners rather than groups. Sometimes there are multiple simultaneous partners: a co-author, with whom I have an agreement about meeting a deadline together; a local writer that I can meet at a coffee shop in town; a colleague willing to Skype on a regular basis.

Another strategy for perseverance that I have found indispensable is a writing log. During fieldwork, I log data collection and analysis, as well as writing time. The log is, first, an organizing device: In this day of many digital storage options and frequent backups, remembering where I saved something is half the battle of getting started the next day. I save a lot of time by noting the path of the last saved version, like "/homelaptop/research/Spain/notes 5 12 12." I also stop every day at a hilltop: i.e., a point from which I can pick up quickly and easily the next time I turn to that project. That might be a question that stumped me; it might be the next item in a list I roughed out; it might be a direction I was trying to go in the prose but ran out of words or time. The hilltop, again, keeps me from staring at the blank screen long enough for panic to rise.

Second, the log is a motivator. Even on days when it feels like I erased as many words as I added, I can see that I made progress. If I have writing time blocked out but I'm not sure where to start on the many projects I am involved with, I can look first at the log and see where I stopped on each of them. I can focus on a particular one or skim them all to pick the one I have the strongest itch (or most pressing need) to get back to. Reading the last few lines I left the time before is always a push to get started (instead of, say, sharpening pencils and cleaning out my e-mail queue a little longer). When weeks or months have disappeared into a fog and I feel like I have not shown up on a page in forever (with the consequent sigh of resignation that there's no point trying to do it on *this* day/*this* week, either), I can look at the log and be pleasantly surprised to see it wasn't really that long ago. I can read the brief note about where I left off and feel a spark of interest, enthusiasm, even confidence: There IS something I was working on; I DO remember it; it IS worth going back to—just for this one hour or day.

I have also used a table form of log, with more specified information items:

Date	Time	Location	Action	Output	Next time
3/1/12	11-1	Dining room table	Mp's, revise perbles	985 wds to page 9	Start at politeness theory
3/4/12	4-6	Community pool	Observed intercultural interaction	brief FN's on iPad, some audio	Expand FNs to 3-5 pps

In this example, I combine some fieldwork (on 3/4) with writing time (on 3/1). The goal with each is to keep track of what I have done, have a clear place to start so I can pick up any project with a minimum of searching and wandering, and most of all: Stick with it.

Silvia's book also has a chapter called "Specious Barriers to Writing a Lot," a spirit I agree with but would frame differently. I do not experience writer's block, in the sense of a blank page that refuses to fill with words. I have my most constant struggles with distractions (the internet slid right into the space left when my children grew up and left home) and with pressures and interruptions that have—and will always have—legitimate claims on my time. Many days, of course, those two are one and the same. Although some of them are relational (friends, family, students) and some environmental (cars, weather, plumbing), the most recalcitrant ones involve writing that is part of the job I am blessed and paid well to do. Reports, reviews, student feedback, and absolutely endless e-mail not only suck up time and energy, they leave me limp and unwell. After several hours of this, can I get right back to a computer screen for my own writing? Or a printed page with a pencil in hand? No. Freaking. Way.

I am embarrassed to say that months have somehow strung themselves together and scampered away with nothing written that was important to me, fiction or science. I always marked off time for writing, at first in my head and then, once calendars came online, electronically. When the day came, though, there was always something more urgent. I convinced myself that tasks would take only a short time to finish, and that once they were behind me I would be able to concentrate and thus write more and better. The tasks didn't take short times, they took over entire days and then weeks. Even worse, this didn't happen once or twice; it happened week in and week out.

I take back the statement that I'm embarrassed, because in fact I know that too many academics do exactly this. The ironic perceptions abound: those of the general public, who think we have "summers off," and our own, that we "have no boss, we're our own bosses." What gets me past that observation is a mantra of people who HAVE written smart, important, lengthy works while holding down a day job to support themselves: Steven King taught high school English while he wrote *Carrie*. Steven E. Wilson was an award-winning, patent-holding eye surgeon when he wrote *Winter in Kandahar*—and still is. Scott Turow wrote *One-L* as a first year law student at Harvard, and his first novels while working as an attorney in Chicago. Perhaps most famously, J. K. Rowling wrote the first Harry Potter book as a single mother, working as a researcher and bilingual secretary for Amnesty International.

The list could go on and on, of course, but I chose these four because none of them worked at menial, mindless jobs while they wrote their fiction and nonfiction classics. They worked at mentally demanding, time and energy-sucking jobs that one can only assume left them exhausted a fair amount of the time, and yet they found time for a writing habit outside the jobs that paid their bills. I do not know what they *didn't* do while they were both paying the bills and writing classics; maybe, as is often assumed about hyper-productive people, they didn't sleep. Maybe, though, they didn't do e-mail. Maybe they let their house stay filthy and fed their kids waffles and Fudgesicles for dinner. Maybe they found a pace they could sustain, finding a time when they could write—early in the morning, late at night, on trains or planes—and they *stuck to that.* Apart from unavoidable emergencies, a level to which they did not allow many day-to-day issues to rise, they did not let their day jobs take over the time when they were writing what they most wanted to write. A friend once nodded sympathetically while I reeled off a list of things I absolutely *had to get done* before I could get back to writing: "Yeah, I hear you. Do *you* hear how many things are getting in the way of your writing?"[18]

That same friend identified one of the things getting in my way: When I decided I did not have time to write on a particular day, it was because I didn't have two or three hours that day. Once I took her suggestion to find 15 minutes to write, and find it every day, I started to see the magic of routine. Yes, I still find some days disappear into an abyss, and yes, the 15 minutes has become an hour or more on at least a few days a week, but weeks and months no longer disappear with no writing at all. I finish more writing projects than before, and even better, I notice a significant decrease in how much

I resent the intrusive needs of others and loathe myself for putting them ahead of my own need to write.

To be clear: In some professions, and academia is certainly one of them, there is writing that pays the bills. If that writing is also that which most fulfills and satisfies you, you are blessed. If there is writing that you profoundly want to do, you should find a way to do that, even if it will not cross an item off the to-do list, fit into that journal article you *must* write to get tenure, or meet the deadline on something you agreed to produce. Perseverance is the secret to joy, as the Alice Walker novel promised. Because it is the key to success and happiness of many kinds, I'm a firm believer in finding something satisfying and pleasurable to balance out the tasks that are not so rewarding in themselves. Most writers I know use a reward system to keep themselves going: For 500 words today they get 30 minutes playing X-Box tonight. When this book is finished, the reward is a trip to Acapulco. I know others who say they respond better to threats of punishment: If I do NOT finish this paper today, I'll have to work on it this weekend instead of going to the Broadway musical in town. Either I write this article this month or I'll lose my job. A new favorite: If I don't send this out by next week I have to write a big check to a political cause I loathe. Although I'm in favor of whatever works, I think that, ideally, writing itself provides enough satisfaction and fulfillment to keep going.

For me, that happened by finding out that there was more room in the ethnographic tent than I thought originally. The final point I want to make about ethnographic writing is specifically about finding that room. If the three important things for real estate are location, location, and location, the equivalent for ethnography is audience, audience, and audience. In many ways, an audience IS real estate.

Audience analysis and adaptation

This section will be brief, because it is both very simple and endlessly complex: All communication depends on a connection between an intention and an interpretation. In writing, that means an author and an audience. Those can be the same person: We may want, or need, to write only for ourselves.

When the audience expands to other people, there is always—or should be—some degree of audience analysis and adaptation. Even if my goal in writing an e-mail to my closest friend is to unburden myself, I will tailor what I'm saying to her as the audience. At minimum, I won't repeat information she already knows ("Jairo is my husband, Gabe and Erica are my children") unless I think I should remind her of it ("I told you what happened last time I went to this restaurant, right?"). Although we are very close, there are things I will not say if I know they will hurt, distract, or offend her. Nonetheless, I can pour my heart out assuming she will read all the way to the end, that she will work as hard as needed to understand what I'm getting at, and that she will always be on my side.

The larger the audience and the more delicate the message, the less I can take any of that for granted. Analyzing the audience becomes more complicated and adapting to them (it) more important, if for no other reason than to get them to keep reading. Ethnography has many audiences: different fields, different journals, different institutions, even different professions. One way to think about audiences is that they are groups of people with particular levels of commitment to understand, accept, and support a particular kind of message. A consistent, but more vivid, way to think about audiences and writing is to imagine an old-time post office, with tall racks of little boxes to distribute mail into. Looking at a large pink envelope with swirling handwriting, you put it in one box, and the smaller, green one with neat printing goes in another, and the business-sized white one with a typed address goes into a third. As people come along to pick up their mail, they take the ones that belong to them and put the ones that do not back in the central box (sometimes the shove back to the box is rough). You pick up the ones that get pushed back and try them somewhere else, and you keep this up until every piece of mail is distributed.[19]

I treasure this image because it keeps me from dividing my work into "good" and "awful." First, I can't tell whether a piece is one or the other until I put it into a slot and let someone else be the judge. Second, when a piece is pushed back to me, I do not necessarily have to conclude that it was awful; it may simply have gone into the wrong slot. Where the metaphor breaks down is that I cannot assume that everything I write can find an audience if I just send it out to enough places. There are some things I want to write that I find out, from sending them around to trusted friends, do not serve any purpose they have. I may need to reframe the argument or the purpose, arrange data and interpretation differently, or simply make what I'm doing more clear. Some of those changes may be major, and I may need to give up on that piece for the time being (I'm not sure I've ever consciously abandoned a piece of writing "forever," although there are some that are still waiting their turn after decades).

Another fact that the mailbox metaphor doesn't quite get at is that there is no substitute for, or shortcut to, audience analysis. One of the most useful assignments I was given as a graduate student was to analyze the most recent 5–10 years of a journal that might be appropriate for my work.[20] Each of us in the introduction to graduate school class read abstracts from one issue of each year of the journal during the time frame, as well as the description for authors of the journal's scope (topics, methods, expectations). Based on that, we wrote a page or so description of the audience for that journal, exchanged them among ourselves, and discussed them. This was a first step to decoding the mysteries of scholarly publication. A later step was to look at publishers' catalogues and book series in the same way:[21] What range of work did each one publish? What was the stated goal or approach of the series? What did my colleagues know about them? What was the fit between what the audience for the series, as envisioned by the publisher, paid attention to and what I did? At least as importantly, what audiences did my employer—actual or desired—recognize as evidence to support hiring or promoting me, or calculating that well-deserved merit raise?

I do not mean to suggest that finding such a fit is inevitable, nor to overlook the frustration and anxiety that the trial and error nature of publication can bring about. Those tend to get better with time and practice, so that the focus for ethnographic writing can be more on the process—and the wider variety of possibilities available than ever of ways to observe, describe, interpret, and evaluate social phenomena—than on where a given piece of work might be published. The writer's end of the deal is to work persistently to anticipate (and when possible, provide) what their desired audience needs to understand, stay interested in, and make use of their work. To do that, writers have to craft their ideas and their data (texts, experiences) into forms that will reach that audience and make good on the promises of the form, the venue, or the occasion. To a writer with broad interests and a lively curiosity, that can feel like a pact with the devil: selling the soul of what got us into ethnography in order to fit a text into 30 manuscript pages, including references and footnotes. Other times, when we are lucky as well as persistent, we get to wake up in the morning looking forward to getting to the screen, the tablet, the camera, or the stage. People respond constructively and positively to what we have produced, and encourage us to take it further. We lead relatively full and happy lives, and have some occasions to feel we have contributed something positive to other people's lives, as well as their theories.

One of the most profound changes in writing practices and ethnography since I started writing this book in 1992 is—you guessed it—the communication explosion called digital media. There is very little about scholarship that has been left untouched by the internet, and I will not try even a brief sketch of the landscape. Instead, I will focus on one form of ethnographic writing that incorporates the three dimensions just discussed—craft, persistence, and audience—in ways relevant to the central issues of this book: silence, the unsaid, and being heard.

What about blogs?

The category of blog, and the activities of blogging, cover as wide a range of possibility as the previous range from quill pen on parchment through the most current version of Word. They go from private online diaries to the scholarly equivalents, in readership and impact, of the *New York Times* (or the *Huffington Post* may now be a better metaphor). As a form of scholarship, they are celebrated for the possibilities they offer of open access, immediate dissemination of information, public engagement, and intellectual discussion. They are just as vigorously disparaged as a frivolous dilution of academic labor, forums for unverified claims masquerading as scholarship, and uncontrolled and counterproductive—even dangerous—attacks on people and ideas. Blogs intrigue me, both for the riches I have found in the thoughtfully done ones and for the vehemence of the debates they spark. Below is a list of some pros and cons relative to the issues this book, and particularly this concluding chapter, have focused on. I should note that I have conflated the idea of a blog as a particular web-based form with certain other kinds of web publications, such as personal or organizational websites that post full essays outside of the structure of a journal.

Giving voice and creating conversation

The technology of blogging is easy to learn and usually free. Blogs give public access to voices that are silenced in other forms and forums, both the authors excluded from traditional scholarship and the kinds of work that traditional scholars want to do but have not had outlets for. Conversation with others interested in similar topics but not physically co-present can happen more easily and can expand networks beyond those people the blogger would ordinarily have contact with. Under ideal—or even good—circumstances, communities can form that are useful to all involved. Participants in such communities can provide feedback on ideas, and answers to questions, more quickly than through traditional channels of scholarly interaction.

The downside is that the blogosphere is both seductive and largely lawless. Keeping up extended conversations online can overwhelm already overcommitted scholars' time, both personal and professional. Blogs may also begin to substitute for more direct contact, in ways that are harmful to ideas and relationships: If spending more time posting online to respond to the work of non-present others means I do not bother to find out what my new colleague down the hall is working on, something precious about scholarly community is at risk. Specifically, I am not doing for my co-present colleagues what senior people did for me 20 and 30 years ago: taking them to lunch; listening to the big picture of how academic life is treating them; offering encouragement, insight, and personal connection that can make that life as productive and pleasant as possible. Online communities are easier than human beings in many ways, but they don't (usually) show up at your mother's funeral.

In addition to giving voice to people with valuable things to say, the comment and hyperlink features of blogs allow for questions, distractions, and attacks motivated by jealousy and animosity rather than truth and/or relevance. The usual social, scholarly, and legal conventions that control digression, not to mention outright spite and slander, may be unenforceable: You can block someone from posting on your blog, but you have no control over what they say on theirs, which might end up circulating further than your own because it's more inflammatory and, thus, juicier. Silence takes on nuances in the blogosphere: Lack of comments and of linking to other blogs might mean that no one is reading, or that readers are too offended or bored to respond. The eternal scholars' weakness of looking at related work first to see "Did they cite ME?" goes on steroids. On blogs, there is almost nothing that *must* go unsaid, which is both a good and bad thing.

Craft

The immense number and variety of blogs on every conceivable topic provide many more models for the adventurous writer to emulate and learn from. When there are responses and interaction, a blog provides ongoing motivation to hone ideas and prose: If I know someone besides me might read something I'm writing, I will do second and subsequent drafts. The process of doing those drafts improves my writing, regardless of how many eyeballs ultimately meet the page or screen. In supportive, constructive, and knowledgeable communities, writers can get more immediate and specific feedback than a review/revise and resubmit/re-review sequence for a journal would provide.

In an electronic world where posts can be short or long, writers can take more chances on new ideas, structures, and genres. Some of those chances may pay off in better writing habits and products in other, more traditional venues. On the other hand, bad examples and bad feedback, including indiscriminate praise, can lead writers down unproductive paths that lead only to rude shocks when they venture outside the blogosphere. Lack of response can be read as approval, or at least lack of objection, giving writers a false sense of security.

Persistence

Blogging is instant gratification for writers committed to writing every day and focused on publishing their work. Setting a goal to post to a blog regularly can provide a short-term deadline that is easier to meet than longer pieces or more distant deadlines ("Finish this book by 2016."). Having even a few committed readers can be powerful motivation to show up on the screen and get something together that is suitable for public eyes to see. The encouragement, reassurance, and accountability of a writing group may be easier to commit to with people who do not—in contrast to the co-present colleague described earlier—also hope for emotional support or require work-related evaluations.

The opposite of all those good things is, of course, equally true: Writing and polishing blog posts can take time that may not directly contribute to achieving longer-term writing goals. The immediate gratification of blog posts may be out of proportion to actual learning and online connections to others (like all immediate gratifications) can be addictive. Once there are commitments to connecting within the blogosphere, they may begin to take on an urgency that is out of proportion to the real rewards and ignorant of the real consequences of neglecting other tasks like, oh, grading and answering e-mail. When blogging is one more item on an overloaded to-do list, it can add more pressure than opportunity. There is a fine line between motivation to reach certain clear, consciously formulated goals and having so many commitments that none of them gets its due.

Audience analysis and adaptation

New audiences, and expanded ones, can be found on the web beyond those available through traditional conference and publication venues. Audience analysis can be done more directly if there is early feedback from desired audiences that shows connections and gaps to their needs and interests, and to other work in the field. In a climate that encourages, and increasingly insists on, publicly engaged scholarship, blogs are a form of public intellectual engagement that more scholars could participate in than those consulted by the media or Congress, or those disposed to be community activists.

On the other hand, as noted earlier, harsh and sometimes ill-informed responses to blogs are hard to avoid and may be distracting, even devastating. New ideas can be nipped in the bud, or opportunities to increase the size and devotion of an audience can take precedence over the ones that would lead to productive theoretical or methodological insights. It may be more difficult to focus on helpful and well-informed feedback if there is also a steady hail of (perhaps ill-founded) rocks and tomatoes. Finally, the question of "what counts" as scholarly contribution rests heavily on divergent opinions on how much credibility and value the institution or discipline accords to material published on blogs. Because it is difficult to predict or prove how much of an audience a blog will reach, the credibility of blog production still generally ranges from slim to none.

In sum, both the promise and the danger of the blogosphere seems to be that everything that once remained unsaid can now be spoken. People, their ideas, their interconnections, and the ways they spend their time, all silenced or hidden in the pre-internet era, now have places to go and things to do. The places are of unlimited size, although audiences and their attention spans are not, and they are potentially public and enduring. Some of the things people can do online are important, and can be done better (more efficiently, more accessibly, more thoroughly) through electronic means than landline telephones and hard copies ever managed.

It struck me as I wrote this final section on blogging that I was finding a grave danger or weakness for every strength I encountered. Maybe one more thing blogging does is to make more obvious something that's true of all communication: For every good thought, word, or deed that happens through communication there is an equal potential for evil. Some of the bad is probably anticipated or intentional; much is neither of those, but still unavoidable. I have explored some of the world of the unsaid in this book: the forms it takes, the reasons people have for not saying, the danger and hurt of not putting something into words or actions, the abundant riches of feeling and subtlety available only through indirectness and silence. That exploration led me, on balance, to a new appreciation for the unsaid and respect for some senses of the unsayable. The social world will always be a place of inequality, insecurity, and human meanness. It will also be the place where poetry, art, and music—all in the form of ordinary communication and relationships—happen every single day. Although blogging clearly gives voice and space and freedom, I think it also underscores a basic truth about communication and human beings: There is much that, for any number of good reasons, is better left unsaid.

Appendix

A very short list of favorite books on ethnographic writing

Becker, H. S. (1986). *Writing for social scientists: How to start and finish your thesis, book, or article.* Chicago: University of Chicago Press.

Cameron, J. (1998). *The right to write.* New York: Jeremy P. Tarcher/ Penguin.

Freedman, D. P., & Frey, O. (Eds.). (2003). *Autobiographical writing across the disciplines.* Durham, NC: Duke University Press.

Goodall, H. L. Jr. (2000). *Writing the new ethnography.* Walnut Creek, CA: AltaMira Press.

Mallon, T. (2001). *In fact: Essays on writers and writing.* New York: Pantheon.

Narayan, K. (2012). *Alive in the writing.* Chicago: University of Chicago Press.

Prose, F. (2006). *Reading like a writer.* New York: HarperCollins.

Richardson, L. (1990). *Writing strategies: Reaching diverse audiences.* Newbury Park, CA: Sage.

Van Maanen, J. (1988). *Tales of the field: On writing ethnography.* Chicago: University of Chicago Press.

Zinsser, W. (2006). *On writing well.* (7th ed.). New York: HarperCollins.

Notes

Preface

1. French (*esprit de l'escalier*) and German (*Treppenwistz*) have words for those clever remarks that do not come to mind in time to utter them (Rheingold, 1988).
2. Although Sissela Bok's work on both lying (1999) and secrets (2011) is more in the realm of philosophy and ethics, she has much to say about communication practices that constitute lies and secrets.
3. See, for example, Anderson, (2006, 373–395); Ellis, C. S., & Bochner, A. P., (2006, 429–449, and other essays in that special issue).

Introduction

1. This summary and application of politeness theory are drawn from the Brown & Levinson (1987) development of ideas formulated early on by Erving Goffman (1959, 1967).
2. There are also social worlds where being a drug addict, and perhaps even being a murderer, is no more awkward for identity and the comfort of others than being left-handed or extremely tall, despite the physical and mental inconvenience those might create for the person possessing those characteristics. I will leave those possibilities for someone else to explore.

3. Quoted in Wilkins & Isotalus (2008, 43).
4. I learned there were two of them: *Alice's Adventures in Wonderland*, published in 1865, and *Through the Looking-Glass, and What Alice Found There*, published in 1871. Wikipedia simply describes them as "similar," though I envision shelves of doctoral dissertations on the differences between them and the reasons there are two.
5. In the early days of communication theory, it was meaningful to talk about "senders," "receivers," and "messages." That model is, at best, inconsistent with the approach I take here, so I'll leave it at an assumption that participants work together to construct meaning without taking on those distinct roles.
6. Fitch (1994); Fitch (1998).
7. Questions of why this family (or friendship, marriage, work group) goes this way and another goes a different way, and when secrets and lies are productive as opposed to destructive, are ones I will happily leave to psychologists.
8. That is the next, more social scientific, book: *Relational Codes in Cultural Contexts*, forthcoming.

Forbidden love

1. A childhood name that distinguished me from an Aunt Kristine that I gave up at age 20.

The lady DEO

1. In Big 10 universities, department chairs are referred to as DEO's—Departmental Executive Officers. Is there no clunkier way to avoid the generic *he* of "chairman?"

A death foretold

1. An earlier version of this essay was published as the Epilogue in Fitch (1998).

Scenes from an intercultural marriage

1. When Jairo read this, he snorted. "We ARE an interracial couple," he insisted. I was stunned and intrigued: Why did I, the white person, see us as intercultural and he, the brown one, see us as interracial? I started to wonder how other people see us. Unlike some other cheeky, odd questions, I have never had the nerve to ask this one.

Alone again, naturally

1. Gilbert O'Sullivan sang a hit song with a title almost identical to the title of this chapter in the 1970s, far more gloomy than the use I am putting the title to here.

Conclusion

1. Richardson (1990); Richardson (1994, 516–529); Van Maanen (1988); Van Maanen (1995).
2. Given the centrality of ethnography to anthropology, the lineage is predictably longer and wider. Rather than try to point to germinal works, I would point simply to Freedman and Frey (2003). The introduction by Ruth Behar describes in useful detail the questions of reflexivity and inclusion of the author that intertwine with serious consideration of writing practices and products.
3. Although this chapter has previous and subsequent iterations, Ellis and Bochner (2000) "Autoethnography, Personal Narrative, Reflexivity: Researcher as Subject," has been cited an astonishing 2,300 times as of March, 2014. That is quite the conversation starter.
4. I have since been dismayed at how many academic writers report exactly the same experiences sometime early in life that had the effect—if not the intention—of convincing them they were terrible, incompetent writers. Even Amy Tan (*The Joy Luck Club, Saving Fish from Drowning*) describes a similar experience that led her to abandon writing for several years. Getting over that

kind of trauma is never quick or easy, and I'm convinced it makes writing, academic and otherwise, a more tortured process for many of us than it needs to be. People, we need to be kind to each other about writing!

5. The original story and user comments can be viewed online at insidehighered.com/views/2006/11/21/caesar.
6. The world as I knew it expanded the day I picked up Barbara Kingsolver's *High Tide in Tucson: Essays from Now or Never* (Harper Perennial, 1995). Once I got past the questions of what is an *essay* and who reads them for pleasure, and is this really the first time I've ever read something like this, I noticed that many literary essays were based on excellent ethnographic work. Thomas Mallon's *In Fact: Essays on Writers and Writing* (Pantheon, 2001) left me well and truly hooked, and since then I've read more nonfiction than fiction for pleasure. I'm shocked at that, but more convinced than ever that good writing is good writing, whether it's Shakespeare or *Sports Illustrated*.
7. Such classes have become far more available in the academic world. My institution has one called "Writing for Learned Journals," and I presume students would be as free to identify *Journal of Contemporary Ethnography* as their target audience as any other. The University of Washington has one called "Writing as Ethnographic Method." Autoethnographic writing is a particular strength of the University of South Florida graduate program. The International Congress of Qualitative Inquiry (www.icqi.org/) offers multiple writing seminars each summer. Sonja Foss and William Waters conduct scholars' retreats (www.sonjafoss.com/html/overview) focused on writing, and there are many highly regarded writing coaches who work online and in person. Some of the excellent books relevant to ethnographic writing are listed in the Appendix for the sake of clarity. Although classes, seminars, workshops and instructors/coaches vary in their approaches and expertise, no one interested in a writing journey needs to travel alone.

8. We were almost all women, which either does or does not suggest women are more likely to feel they have to ask permission than men are. We also noted many times that even the full professors among us were asking permission as earnestly as anyone else.
9. A very smart social scientist friend once looked at me in disbelief when I said "creative nonfiction." "Is that really something your people believe in?" she asked. "Do you *really* not hear those as contradictory?" I loved the reference to "your people"—the exotic tribe of ethnographers.
10. A journalist suggested, during a guest lecture to one of my classes, that these might be different standards. "Something may be *accurate* without being strictly *true*," he said. That view got him in so much trouble that I shudder to repeat it, let alone suggest I would adhere to it. I have no other explanation for the conversational details, for example, in the essays ofPart 1, however: I did not make any of them up, but I know I did not remember them word for word, either.
11. *Alive in the Writing: Crafting Ethnography in the Company of Chekhov* (University of Chicago Press, 2012). Narayan also highly recommends Theodore Cheney, *Writing Creative Nonfiction: Fiction Techniques for Crafting Great Nonfiction* (Ten Speed Press, 2001).
12. Tharp (2003).
13. Cameron (1992/2002).
14. Morning pages is essentially freewriting, a very common recommendation for writers to build and maintain good habits of persistence and to counteract writer's block.
15. A powerful phrase from 12-step programs such as Alcoholics Anonymous that emphasizes the strength of interpersonal bonds to help people accomplish things they cannot do alone.
16. Silvia (2007).
17. There is a fifth, optional guideline: Drink coffee.

18. Naomi Greyser: Remember that conversation? Thank you.
19. Marilyn Abildskov offered this image in a writing class, to talk about publishing.
20. Thank you, Tom Scheidel.
21. Without Left Coast Press's commitment to qualitative and ethnographic research methods, you might not be reading this book, and I would not have had the best time of my professional life writing it.

References

Anderson, L. (2006). Analytic Autoethnography. *Journal of Contemporary Ethnography, 35*(4), 373–395.

Basso, K. (1970). "To give up on words": Silence in western Apache culture. *Southwestern Journal of American Folklore, 88*, 213–230.

Berlant, L. (Ed.). (2004). *Compassion: The culture and politics of an emotion*. New York: Routledge.

Bok, S. (1999). *Lying: Moral choice in public and private life*. New York: Vintage.

Bok, S. (2011). *Secrets: On the ethics of concealment and revelation*. New York: Vintage.

Brown, P., & Levinson, S. (1987). *Politeness: Some universals in language usage*. New York: Cambridge University Press.

Caesar, T. (2006). Who's the boss? *Insidehighered.com*. Retrieved from www.insidehighered.com/views/2006/11/21/caesar#sthash.PlzwMsJE.dpbs (accessed April 21, 2014).

Cameron, J. (1992/2002). *The artist's way*. New York: Jeremy P. Tarcher/Putnam.

Carroll, L. (1865). *Alice's adventures in wonderland*. Retrieved from www.gutenberg.org/ebooks/11 (accessed April 21, 2014).

Cvetkovich, A. (2012). *Depression: A public feeling*. Durham, NC: Duke University Press.

de Botton, A. (1993). *On love*. New York: Grove Press.

Ellis, C., & Bochner, A. (2000). Autoethnography, personal narrative, reflexivity: Researcher as subject. In N. Denzin & Y. Lincoln (Eds.), *Handbook of Qualitative Research* (pp. 733–768). Thousand Oaks, CA: Sage.

Ellis, C. S., & Bochner, A. P. (2006). Analyzing analytic autoethnography: An autopsy. *Journal of Contemporary Ethnography, 35*(4), 429–449.

Erdrich, L. (2009). *The last report of the miracles at Little No Horse*. New York: HarperCollins.

Eugenides, J. (2007). *Middlesex*. New York: Picador.

Fitch, K. (1994). Culture, ideology, and interpersonal communication research. In E. S. Deetz (Ed.), *Communication Yearbook 17* (pp. 104–135). Beverly Hills, CA: Sage.

Fitch, K. (1998). *Speaking relationally: Culture, communication, and interpersonal connection*. New York: Guilford.Freedman, D. P., & Frey, O. (Eds.). (2003). *Autobiographical writing across the disciplines*. Durham, NC: Duke University Press.

Goffman, E. (1959). *The presentation of self in everyday life*. Garden City, NY: Doubleday-Anchor.

Goffman, E. (1967). *Interaction ritual: Essays on face-to-face behavior*. New York: Anchor.

Gregg, M., & Seigworth, G. J. (Eds.). (2010). *The affect theory reader*. Durham, NC: Duke University Press.

Jaworski, A. (Ed.). (1997). *Silence: Interdisciplinary perspectives*. Berlin: Mouton de Gruyter.

Katriel, T., & Philipsen, G. (1981). "What we need is communication": "Communication" as a cultural term in some American speech. *Communication Monographs, 48*, 301–317.

Lubrano, A. (2005). *Limbo: Blue-collar roots, white-collar dreams*. New York: Wiley.

Lutz, C. (1988). *Unnatural emotions: Everyday sentiments on a Micronesia atoll and their challenge to Western theory*. Chicago: University of Chicago Press.

McEwan, I. (2007). *On Chesil Beach*. New York: Anchor.

Nakane, I. (2007). *Silence in intercultural communication.* Amsterdam: John Benjamins.

Rheingold, H. (1988). *They have a word for it.* Los Angeles: Tarcher/St. Martin's.

Richardson, L. (1990). *Writing strategies: Reaching diverse audiences.* Newbury Park, CA: Sage.

Richardson, L. (1994). Writing: A method of inquiry. In N. K. Denzin & Y. Lincoln (Eds.), *Handbook of qualitative research* (pp. 516–529). Thousand Oaks, CA: Sage.

Silvia, P. (2007). *How to write a lot.* Washington DC: American Psychological Association.

Tannen, D., & Saville-Troike, M. (Eds.). (1985). *Perspectives on silence.* Norwood, NJ: Ablex.

Tharp, T. (2003). *The creative habit: Learn it and use it for life.* New York: Simon & Schuster.

Van Maanen, J. (1988). *Tales of the field: On writing ethnography.* Chicago: University of Chicago Press.

Van Maanen, J. (Ed.). (1995). *Representation in ethnography.* Thousand Oaks, CA: Sage.

Wilkins, R., & Isotalus, P. (Eds.). (2008). *Speech culture in Finland.* Lanham, MD: University Press of America.

Index

About the author

Kristine L. Muñoz is Professor of Communication Studies and Latin American Studies at the University of Iowa. She received her PhD from the University of Washington in 1989. Her research and teaching are centered in the ethnography of communication, based on fieldwork in Colombia since 1983 and in the UK, Spain, and the US Midwest since 1999. This work has been supported by a Fulbright Award, a Leverhulme Grant, a University of Iowa Global Scholar Award, and the European Social Research Council. She has published four books, and 40 articles and book chapters *in Communication Monographs, Communication Theory, Human Communication Research, Communication Theory* and other communication-based and interdisciplinary journals. She edited *Research on Language and Social Interaction* from 2005 to 2009, and has served on numerous editorial boards. Her book, *Speaking Relationally,* received the Gerald R. Miller Award for Outstanding Publication in Interpersonal Communication Research, and her article, "Cultural Persuadables," won the Outstanding Scholarship in Language and Social Interaction award in 2008. She served as Research Board Director of the National Communication Association from 2011 to 2013.

